Political Campaign Debates

Political Campaign Debates

Images, Strategies, and Tactics

Myles Martel

Longman

New York & London

Political Campaign Debates
Images, Strategies, and Tactics

Longman Inc., 1560 Broadway, New York, N.Y. 10036
Associated companies, branches, and representatives
throughout the world.

Copyright © 1983 by Longman Inc.

Developmental Editor: Irving E. Rockwood
Editorial and Design Supervisor: Joan Matthews
Production Supervisor: Ferne Y. Kawahara
Manufacturing Supervisor: Marion Hess
Composition: Kingsport Press
Printing and Binding: Fairfield Graphics

Library of Congress Cataloging in Publication Data

Martel, Myles.
   Political campaign debates.

   (Longman professional studies in political
communication and policy)
   Bibliography: p.
   Includes index.
   1. Campaign debates.   I. Title.   II. Series.
JF2112.D43M37   1983   324.7'2   82–20862
ISBN 0–582–28366–3
ISBN 0–582–28367–1 (pbk.)

MANUFACTURED IN THE UNITED STATES OF AMERICA
Printing: 9 8 7 6 5 4 3 2 1   Year: 91 90 89 88 87 86 85 84 83

Lovingly dedicated to Susan and David

Contents

Foreword

Myles Martel brings to this study of the political campaign debate both the practical insights of a seasoned insider and the analytical sophistication of an experienced researcher. The author has advised a number of candidates, including Ronald Reagan, as to the strategies and tactics of such debate, and the book is replete with examples from his own experience. But although elements of both are present, this is neither a case study nor a "how to guide" to successful debating. What Dr. Martel has produced instead is a thoughtful examination of the place and practice of the debate in political campaigns for all levels of public office. Both the substantive breadth of his approach, touching on all aspects of campaign debates, and his ability to generalize across electoral levels, contribute to the importance of Martel's work.

Political Campaign Debates draws on an extensive series of oral history interviews, three surveys of participants in congressional debates, and systematic analysis of several specific debates to identify and assess the significance of factors contributing to the decision to debate, to the establishment and pursuit of particular debate goals, and to the selection of formats, rhetorical styles, and other tactical devices. The book then focuses on what Martel terms "metadebating," the tactics of public posturing over the very holding of debates, before concluding with the author's recommendations for enhancing the utility of campaign debates.

The cogent analysis of this book recommends it to the scholar and teacher; the author's ability to draw important practical lessons from the multiplicity of seemingly divergent campaign debates recommends it to the practitioner; and the impressive array of examples and Martel's readily accessible writing style recommend it to anyone with an interest in political debates or political campaigning generally.

The monographs in this series are intended to illuminate the theoretical and structural foundations of the process of political communication. In *Political Campaign Debates* Myles Martel clearly fulfills this purpose.

Jarol B. Manheim

Preface

In 1976 I was selected to serve as a debate adviser to two candidates, both challengers, one running for Congress, the other for the Pennsylvania General Assembly. No credentials qualified me uniquely for this position other than eight years as a college debate coach and two years as a speechwriter for a congressman. Once situated in my new role, I learned quickly that there was a vast difference between political and academic debate; any attempt to force the academic model on a campaign was, at best, naïve and, at worst, politically dangerous.

Not long after, I became interested in conducting research on political campaign debates. I soon learned that little had been written about them except for a host of studies which examined the effects of the 1960 and 1976 presidential debates. No work, therefore, discussed thoroughly the decision to debate; the candidate's goals, strategies, or tactics; the format; or the "debates" about debates waged in the media. Hence, the impetus for this book.

My subsequent experience as a debate adviser at all major levels—gubernatorial, congressional, senatorial, and presidential—has put me in contact with scores of candidates, advisers, and campaign consultants. While so many have impressed me with their intelligence and political acumen, I have been equally impressed by their lack of understanding of political debates—by their tenacious attachment to tireless axioms, bromides, and superficial notions regarding both images and issues. The formulation of a coherent debate strategy with complementary tactical options appeared novel or alien to most; the specific performance requirements which television in its potency as a political medium imposes on candidates seemed elusive, if not ethereal.

In speaking with civic-minded persons such as debate sponsors, journalists, and academics, I was taken by their insensitivity to—even disdain for—the candidate's strategies. In their zeal to promote the public interest, they seemed woefully unclear regarding what "the public interest" was. And in a related vein, they could not defend convincingly their all too popular notion that the candidate's interests were necessarily inimical to the public's.

Political Campaign Debates examines the political debate process in a way which should illuminate the interests of the candidates, sponsors, and the electorate. This book is fully intended to assist these parties in enhancing the role of debates in the political process. Indeed, debates are here to stay. To live with them requires more than passive tolerance; it requires active understanding.

Myles Martel

Acknowledgments

Over the past six years many loyal and talented persons helped bring this book to fruition. In addition to the many persons noted on the list of interviews appearing in the bibliography, I wish to express particular gratitude to the following:

Frank Ursomarso for his boundless friendship, enlightening interviews, and consistently excellent advice;

Ralph Towne for helping me define the scope of this undertaking and for stressing its importance;

John Field for his steady support and insightful editorial advice;

President Ford, Jim Karayn, Mike Duval, and Dick Cheney for sharing generous amounts of time to educate me during the early stages of this research and for being "on call" ever since;

Lee Mitchell, Carolyn Keefe, Diane Casagrande, Stan Kelley, Kurt Ritter, Justin Green, Marc Ross, Herb Simons, Fred Stern, Sid Waldman, and Kathy Cramer for their thoughtful reactions to various portions of the manuscript;

Les Houtz for his gifted insights as a political scientist and critic, and for his commitment to see this project through;

Joe Cassel, Pat McLane, and Denise Neary for their persistently thorough research assistance;

Arlen and Shanin Specter, Gordon Woodrow, Carter Clews, Bill Scranton, Jeff Peters, Barry Goldwater, Jr., Signy Ellerton, Ben Key, Dick Schulze, Joe Westner, Pete Wilson, Bob Goodman, Loren Kaye, David Caplan, Bob Arnhym, Otto Bos, Bill McLaughlin, Ray Shamie, Dennis Rochford, and Lori Forman for providing me with a real-life campaign laboratory to test many of the concepts discussed herein;

Henry and Bob Pollak, W. W. Keen Butcher, Bill Morehouse, and Rich Branton for helping me to secure logistical support and funding for this research;

Alice Ives and John Vlandis, my high school and college debate coaches, who helped cultivate within me a passion for analysis and argument, including a devoted interest in public policy issues;

Shirley Noble, Barbara Hoffman, and Elizabeth Popper for typing the manuscript so ably under uncommon pressure;

The staffs of the Haverford College and Bryn Mawr libraries for welcoming me into an ideal writing environment;

Jarol Manheim for his penetrating reviews and invaluable encouragement;

Irv Rockwood, my unflappable editor, whose contagious calm and editorial sensitivity added sanity and substance to this project;

David Estrin and Joan Matthews, Irv's colleagues at Longman, who coordinated the many logistical details associated with this book with professionalism and refreshing good humor.

Finally, I wish to express special appreciation to President Reagan, who granted me the honor to serve as his debate adviser and to Jim Baker, Kathy Camalier, Bill Carruthers, Dave Gergen, Dick Wirthlin, Richard Beal, David Stockman, and Frank Hodsoll, with whom I served during the 1980 presidential campaign and who have since been most supportive of this research.

Introduction

Since the drafting of the Constitution, debate has been a respected method for addressing public policy issues of all types and magnitude. Political campaign debates, a variation of the legislative debate tradition, have earned historical significance because of the Lincoln-Douglas debates of 1858 and have attained contemporary significance since the 1960 televised presidential debates between John F. Kennedy and Richard M. Nixon. The 1960 presidential debates were the first such encounters of their kind between the nominees of the Democratic and Republican parties and drew some 100 million viewers, to that point the largest television audience ever.[1] Sixteen years later, before an audience of at least 70 million viewers, Gerald Ford became the first incumbent president to debate his challenger, Jimmy Carter. Four years later history would, in a sense, repeat itself when Carter, the incumbent, debated Ronald Reagan before 100 million viewers.[2] On the congressional level, too, campaign debates appear to be gaining significance: in 1976, 53% of all candidates seeking reelection debated; in 1980, the figure jumped to 65%.[3]

Political campaigns in this country have been called "a continuing source of dissatisfaction to friendly students of American political life," and indicted for not providing the enlightened campaign discussion that might "help voters make rational decisions."[4] Indeed, many campaigns have been and continue to be exploitive, focusing on cosmetics and hoopla—seldom offering a serious discussion of the issues. In particular, the thirty or sixty second spot television or radio commercial has drawn heavy and often justifiable criticism for superficiality and attempted manipulation. While campaign budgets normally treat the spot commercial as *the* priority item, the electorate often learns little about the candidate through them; in fact, the candidate may not even appear or speak during the commercial. Moreover, if issue positions are presented, they are normally couched in calculated ambiguity.

In contrast, political debates may offer three distinct values for the electorate: (1) they can be a significant means by which the electorate can compare up close the candidates' personalities and issue positions, especially since voters generally avoid information presented by the candidate they do not at least initially favor; (2) despite the possible extensiveness of the candidates' preparations, debates can result in exchanges more spontaneous and more revealing than, for instance, stump speeches or spot commercials; and (3) debates can stimulate interest in elections.[5]

However, campaign debates are hardly immune from criticism either; they often draw more heavy criticism than the spot commercials, for few forms of public communication on the campaign landscape are as prominent as a "great debate."

One of the more frequent objections against political debates is that they are not debates at all, at least in the traditional sense. Professor J. Jeffrey Auer suggests that a true debate contains five essential components: (1) a confrontation, (2) in equal and adequate time, (3) of matched contestants, (4) on a stated proposition, (5) to gain an audience decision.[6] Most political campaign debates do involve a confrontation in essentially equal, but usually not adequate, time, to gain (or, perhaps, contribute to) an audience decision (albeit delayed), and, more often than not, there is at least a basic matching of candidates. However, there is hardly ever a stated proposition.

It is this failure to have a "stated proposition"—that is, to have a focused controversy about which candidates can argue—that mainly removes political debates from the classical debate tradition. However, the dominant proposition in any debate is implicit and always the same: Candidate A would fit the role requirements or criteria perceived by the audience for the office being sought more impressively than Candidate B, his opponent.

A definition of a political campaign debate seems in order, since the definition of a traditional debate does not apply. A political campaign debate is *the joint appearance by two or more opposing candidates, who expound on their positions, with explicit and equitable provisions for refutation without interruption.* This definition excludes joint press conferences and so-called candidate nights or forums wherein each candidate argues only those questions addressed to him and has no specified opportunity to react to the opponent's responses to his questions.

Another popular complaint regarding campaign debates is that they emphasize images over issues or substance. Candidates, critics contend, are far more interested in putting up a good front—in making an overall positive impression—than in providing enlightening interpretations of public policy alternatives. In essence, this argument is correct, but before the role of image and campaign debates can be properly understood, it is necessary to note the five major weaknesses of the popular thinking regarding images versus issues: (1) critics seldom, if ever, define "image"; (2) nor do they differentiate clearly "image" from "issues" or "substance"; (3) the actual dominance of "image" factors over "substance" factors in debates has not been established empirically; (4) while "image" may normally register a negative connotation, it has not been proven as an impediment to the voter's rational decision-making; (5) there is no evidence that debates are any more prone to image promotion than other forms of campaign communication.

Image is indeed the common denominator in political debates; normally, everything else is subordinated to its development. For this study I define image as *a collage of selective conscious and subconscious perceptions that the audience draws from the candidate's physical and vocal cues* (overall appearance, gestures, facial expression, tone of voice, etc.) and from his statements. In fact, the candidate's issue positions are intrinsically images: they are not realities per se but are instead verbalized abstractions of realities. Hence, the audience receives a secondhand image, the candidate's image of a reality adapted to them.

But more important, the candidate's formulation of an issue position is often based on, or at least articulated to project, the trait the position helps communicate, e.g., strength, compassion, or knowledgeability. When, for instance, during a debate a candidate takes a forceful stand against a particular trade agreement between the United States and the Soviet Union, he may feel that the merits of the proposition warrant the stance, but he also may regard his position as a significant vehicle for projecting strength.

Despite the primacy of image in campaign debate, such an orientation is not ipso facto manipulative. To put this issue in perspective, it might be helpful to ask this question: When a person seeking a job wears his best suit for the interview, attends more meticulously than usual to grooming needs, and demonstrates more poise, better listening habits and closer attention to what he says than usual, is he being unduly manipulative? Of course not. Job interviews are imbued with image-oriented rituals rooted in the applicant's needs for survival and success. Campaign debates, too, are forms of job interviews imbued with image-oriented rituals which we need to understand before passing judgment. In fact, as far back as 2500 years ago, Aristotle wrote that the obligation of a speaker is to acquire the "faculty or power of discovering in the particular case what are the available means of persuasion."[7] It would be foolhardy then, for any politician not to subscribe to Aristotle's dictum which includes the need to adapt to whatever medium of communication is being used. In the case of political debates, the major medium is television. And there is no disputing the fact that television, particularly in its capacity to present the candidates up close, is a medium that accentuates the formation of images.

In addition to the image implications of the piercing eye of the television camera, images are also accentuated by another reality: Debates ordinarily feature exchanges regarding public policy issues with which a large percentage of the population is moderately to poorly informed. When the public is more informed about and more interested in the issues, it is more likely to attend to the merits or demerits of the issues; when less informed, it will be more inclined to draw inferences about the candidate's personality, character, and leadership. Thus, culpability for superficiality or manipulation cannot be placed squarely on the candidates; some of the onus must be assumed by the electorate and by the other sources on which it relies for information regarding candidates and the issues.

In a related vein, regardless of whether or not image manipulation is justifiable, an equally pertinent question is whether or not it is even likely to be effective. During a televised debate can a candidate project inauthentic image traits and be believed? Very unlikely. Close-up shots of candidates are conducive to sensitizing viewers to the harmony between the candidate's verbal and nonverbal communication. If, for instance, a candidate's words of compassion are not complemented by his tone and bearing, he is sending conflicting messages. Research indicates that in such instances people tend to rely more on the source's nonverbal cues than on the spoken words.[8] Norman Cousins describes well the difficulty facing a candidate who might seek to manipulate his image:

> No amount of TV makeup can change the way a man's eyes move, or the way his lips are drawn under surges of animus or temper. When the camera burrows into a man's face, the fact that some wrinkles may be covered up by pancake makeup is not as important as the visibility of the emotions that come to the surface. The strength of the TV debates derives less from what is hidden than from what is impossible to conceal.[9]

Compounding their imprecision in discussing image, critics of debates can be faulted on two additional counts: (1) they fail to appreciate both the political realities and complexities of political debates, a point that will be expanded on throughout this book; (2) they are prone to making superficial judgments regarding not only who won and lost, but are just as superficial in analyzing why. In this latter regard, many an authoritative work has attributed Richard M. Nixon's weak performance in his first 1960 presidential debate either to his poor shave, wan appearance, perspiring brow, shifty eyes—or to any combination of these factors. Yet no empirical research supports such a conclusion. But more important, the logic behind such thinking, regardless of its popularity, is decidedly primitive; it assumes that one or a few physical cues constituted sufficient cause for influencing millions of Americans to respond more favorably to Kennedy's performance. Realistically, the debate's outcome was, as is the case with any debate, rooted in an amalgam of physical, vocal, and verbal cues resulting from discrete strategic and tactical plans formulated by each candidate.

The value of this book to students and journalists, as well as to candidates and their advisers, is rooted in three principal and unique factors: (1) it dissects the entire debate process, from the contemplated decision whether or not to debate to the media coverage following the debate; (2) it treats debates at all major levels of government, i.e., presidential, senatorial, congressional, gubernatorial, and mayoral; (3) it focuses pointedly on the interests of the three principal parties, the candidates, the sponsors, and the electorate.

The book is divided into six chapters. Chapter 1 features a case study of the 1980 presidential debates, one of the more significant and fascinating examples to be drawn from American history. Chapter 2 discusses the factors involved in deciding whether or not to debate, examining closely such axioms as "don't debate if you're ahead in the polls" or "if you're an incumbent." Chapter 3 discusses the candidate's goals and strategies, identifying the preeminence of image in the debate planning stages. Chapter 4 presents a comprehensive discussion of the tactical options available to the candidates to help fulfill their designated goals and strategies. Chapter 5 focuses on the debate format, paying particular attention to the rhetorical and political implications of their many features. Chapter 6 treats metadebating, the "debates" about debates waged in the media. The Epilogue offers recommendations for improved debates drawn from both my research and campaign experience.

This study is based on four principal sources in addition to the current literature on political campaign debates: (1) oral history interviews with eighty-three people intimately associated with major political debates held since World War Two, (2) Congressional Debate Surveys conducted in 1976, 1978, and 1981, (3) analyses of videotapes, audiotapes, and manuscripts of forty-nine political campaign debates, and (4) my experience as a debate adviser to presidential, senatorial, congressional, and gubernatorial candidates.

The oral history interviews, the first known research of this kind on political campaign debates, were conducted with the candidates themselves and their advisers and negotiators; with network executives (the sponsors); and with panelists and moderators. Each interview was tape recorded, transcribed, and analyzed.

The Congressional Debate Survey (CDS) was expanded from a pilot study in 1976 to a full-scale research project in 1978 and 1981. Five researchers were trained to conduct focused interviews with 183 randomly selected Congressional candidates or their advisers in 1978, and in 1981 with 90 Congressional and gubernatorial candidates. The interviews determined candidates' reasons for or against debating, the number of debates, the nature of the format, the amount of media coverage, and the perceived importance of the debate to the election.[10]

Over the past six years, I have assembled a large collection of audiotapes, videotapes, and manuscripts of debates on all major levels. These have been more helpful than anything else in providing me with insights about and examples of candidates' strategies and tactics, their interaction with panelists and moderators, and the implications of formats on their performances.

My experience as a debate adviser to political candidates at every major level, including most recently to Ronald Reagan, has provided me with an extraordinary opportunity to witness firsthand how debates are approached in major campaigns, including particularly the opportunity to test many of the insights I have gained since this study began in 1976.

NOTES

1. For a concise summary of the viewership data regarding the 1960 and 1976 presidential debates see: *With the Nation Watching,* Report of the Twentieth Century Fund Task Force on Televised Presidential Debates (Lexington, Massachusetts: D.C. Heath, 1979), pp. 42–43.

2. "The 1980 Presidential Debates: Behind the Scenes," booklet published by the League of Women Voters Education Fund, 1981, p. 1.

3. Based on research conducted by the author.

4. Stanley Kelley, Jr., *Political Campaigning: Problems in Creating an Informed Electorate* (Washington, D.C.: The Brookings Institution, 1960), p. 1.

5. For excellent discussions regarding the value of political debates see: Steven H. Chaffee and Jack Dennis, "Presidential Debates: An Empirical Assessment" in *The Past and Future of Presidential Debates,* ed. Austin Ranney (Washington, D.C.: American Enterprise Institute, 1979), pp. 75–102; Stanley Kelley, Jr., "Campaign Debates: Some Facts and Issues," *Public Opinion Quarterly* 26 (Fall 1962), pp. 351–366; *With the Nation Watching,* op. cit., pp. 41–49.

6. J. Jeffery Auer, "The Counterfeit Debates," in *The Great Debates: Kennedy vs. Nixon, 1960,* ed. Sidney Kraus (Bloomington, Indiana: Indiana University Press, 1962), pp. 147–148.

7. Aristotle, *The Rhetoric,* trans. Lane Cooper (New York: Appleton-Century Crofts, 1932), p. 7.

8. See: Albert Mehrahian, *Silent Messages* (Belmont, Calif.: Wadsworth, 1971), pp. 40–56. For an understanding of the cognitive processes used in interpreting conflicting or inconsistent messages, see: D. E. Bugental, "Interpretations of Naturally Occurring Discrepancies Between Words and Intonation: Modes of Inconsistent Resolution," *Journal of Personality and Social Psychology* 30 (1974), pp. 125–133.

9. *Saturday Review,* November 13, 1976, p. 4.

10. The 1980 Congressional Debate Survey (CDS) is the major source of statistical information for this book. The research proceeded in two stages. First, telephone calls were made to the offices of all incumbents included in the sample to determine if there had been a debate in the general election campaign. We read to each respondent the definition of debate we were using in the study: an occasion where two or more opposing candidates appear jointly with an opportunity to explain their positions with explicit provisions for refutation without interruption. Once we were convinced that there had been a campaign debate, we interviewed a staff member who had been involved in the debate process.

In the second stage of the research we attempted to contact the losing candidate (or a staff member) in each campaign where a debate had occurred. First we confirmed that there had been a debate. On several occasions the losing candidate asserted that although there had been a joint campaign appearance, the event did not qualify under our definition of debate. In these cases, in order not to overestimate the occurrence of campaign debates, we coded the race as "no debate." If the losing candidate confirmed the occurrence of a debate, we requested permission to mail the same questionnaire that was being sent to the winners. After allowing several weeks for return of the questionnaires, we visited incumbents' offices in Washington and telephoned losing candidates across the country to encourage nonrespondents to reply.

The response rate for incumbents was surprisingly high. All 34 Senate offices and 69 of the 79 House offices responded to our initial telephone request for information about campaign debates. Using these responses, we mailed questionnaires to the 22 Senate incumbents and 46 House incumbents who reported that they had debated. The questionnaires were returned by 37 of the 46 House members (80%) and 13 of the 22 Senate members (59%). Return rates from losing candidates were lower: 32 of 46 in the House (70%) and 8 of 22 in the Senate (36%).

1

The 1980 Presidential
Debates

The 1980 presidential debates were state-of-the-art examples of the extent to which candidates and their advisers take pains to minimize risks and maximize the gains related to every aspect of the debate process. Indeed, the 1960 and 1976 presidential debates and television's escalating primacy as a medium of political communication reinforced the sheer vastness of the stakes and the axiom "be prepared."

This drama of the behind-the-scenes events in Reagan's, Carter's, and Anderson's camps is a case study in image-oriented strategy fashioned and wielded by the best political thinkers in the business and sets the stage for many of the concepts discussed in this book. Specifically, this chapter traces the genesis of the debates, clarifies the rationales for the candidates' decisions to debate or not, describes their strategies and tactics and practice sessions, analyzes the rhetorical implications of the formats, highlights the major aspects of the debates themselves, and discusses their effects.

Genesis

The League of Women Voters, encouraged by its success in sponsoring the 1976 presidential debates between Gerald Ford and Jimmy Carter, moved early to claim sponsorship for the 1980 debates. In the spring of 1979, the League of Women Voters Education Fund received assurances from both the Democratic and the Republican National Committees that there would be no objection to the League attempting to arrange a series of presidential debates. The League's hopes were later buttressed by a Federal Election Commission ruling issued in March 1980 that allowed organizations like the League to use corporate, union, and foundation contributions to help finance events featuring candidates for national office. In July 1980, the League began contacting leading journalistic organizations to solicit recommendations for a panel of respected reporters.

On August 19, 1980, the League invited Ronald Reagan and Jimmy Carter and their running mates to take part in a series of four debates:

September 18th:	Baltimore, Maryland
October 2nd:	Louisville, Kentucky
October 13th:	Portland, Oregon
October 27th:	Cleveland, Ohio

League Education Fund Chair Ruth Hinerfeld explained that the choice of four debates had been influenced by the 1976 debates, and were selected mainly because of "geographical diversity" and the availability of League facilities and supporters.

The most controversial and politically sensitive aspect of the League's invitation was its approach to the third-party candidacy of John Anderson. The League had announced on August 10 that non–major party candidates would be allowed to participate if they were constitutionally eligible to serve as president, on the ballot in a sufficient number of states to have a mathematical possibility of winning the presidency, and if by September 10 they could demonstrate a voter support level of 15% in prominent nationwide public opinion polls. Anderson met the first two criteria, and his poll ratings, although only 10% at the time, were steadily climbing, thus making it likely that he would qualify for the proposed September 18 debate. By September 9, Anderson's ratings had hit the required 15% level, and he was formally invited to the first debate, rescheduled for September 21.

The League's decision to adopt a 15% poll rating as a requirement for participation was criticized by some for being arbitrary and for placing undue emphasis on public opinion ratings, which fluctuate rapidly in the course of a campaign and are subject to measurement error and variation in techniques. The League's defense was that to maintain its own reputation and the Federal Election Commission's recognition of it as a nonpartisan group, it had to select an easily understood objective indicator—one that would eliminate even the appearance of bias on their part. The League contended that relying on five separate polls reduced the problems arising from variations among polling techniques and imprecision. The 15% cutoff, although admittedly arbitrary, was chosen only after a study of the relationship between preelection polls and final outcomes in previous presidential elections. In the League's view, a minor party candidate able to attain a 15% level of support was, if not a credible contender, at least "a significant force in the election" whose voice should be heard.[1] Whether presidential debates should be the forum for that voice will remain a major issue facing parties involved in the American political process.

The Decision to Debate

The Carter camp reacted negatively to the League's initial announcement. It was perturbed by the League's failure to include a site in the deep South and by their selection of Louisville for only the vice-presidential debate.

Nothing, however, bothered the Carter camp as much as their belief that the League had given John Anderson's campaign a major boost. As early as May, Carter had said that he would not engage in a three-way debate involving Anderson. In June he had softened his position slightly, stating that he might agree to a three-way debate if the first debate of the campaign would be a one-on-one with Ronald Reagan. But now, because of Anderson's eligibility to participate, the League had made it especially difficult for Carter to avoid a three-way debate. Carter had good reason to prefer a two-man format. Anderson was expected by each of the candidates' pollsters to drain more votes from Carter than from Reagan. Carter thus had no interest in appearing in a debate that would not only give Anderson much-needed exposure, but would also present him to the American public on an equal plane with the two major-party nominees.

The Carter camp, therefore, decided that its candidate would not debate if Anderson were included. Among Carter's major advisers, only Stuart Eizenstat argued that Carter should accept the League's invitation. He contended that Carter had already refused to debate Edward Kennedy in the Democratic primaries and should not risk acquiring or reinforcing the image of a man afraid to confront his opponents. Eizenstat also expected that Carter would perform well in the debate.[2] The remainder of Carter's inner circle, however, agreed with Carter's pollster Pat Caddell's argument that the public outcry over Carter's avoiding the debate would soon subside and be forgotten by Election Day, still six weeks off.

To reduce the political damage to Carter, his advisers decided on a two-pronged strategy. First, Carter and his spokesmen would imply that the League's standards for including Anderson were set in a partisan and arbitrary fashion, and that a two-way debate between Reagan and Anderson would be merely a debate between two partisan Republicans. They hoped to thereby cast doubt on both the neutrality of the League and the signifance of the debate. Second, the Carter campaign would encourage other organizations to issue invitations for face-to-face debates with Ronald Reagan. This ploy allowed Carter's camp to turn the tables on Reagan, portraying him as the one who was avoiding debates. The National Press Club, among others, quickly took the cue, and on August 25 announced its willingness to sponsor a two-man debate. Carter accepted on August 26, and, as expected, Reagan declined the following day.

Reagan's advisers never seriously considered Carter's offer of an initial two-man debate. They knew as well as Carter that boosting Anderson's campaign would cost Carter far more votes than Reagan. Moreover, by championing Anderson's inclusion, Reagan could present himself as being "fair" to the electorate while implying that Carter was afraid to debate Anderson. Reagan, therefore, took the position that in fairness to the League and to John Anderson, he could not debate Carter in any other forum until after the first scheduled debate. This allowed him to take full advantage of the opportunity the League was offering him now, while holding onto the option of accepting another forum at a later date.

When Carter formally refused the League's invitation on September 9, three hours after Anderson had been invited to participate, the Reagan camp faced a tougher decision. Should Reagan debate Anderson alone? There were several disadvantages to doing so. Of primary concern was the "gaffe" issue, since within the past month Reagan had made several ill-advised statements during his speeches and press conferences. A second concern, voiced by Jim Baker, the head of Reagan's debate task force, was whether debating Anderson would be "putting yourself in the category of a token candidate when you go out and debate a token candidate and let the President of the United States sit on the sidelines."[3]

Despite these reservations, Reagan decided to accept the League's invitation. I argued that although Reagan might gain little by debating, he could lose more by refusing, especially since he had spent the past month championing Anderson's participation. As David Gergen, a key Reagan adviser, said later, "to appear to be ducking a debate would be more damaging than the debate itself."[4] I also noted that Reagan would "strike a pleasing contrast against Anderson who comes off as too intense and even cocksure."[5] A solid performance might also put an end to the gaffe issue for Reagan. Moreover, at this point Ronald Reagan still needed exposure. According to Richard Wirthlin, Reagan's pollster and chief strategist, "from a perceptual point of view, Reagan was known but not well known. Fully 40% of the electorate said that they knew very little about Ronald Reagan and what he stood for."[6]

For Anderson, the decision to debate was almost automatic. As Bob Walker, a key Anderson aide, told me, "Unless we had been included in the first debate, the Anderson campaign would have been doomed."[7] By September 16, Anderson's campaign was a half-million dollars in debt. David Garth, the prominent campaign strategist who had been given complete control of Anderson's campaign in late August, was transforming the focus of the campaign from a grass-roots approach to qualify for state ballots to fundraising activities to underwrite a media-based campaign. Anderson desperately needed the free exposure of a presidential debate to stimulate campaign contributions. Anderson also expected that he would more than hold his own with Reagan in the debate. Anderson's oratorical skills were highly regarded, and his previous performance in the Republican primary forums had given him confidence that his sharpness, knowledge of issues, and command of detail would contrast well with Reagan's approach and positions.[8]

Strategies

John Anderson's strategy for the debate was difficult to define and to execute. Public opinion polls showed that most of his support came from voters who would otherwise have supported Carter. If Anderson was to improve his standing significantly, he would have to do it by taking votes away from Carter. How could this best be done? An all-out attack on Carter had several disadvantages. First, attacking the President when he is not present to defend himself might be perceived as unfair. This potential problem, however, could be reduced somewhat by focusing the attack on Carter's record and policies rather than on the man himself. Complicating this strategy was another constraint, expressed by Anderson to columnists Evans and Novak: "If I attack Carter, I begin to look like a pale imitation of Ronald Reagan, and I'm not that, I'm not that."[9] Anderson's remaining options were simply to "sell" his own positions, avoiding any major attacks on Carter or Reagan, or to concentrate his fire on Reagan. A few days before the debate, Anderson announced that he intended to attack Reagan hard—to emphasize the differences between them. Anderson wanted to make it clear to those who were dissatisfied with Jimmy Carter's performance but still doubtful about Ronald Reagan that there was an alternative.

Reagan's goal for this debate was to perform "very respectably"—to present a "respectable" answer to each question, to remain presidential—against the man considered to be one of the House of Representatives' outstanding orators. As the strategy was developed, Reagan was expected to do well against Anderson. He had, it was generally agreed, outperformed him during the New Hampshire and Illinois primary debates.[10]

Reagan's specific goals were to emphasize Carter's incompetent leadership and to project his own "reasonableness, moderation and sensitivity," especially since a significant portion of the electorate believed he possessed the opposite traits. As stated in a pre-debate memo prepared by Richard Wirthlin and Richard Beal, his assistant, "it is more important in the debate to show the Governor's judgment, sense of balance and moderation and control than to explain his position on each and every issue."[11] Toward this end our greatest hope strategically was for Anderson to attack Carter harder than Reagan. Such a scenario would allow Reagan to minimize defending his own positions, to pay less attention to Anderson's, and to focus on the salient negative aspects of Carter's record. In fact, several conversations with Reagan were aimed at developing a "pass through" strategy which would have him talking "through" Anderson to take on Carter's record.[12]

Two more related tactical issues also surfaced before the Baltimore debate. First, to what extent should Reagan stress Carter's absence? Second, how forceful should Reagan's anti-Carter attacks be? Our concern for a possible voter backlash prompted us to counsel Reagan not to overplay Carter's absence and to temper his anti-Carter attacks. The risk of overplaying Carter's absence was, however, effectively reduced when the League decided against placing a lectern in the center of the stage to symbolize Carter's absence.

The most controversial tactical issue raised before the debate concerned whether or not Reagan should during his closing address challenge Carter to a one-on-one debate. Reagan's advisers had initially wanted to avoid a debate, not wanting to risk their comfortable lead over Carter. However, Reagan's gaffes in early September had weakened his position and thereby led some of his advisers to conclude that a dramatic event such as a debate challenge to Carter was necessary to reverse the downward slide of the campaign. The final decision, though, was against issuing the challenge.

Candidate Preparations

Anderson entered the debate with a minimum of preparation. He was confident that he knew the issues well enough to dispense with issue-briefings. Despite the requests of his staff, he also refused to engage in simulations or formal practice sessions. In fact, he held only two brief meetings with the staff before the debate in which they provided him with two to three minute answers to likely questions. Bob Walker of Anderson's campaign told me that the predictable nature of Reagan's responses lessened the need for extensive practice. Anderson did, however, watch videotapes of the Republican primary forum in Iowa, where he had done well, and of the March forum in Illinois, where he appeared nervous and defensive.

Reagan's preparation was far more elaborate. A Debate Task Force was formed in mid-August by James Baker, Gerald Ford's campaign manager in 1976 and George Bush's in 1980. The Task Force was Baker's first major campaign project—an opportunity for him to display his political prowess to the major Reagan advisers who, until the convention, knew him as the general in the enemy camp. A tough but amiable master organizer with impressive political acumen and negotiating skill, Baker convinced other senior Reagan advisers of the importance of forming a debate team composed primarily of people not intimately involved in the day-to-day management of the campaign. In that way, the Task Force could devote most of its energy to the debates.

Members of the Task Force, in addition to Baker, included Bill Carruthers, Frank Ursomarso, David Gergen, Frank Hodsoll, and me. Carruthers, a top-notch Hollywood television producer who had served as Gerald Ford's media adviser in 1976, and who was serving in a similar capacity for Reagan, would take charge of technical preparations and would become one of Reagan's negotiators with the sponsor of both debates, the League of Women Voters. Ursomarso, an accomplished advance man for Ford and Nixon who had headed the advance operation for the 1976 presidential debates, would do the same for the 1980 debates. Gergen, who had served as head of the White House Office of Communications under Ford, would head up the preparation of Reagan's briefing materials. Hodsoll, a former State Department official (Deputy U.S. Representative for Nonproliferation of Nuclear Arms) and an exceptional administrator with a well-disciplined legal mind, would manage the research and the administration of the debate preparations. I had served as a debate adviser to several candidates and was brought to Baker's attention by Ursomarso and Carruthers whom I met while conducting research for this book. My main responsibilities involved defining and briefing Reagan on the strategic and tactical options available to him and critiquing the presentational aspects of his practice debates.

At the outset, the Task Force faced the possibility that all its work might be in vain, for there was no clear assurance that Reagan would be willing to devote much of his time to debate preparations. He had, after all, prepared very little for the Republican primary debates, but did well in them anyway.

On September 18, we began three days of intensive meetings with Reagan at his home. Originally, formal briefings were planned for each morning, and practice question and answer sessions for the afternoons. However, we soon discovered that Reagan felt most comfortable in and derived his greatest stimulation from the question and answer sessions critiqued by his advisers. As a result, we spent the afternoon of the first day and the entire preparation time of the next two days in his garage, a building Carruthers had converted into a professional quality television studio. The studio, a 20-foot by 30-foot carpeted room that would also be used for the Cleveland debate, was complete with eighteen theatrical lights, two television cameras, two monitors, a replica of the lectern to be used in Baltimore, two professional cameramen, and a lighting expert.

The initial sessions involved questions posed to Reagan by major advisers and key aides acting as panelists. Participating in at least one session were economic and domestic policy advisers Martin Anderson, Alan Greenspan, William Simon, and Caspar Weinberger; foreign policy and military advisers Richard Allen, William Van Cleve, and Stefan Halper; Senators Howard Baker (R., Tenn.) and John Tower (R., Tex.); Representatives Margaret Heckler (R., Mass.) and Richard Cheney (R., Wyo.); Professors Jeanne Kirkpatrick (Georgetown University) and Michael Boskin (Stanford University), and journalists George Will and Pat Buchanan. Following each question or round of questions, Reagan's responses were critiqued by panelists and other advisers for accuracy, completeness, strategic and tactical soundness, and persuasiveness.

On September 19, two days before the Baltimore debate, John Anderson's stand-in arrived on the scene. David Stockman, a bright, articulate two-term Congressman from Michigan who had once served as John Anderson's administrative assistant, impressed all of us with a realistic portrayal of his former boss. The air of competition imposed by Stockman's role helped make Reagan's answers more pointed and his style more self-assured.

One of the discussions leading up to the debate with Anderson concerned whether Reagan should arrive in Baltimore by car, helicopter, or airplane. Following Carruthers' advice, an airplane was chosen because it was regarded as a "more presidential" means of transportation. Indeed, this decision illustrates the understanding within the Reagan camp—and certainly within the Anderson and Carter camps as well—that the debate was an event whose implications far exceeded what a mere exchange of verbal blows between the candidates seemed to represent.

The Debate Format

The format negotiations for the Anderson-Reagan debate were relatively uncomplicated, since Anderson's negotiator, Mitchell Rogovin, did not want

TABLE 1.1   Reagan vs. Anderson, Baltimore Debate, September 21, 1980

Each of the candidates was required to respond to the same question. The format of a question round was as follows:
   Question No. 1: 30 seconds
   Candidate A response: 2:30
   Question No. 2 restated to Candidate B: 30 seconds
   Candidate B response: 2:30
   Candidate A rejoinder: 1:15
   Candidate B rejoinder: 1:15

There were no opening statements, and closing statements were limited to three minutes per candidate.

Panelists: Bill Moyers, PBS, moderator
         Charles Corddry, *Baltimore Sun*
         Soma Golden, *New York Times*
         Daniel Greenberg, syndicated columnist
         Carol Loomis, *Fortune* magazine
         Lee May, *Los Angeles Times*
         Jane Bryant Quinn, *Newsweek* magazine

to place a demand on the negotiating table that might prompt Reagan's withdrawal from the debate. As he told me, "We would have debated the 50¢ gas tax for an hour if that's what they wanted."[13] He did seek a ninety-minute debate to increase Anderson's exposure and to highlight his expertise, and to place a greater energy burden on the sixty-nine-year-old Reagan. However, Rogovin settled quickly for an hour-long debate, although it would reduce the possibility that Reagan might commit a gaffe or be caught uninformed.

The League proposed that each of six journalists ask one question, to be repeated for each candidate. (See Table 1.1.) The format represented a slight advantage to Reagan. The Anderson camp would have preferred a greater number of questions to display its candidate's command of detail, and to present more opportunities for a Reagan gaffe. However, it did not push this demand in the negotiations, and agreed to accept the League's format. As Jim Baker said later, "We got what we wanted in the Anderson debate. They (Anderson's people) wanted that debate so bad that there was very little negotiation."[14]

The Debate

During the debate, Anderson's attacks on Reagan were more restrained than he had announced they would be and than Reagan's advisers had expected. He focused on drawing a contrast between himself and Reagan based on the issues, rather than on attacking Reagan personally. In part, this approach may have been spurred by his recognition that Reagan's genial personality made him difficult to attack (as Jimmy Carter was to learn five weeks later). Anderson also may have decided that it was more important for him to establish his own credentials, to sell himself as a serious candidate, than to attack Reagan.[15]

Anderson did take advantage of every opportunity to distinguish himself from Reagan on the issues. The first question, about inflation, elicited the charge that Reagan's across-the-board tax cut proposal was "irresponsible."[16] In rebuttal to a Reagan answer on energy policy, Anderson said that Reagan "has demonstrated, I think, a total misunderstanding of the energy crisis . . ." Finding that he and Reagan agreed on the next question, on military manpower, Anderson changed the subject: "Unlike Governor Reagan, I do not support a boondoggle like the MX missile." In replying to a question about his own economic assumptions, Anderson inserted George Bush's characterization (raised during the primary) of Reagan's economic program as "voodoo economics." Reagan, meanwhile, was ignoring the attacks, as he had been advised to do. It was strategically wise not to engage John Anderson any more than necessary.

At the end of the debate, both sides had cause to be pleased. Anderson had received the exposure that he needed, and campaign contributions increased dramatically in the days immediately following the debate.[17] The *Washington Star* reported that a panel of debate experts judged Anderson to have outperformed Reagan.[18] Several public opinion polls found that the general public, by a slight margin, also thought that Anderson had "won." Unfortunately for Anderson, however, the debate marked the high point of his campaign, for within a few days his public opinion ratings experienced a steady decline that he could not reverse. The Reagan forces saw the debate as an important victory for their candidate. Jim Baker, pointing to the successes yielded by the debate, explained, "we wanted [Anderson's] campaign to be legitimized and upgraded, and we also wanted whatever forum we could find to dispel the notion that the Governor was a dangerous bomb-thrower."[19] The debate also put the gaffe issue some distance behind Reagan, and at least temporarily placed Jimmy Carter in an uncomfortable position due to his failure to participate.

A Second Debate?

No one was sure following the Reagan-Anderson debate whether or not there would be another debate in the 1980 campaign. Anderson was, of course, anxious to debate, but the Carter and Reagan camps were interested only under certain conditions. Carter was standing by the position that he had adopted in June, that he would consider joining Anderson and Reagan in a three-way debate, but only after a one-on-one encounter with Reagan. The League, fearful that there might be no further debates, or that Reagan or Carter might agree to meet under another organization's sponsorship, decided to modify its original position. On September 25, the League offered to sponsor a two-man debate if both candidates would agree to include Anderson in a third debate. Carter accepted immediately, but the Reagan camp declined, insisting that Anderson deserved to be included in any debate.

Concurrent with the League's new offer was its invitation to the three vice-presidential contenders to debate in Louisville. Carter's and Anderson's running mates, Walter Mondale and Patrick Lucey, accepted, but Reagan's running mate, George Bush, declined. Mondale then withdrew, effectively cancelling the debate.

By the end of September, Reagan's advisers had decided that a one-on-one with Carter was not, at least at that point in the campaign, in Reagan's best interest. The consensus among his advisers throughout the campaign had been that a direct confrontation with Carter should be avoided. Reagan had started out with a thirty-point lead over Carter, and had no reason to hazard it in such a high-risk situation as a debate. This decision against a one-on-one debate was made despite a discouraging downtrend in Reagan's lead: NBC had Reagan leading Carter by only ten points on September 24, while CBS had him leading by six. However, having criticized Carter for his refusal to debate, Reagan could not now afford to be seen as ducking a debate. Therefore the Reagan camp made a counterproposal: a round-robin series of three, two-man debates in which each candidate would meet each of his rivals. The order of the debates would be determined by lot. As expected, Carter rejected this proposal, but it did have the effect of protecting Reagan's public image and delaying the decision about facing Carter in a one-to-one debate.

The next step came from the League, which announced on October 14 that it would reassess John Anderson's "significance" as a candidate. Relying on the latest polling data, the Education Fund declared three days later that Anderson no longer met the minimum standard of 15-percent support, and announced that it would attempt to sponsor a two-man debate between Carter and Reagan.

The Decision to Debate

By mid-October the calculations in both the Reagan and Carter camps were changing. Reagan's camp was now starting to react favorably to the debate, while Carter's was backing away.

Among Reagan's top advisers, only Richard Wirthlin and William Timmons argued that Reagan should decline the League's invitation. Wirthlin's polls, which were being conducted daily, showed Reagan with only a 6-percent lead over Carter. However, Wirthlin was confident that this lead would increase over the remaining weeks, and did not want to risk a major setback in a debate, expecially one that would occur so late in the campaign. In Wirthlin's words, "By the 16th of October, when the decision to debate was made, we were starting to pull ahead of Carter, and once I saw that light, I felt confident that we were going to win the election. . . . I felt we could beat Carter without the debate."[20]

Wirthlin was confident because the campaign appeared to be unfolding just as he had planned.[21] His strategy, spelled out in an October 9 memorandum, had been to have Reagan appeal to his natural conservative and Republican base from the convention until mid-September. This was Reagan's so-called "gaffe period," but Wirthlin was willing to accept some negative press early in the campaign as a necessary cost of shoring up Reagan's base. The Baltimore debate occurred at the end of this phase, and contributed to the major goal of Stage II in Wirthlin's campaign, which was to extend Reagan's appeal to moderates and independents. This stage was scheduled to last from mid-September to mid-October. Finally, Reagan in the last two weeks of the campaign, after establishing himself as a credible candidate, would turn to an attack on Carter. Wirthlin, eyeing a 6-percent Reagan lead in mid-October, was sure that the attack phase of the campaign had recently gotten an unexpected boost when Carter's strident attacks on Reagan had raised the issue of a "mean streak" in Jimmy Carter. With everything going Reagan's way, Wirthlin saw no need for a debate.

Reinforcing Wirthlin's position, Timmons argued that Reagan's great organizational advantage over Carter made a debate unnecessary. The Reagan campaign had saved $6 million of its $15 million media budget for the final ten days, and had far more local workers to bring out the vote on election day than Carter had. A two-man debate might also diminish John Anderson's position further, which could hurt Reagan. Finally, Timmons argued that a debate late in the campaign might spur public interest in the election and increase the turnout of marginal voters, who would more likely harm Reagan.[22]

The other Reagan advisers favored a debate. They were less inclined to rely heavily on Wirthlin's figures, especially since most of the national polls showed Reagan in a decline and the press was making much of the downturn. Several of Reagan's key advisers felt that some dramatic development was needed to reverse the negative press coverage. Also, it was feared that Carter might pull an "October Surprise" for example, a dramatic announcement about the Iranian hostage situation. A debate late in the campaign would assure that Reagan would not be crowded out of news coverage in the critical final days of the campaign. Finally, it would have been extremely difficult for Reagan to justify a refusal to debate Carter now that Anderson was no longer a factor.

Reagan's advisers also acknowledged the potential benefits to a debate. According to Baker, Reagan still had not completely shed his foreign-affairs image problems:

> We were getting killed with the war issue, and the only way you can dispell that is to get him before a large group. But you can't buy enough time to do

that, and Wirthlin's argument was that we just ought to buy 30-minute segments and go that route. Eventually the campaign came down on the other side of it, and we decided that we ought to go ahead and debate.[23]

This decision was made easier by the events of October 16, the day of the Alfred E. Smith dinner in New York City where both Reagan and Carter appeared. There Reagan clearly outshone Carter in his speech, apparently adding to his confidence that he could handle Carter in a debate.[24]

The next day, after hearing the pro and con arguments of his advisers, Reagan made his decision: "Well, everything considered, I feel I should debate. If I'm going to fill the shoes of Carter, I should be willing to meet him face-to-face."[25] According to Wirthlin, Reagan made his decision not so much on the basis of political calculations, as "on the basis that it was the 'fair thing to do.' "[26] Baker also believes that Reagan had largely decided to debate Carter before hearing the pros and cons presented by his advisers:

> I'm convinced without really knowing for sure, that he, himself, pretty much decided out there that he ought to debate and that generated questions to Spencer [Stuart Spencer, an adviser who travelled with Reagan], who then picked up the phone and called me and said, "Let me have a memo on debate pros and cons."[27]

Reagan's decision gave the Carter forces the opportunity they had been looking for throughout the campaign. However, a pre-debate memo by Patrick Caddell, Carter's pollster, indicates clearly that the Carter forces no longer saw the debate as an opportunity:

> The debate on October 28 offers some advantages and is fraught with great risks. The risks far outweigh the possible advantages. . . . There is a 75% chance that Carter will 'lose' the debate even if he 'wins' on points, á la Anderson. There is only at best a 25% chance that the President will 'win' in real and hard terms.[28]

Caddell's analysis of his own polling data led him to conclusions contrary to Wirthlin's. Caddell believed that Carter was gaining ground on Reagan, and would continue to improve his position over the next few weeks. A debate, he felt, might allow Reagan to break Carter's momentum, particularly since, in Caddell's words, "Debates are the vehicles of challengers."[29] Without a debate, Caddell thought that the public's doubts about Reagan on the war and peace issue might be strong enough to give Carter the election. He further contended that if Reagan could use the debate to dispel the doubts about his own personality and to focus attention on the Carter record, he would be nearly impossible to defeat.

Despite these calculations, Carter accepted the League's invitation to debate. After the election, Caddell explained: "Well, we had already committed to a debate. Our problem was after the Reagan campaign had accepted, we could not then get up and say, 'By the way, we've been kidding all this time; we're not going to have a debate,' without really being chewed up."[30]

Strategies

Reagan's main strategy is captured in the opening paragraph of the strategy memorandum prepared for him:

> If the Governor succeeds Tuesday in making Jimmy Carter's record the major issue of the debate and the campaign, we will succeed in the debate and win the general election.
>
> If, however, Carter makes Ronald Reagan the issue of the debate and the campaign, we will lose both.[31]

Of Reagan's two major goals—dispelling doubts about himself and attacking the Carter record—top priority was given the former. This decision was based in part on the belief within the Reagan camp that "The Governor has already built a coalition large enough to win the presidential election . . ."[32] Reagan's advisors thought that it was not necessary to try to undermine Carter's coalition further by a vigorous attack; rather, Reagan should use the debate to reinforce a positive perception of himself by those already intending to support him or leaning in his direction. As stated in another strategy memorandum: "The goal of this debate is to *perform very respectably.* Therefore we do not seek to hit a home run or to win the World Series."[33]

Consequently, Reagan's advisers concentrated on one major question: How can Reagan best counter Carter's apparent success in recent weeks in portraying Reagan as dangerous—as far too inclined to use military force before exhausting diplomatic initiatives. Dozens of meetings and general conversations focused on whether or not Reagan should explicitly attack Carter for exploiting this fear tactic. Might not such an approach project undue defensiveness or result in effective counterargument by Carter? No agreement was reached within the Task Force on this question. Reagan felt, and no one within the inner circle disagreed, that he could defuse his "dangerous" image by remaining good-natured and "presidential." This could be accomplished by focusing as much as possible on Carter's domestic failures rather than on defense and foreign policy issues, and by allowing Carter to establish the attack tone of the debate. In this latter regard, Reagan was advised not to surpass, but to respond in kind, to the tone and degree of attack leveled by Carter. Attacking too hard, most advisers felt, could result in voter backlash and reinforce the "mad bomber" perception.

The specific tactical advice given to Reagan in his debate preparations followed from these considerations. Reagan was advised to avoid defensiveness in responding to Carter's attacks, and instead to project righteous indignation. Rather than presenting an extended defense of his own positions, he should turn as quickly as possible to Carter's record. At all times, whether on the defense or the attack, Reagan should remain good-humored and restrained. Contrary to our strategy, however, several of the memoranda received from prominent Republicans advocated a "no holds barred" attack on Carter's record, anticipating that Carter would direct such an attack against Reagan—

which, in fact, he did not do. No one on the Debate Task Force (myself included) expected Carter to direct such an assault. We believed that he would attempt, instead, to soften his recently publicized reputation for "meanness."

Carter's strategy memoranda show that his advisers were making many calculations similar to Reagan's. Samuel Popkin, a political scientist from the University of California at San Diego, wrote in a memorandum to Patrick Caddell:

> If the debate talks about four years of inflation and unemployment the election becomes a referendum on the Carter Presidency. We want a vote between two futures, not a vote of approval or disapproval on the last four years. . . . We want people to walk into the voting booth wondering about the next four years under a seasoned, tried-under-fire Carter . . . versus the next few years under a man with dangerous tendencies, dubious judgment . . . who doesn't understand the 80's.[34]

However, Carter's advisers recognized that it would not be easy to attack Reagan directly on these points. For one thing, as Popkin noted, "It is impossible both to look Presidential and to attack Reagan."[35] Thus, Carter's advisers recognized, as did Reagan's, that an aggressive attack might revive the "meanness" issue. They also acknowledged that Reagan would not be an easy target. As Patrick Caddell noted pointedly in his strategy memo:

> There is a temptation to pin Reagan down by firing direct challenges at him. . . . Examination of his past debates, however, shows him to be skilled at evading challenges with a variety of diversionary tactics. . . . We do not need to catch Reagan and we couldn't if we wanted to.[36]

Rather than trying to force Reagan to defend his past statements, Carter's strategy was "to educate the audience about Reagan's elusiveness." In Caddell's words, "We want to give Reagan enough rope to hang himself with foolish, simplistic answers, and not let him get away with meaningless, high sounding homilies." Carter's task was to argue, not that Reagan's specific policies were inappropriate, but that his answers were vague, simplistic, and evasive. "Ideally the audience should be drawn into an amiable game in which each of Reagan's responses is watched closely to see if he ducks or doesn't understand another issue."[37]

Carter was advised to focus as much as possible on foreign affairs, in particular on the issue of nuclear proliferation. Carter's advisers knew, however, that Reagan would try to focus the debate on the economy, so they devised a defense for this issue. When pressed, Carter would make a brief defense of his economic policies involving three major points: the economic problems the country is facing are worldwide and unprecedented, the situation is improving, and we have learned from experience. The heart of the response, however, was to meet attack with attack. Carter was instructed to turn quickly to Reagan's economic proposals, and attempt to put Reagan on the defensive here, on his own chosen ground.[38]

Reagan's Preparations

The Task Force's first meeting with Reagan in preparation for Cleveland was held on October 25, four days before the debate. I began the session by presenting him with a 40-minute, videotaped debate profile of Jimmy Carter based principally on excerpts drawn from the 1976 presidential debates. This program was intended to be educational and motivational. Educationally, it conveyed to Reagan (and to Congressman Stockman, now the Carter stand-in) what I perceived as Carter's meanness toward Ford, his evasiveness, proneness to attack, and penchant for specifics. Motivationally, it was intended to instill a fighting spirit in the governor, who is not naturally combative. In fact, his good-naturedness probably accounted for his treading a bit too lightly on Carter's record during the Baltimore debate.

Shortly after this presentation, Wirthlin, Baker, and I briefed the governor on strategy and tactics. The seven points stressed most were:

1. Keep the debate focused as much as possible on Carter's record. Meet offensive with offensive. Don't feel obligated to defend particulars of your position.
2. Show righteous indignation in responding to:
   a. Carter's attacks or innuendos that you are dangerous.
   b. Attacks directed at your California credentials. Looking directly at Carter in such instances may be very effective.
3. Humor or a confident smile can also disarm Carter when he thinks he's got you where he wants you.
4. When Carter is speaking—expecially when he is attacking you—look at him or take notes.
5. Wherever possible, weave your major theme into your responses: "Jimmy Carter has had his chance and has blown it (relate to examples that fit question); I offer promise—hope."
6. Conclude your responses with an attack line against Carter or a people-oriented line based on your proposals.
7. Show compassion by drawing from experiences on the campaign trail. . . .[39]

The remaining two and a half days before the Cleveland debate were devoted principally to practice sessions. Carruthers served as moderator while Reagan's major economic, domestic, and foreign policy advisers (including several from outside the campaign staff) played the role of panelist along with Martin Anderson, Hayden Bryan, and me. Anderson was Reagan's chief domestic adviser in the campaign, while Bryan (who took a vacation leave to work on the debate preparations) was a policy analyst for the Labor and Human Resources Committee of the U.S. Senate. Baker chaired the critique sessions which generally followed each round of questions.

As was the case leading up to the Baltimore debate, Reagan was at his best when Stockman (Carter's stand-in) was doggedly on the attack. Particularly during the Sunday practice session, Stockman's taunting could not throw Reagan off balance. Reagan displayed impressive equanimity, increasing responsiveness, and a greater willingness to attack Carter's record. Moreover, there were no gaffes during this or any other session; in short, Reagan appeared ready for Carter.

On Monday, October 27, the morning before the debate, the atmosphere became tense. Not only did the stakes of the debate seem more pronounced than ever, but Reagan was having difficulty hitting his stride. The uncertain Iranian hostage crisis was apparently wearing on him. And compounding these pressures was the burden of reviewing refined position statements on Iran and SALT II which had been prepared throughout the day by his major advisers.

Following a lengthy lunch the same day with former President Ford, Reagan returned to the studio for the last practice session before Cleveland. It, too, was unimpressive, leaving the team with an uneasy feeling about how he would perform in Cleveland. Reagan, however, appeared less worried, remarking in typical good humor that a perfect dress rehearsal was always the best way to ruin the opening night.

Carter's Preparations

Jimmy Carter had, of course, participated in three presidential debates during the 1976 campaign. Despite this experience, Carter's top adviser, Hamilton Jordan, urged substantial preparation for the Cleveland debate, and Carter, though he disliked debate practice, agreed. Three practice sessions were scheduled, the first being held on Sunday, October 26, at Camp David. As usual, Carter relied heavily on a small group of loyalists. Media adviser Gerald Rafshoon set up two lecterns, cameras, and lights. Also present at this and subsequent practice sessions were pollster Patrick Caddell, press secretary Jody Powell, Jordan, and domestic policy adviser Stuart Eizenstat. Rosalyn Carter also attended one of the practice sessions in Cleveland. The Camp David session lasted approximately 90 minutes, while the two Cleveland sessions were one hour each. The Cleveland hotel room was supplied with practice equipment, including lecterns, cameras, lights, and videotape facilities.[40]

Samuel Popkin served as a stand-in for Reagan in each practice session, while Jody Powell played the panelists' role in questioning Popkin and Carter. Popkin had mastered many of Reagan's standard lines, and he launched into a blistering attack on Carter. Popkin reported that Carter seemed surprised to find himself under attack, adding:

President Carter tried turning the presidential eyebrow on me, and I just skipped right past it. After all, it's every professor's dream to lecture the President of the United States. . . . He didn't have the presidential aura—he stumbled and sputtered a little bit, and gave me lots of openings to come back at him with real Reagan rhetoric.[41]

In the last session in Cleveland, Carter finally had an impressive workout and convinced his advisers that he was ready for Ronald Reagan.

Carter supplemented the debate practice by watching videotapes of himself and Reagan in debate, and studying briefing books prepared under the supervision of Stuart Eizenstat, his domestic policy adviser, and Zbigniew Brzezinski, his foreign affairs adviser.

On the morning of the debate, Carter, rather than resting for the most important event of the campaign, rose early to jog in a heavy downpour. The television cameras were poised to greet him at the end of his daily regimen and captured an out-of-breath and drenched President, hardly an image to complement the one he wanted to project during the debate.

The Debate Format

Negotiations over the format did not proceed as smoothly as they had for the Reagan-Anderson debate. Like Anderson, Carter wanted a long (two-hour) debate while Reagan preferred a shorter, one-hour format. Carter's negotiators also fought for surrebuttals and follow-up questions, which they thought would serve to Carter's advantage as the more informed candidate. The date of the debate became a significant but temporary issue. Reagan's camp wanted a late debate, in fact as late as election eve, to maximize the expected positive impact of Reagan's performance. Carter's wanted an early debate, which would reduce Reagan's time for preparation, give the Carter forces more time to capitalize on any misstatement that Reagan might make, and provide more time for any positive impact of Reagan's performance to diminish.[42] The LWVEF urged that the debate format dispense with panelists and use just a moderator, as had been done in the Illinois Republican Forum. This suggestion was abandoned when both candidates insisted on the customary panel of journalists. The candidates' dissatisfaction with the performance of similar panels in the past was apparently no match for their fear of a largely unstructured encounter.

The format finally agreed upon is the most complex ever devised for a presidential debate. (See Table 1.2.) The hour-and-a-half length was a compromise. The inclusion of follow-up questions in half the debate was a plus for Carter. The date, an exact week before the election, served Reagan's advantage.

The Debate

Carter successfully concentrated on the war and peace issue. In response to the opening question on foreign policy, Carter implied that Reagan's foreign

TABLE 1.2   Reagan vs. Carter, Cleveland Debate,
October 28, 1980

Format I

Four first-round questions:

Question to Candidate A:	:30
Candidate A response:	2:00
Follow-up question:	:30
Candidate A response:	1:00
Same question to Candidate B:	:30
Candidate B response:	2:00
Follow-up question:	:30
Candidate B response:	1:00
Candidate A rebuttal:	1:00
Candidate B rebuttal:	1:00
TOTAL	10:00

(4 × 10 minutes = 40 minutes)

Format II

Four second-round questions:

Question to Candidate A:	:30
Candidate A response:	2:00
Same question to Candidate B:	:30
Candidate B response:	2:00
Candidate A rebuttal:	1:30
Candidate B rebuttal:	1:30
Candidate A surrebuttal:	1:00
Candidate B surrebuttal:	1:00
TOTAL	10:00

(4 × 10 minutes = 40 minutes)

Closing Statements

Candidate A:	3 minutes
Candidate B:	3 minutes
Moderator close:	.5 minute

Panelists: Howard K. Smith, moderator
Harry Ellis, *Christian Science Monitor*
William Hilliard, *Portland Oregonian*
Marvin Stone, *U.S. News and World Report*
Barbara Walters, ABC News

policy positions are "neat and plausible and wrong," and continued by saying that "Governor Reagan has traditionally advocated the injection of military forces into troubling areas. . . ." Throughout the debate, Carter continually refocused on foreign affairs, saying such things as: "the control of nuclear weapons . . . is the most important single issue in this campaign"; "inflation, unemployment, the cities, are all very important issues, but they pale into insignificance in the life and duties of a president, when compared with the control of nuclear weapons"; and "the most important crucial difference in this election campaign . . . is the approach to the control of nuclear weaponry."

In general, Carter was able to control the issues covered in the debate, keeping Reagan on the defensive not only on foreign affairs issues but also on Social Security, energy policy, and the Equal Rights Amendment. Reagan spent much of the debate explaining that his views were not "very dangerous, disturbing," and even "radical" as Carter claimed. Carter therefore survived the debate with a minimum amount of attention focused on his economic record.

Carter was also able to include well expressed special appeals to key constituencies such as Blacks and Hispanics, Women, Jews, and the South. Reagan failed to make these specific appeals. Throughout the practice sessions for both debates, I noticed that Reagan rarely referred to specific target audiences and interest groups, or to George Bush, his running mate. As a consequence, I received permission from Jim Baker to place a list on Reagan's podium that might prompt him to incorporate targeted appeals into his responses. Some of the words on the list were: blacks, unemployed, poor, senior citizens, Israel, young marrieds. Seldom, however, did his responses during the practice or actual debates contain such appeals.

Carter's advisers claimed to be pleased with his performance. The President, said Patrick Caddell, "didn't do everything I wanted him to do, but he did 75% of it."[43] It is doubtful, however, that Caddell was as satisfied as he appeared to be. His pre-debate strategy memorandum had stressed that Carter would "truly win" the debate if he could present Reagan as an unreasonable and dangerous candidate. A close debate victory for Carter, in which Reagan came off as a responsible and credible opponent, would in fact be a loss for the President in the wider context of the campaign. As Caddell said later, "You have to score a knock-out, and there was no way to do that with Reagan."[44]

Reagan avoided a knock-out and achieved his own goal of a respectable showing by following his strategy closely. He maintained his genial personality throughout, and deflected Carter's attack with a combination of humor and righteous indignation, saying with a smile, "That is a misstatement, of course, of my position"; "Well, that just isn't true"; and "Barbara, you've asked that question twice. I think you ought to have an answer." However, the best example of this tactic was Reagan's use of the line, "There you go again," when responding to a potentially damaging attack by Carter. Reagan had been advised during the strategy sessions and the videotape analysis of Carter's debate style to use lines that could dramatically differentiate himself from Carter, especially since this was one of Carter's own pronounced tactics against Ford during the 1976 debates. "There you go again," crafted by Reagan himself, successfully elevated him without projecting himself as unduly strident or defensive.

Reagan scored several other tactical victories over Carter. He took initial control when the two men walked on stage, catching Carter by surprise by walking over to him to shake his hand. As the debate ended, he again took the initiative by crossing the stage to shake Carter's hand, once again surprising the President.

Reagan also benefited during the debate by a single poorly chosen comment of Carter's. In his explanation of the importance of nuclear non-proliferation Carter stated: "I had a discussion with my daughter Amy the other day before I came here, to ask her what the most important issue was. She said she thought nuclear weaponry." The ridicule to which Carter was subjected could have been avoided had he taken the advice of his staff. Carter tried out a line similar to this in his practice sessions, and in the words of a Carter aide "every single person in the room said, 'No Amy! No Amy! This is a debate, not a town meeting.' "[45]

Undoubtedly, the most effective speech of the debate was Reagan's closing statement in which he asked his five rhetorical questions. These, Reagan believed, captured the essence of his audience's attitudes about their lives during Carter's four years as President and gave him psychological control over the close of the debate:

> Next Tuesday, all of you will go to the polls, and stand there in the polling place and make a decision. I think when you make that decision it might be well if you ask yourself, are you better off than you were four years ago? Is it easier for you to go and buy things in the stores than it was four years ago? Is there more or less unemployment in the country than there was four years ago? Is America as respected throughout the world as it was? Do you feel that our security is as safe, that we're as strong as we were four years ago?

With these few lines Reagan did much to neutralize the issue advantage Carter had enjoyed in the debate and to turn the attention of his audience to the record of the Carter administration.

Postdebate Influence

A prevailing perception on both sides was that the media's reaction to the debate would be at least as important as the viewers' immediate reactions. This perception was reinforced by research conducted after the second presidential debate in 1976 wherein President Ford committed his infamous gaffe about Eastern Europe. The research revealed that immediately following the debate, Ford was perceived as the winner, but due to the media's play of the gaffe, Carter soon surpassed him.[46]

The Reagan campaign's concern for potential media influence of the debate results prompted the organization of an extensive surrogate effort. Led by veteran political consultant Clifford White, it involved making available to the media leading, credible Reagan advocates who, after being briefed by surrogate team leaders, would tell reporters that Reagan won, often citing reasons congruent with Reagan's debate goals. For example, following the second debate, the most frequent reaction to Reagan's performance was that he projected himself as "reasonable" and "presidential"—remarks that sought to diminish the widespread and gnawing perception that he was dangerous.

The effort by the Reagan forces to control the post-debate media influence included the establishment of a special Debate Operations Center at Reagan's National Headquarters in Arlington, Virginia. During and immediately following the debate, approximately fifty researchers monitored closely Reagan's and Carter's remarks for errors or omissions that might draw the media's attention. If, for instance, Carter had made a major factual error or the quality of Reagan's debate performance was in question, a representative of the Center would present a reaction to the press. However, since Reagan and his major advisers were confident, if not jubliant, about his performance, they considered it unnecessary to continue the debate in the press.

The surrogate efforts of the competing candidates in Baltimore and Cleveland is a study of striking contrasts. Reagan's surrogates took control of the media in Baltimore. Anderson's effort was far less organized, possibly because he may have had difficulty securing well-known, qualified people to comment on his behalf. Following the Cleveland debates, however, the thick air of competition between Carter and Reagan on stage was carried to the post-debate interviews where representatives from both camps vied for maximum coverage.

The competition occurred not only *after* the debate. Patrick Caddell's strategy memorandum shows that he thought it necessary to lobby the press long before the debate began:

> The more crucial and dangerous game is that with the press. They have an inordinate role in convincing the public not only who won on "points" but more critically, on the nature of the debate itself. . . . Thus we cannot let the press go into the debate with the single notion of looking just for a winner and loser. . . . We must make an all out effort to educate the press to the question of: (1) Will Reagan be specific? (2) Will he flip-flop? (3) Will he know what he is talking about? . . . We have to emphasize that such is the criteria we are looking to for "winning" and hurting Reagan. It must seep into their psyche as well.[47]

From the standpoint of the Carter camp, the most influential post-debate event was a disaster. ABC television conducted a call-in telephone poll at the conclusion of the debate. Viewers could telephone a special number as many times as they wished, at the cost of 50¢ per call, to vote for the candidate who "gained the most" or "did the best," as the question was phrased at different times. Although Carter aides were quick to assail this methodology—and justifiably so—tens of millions of Americans saw Reagan outdistancing Carter in the poll by a two-to-one margin before they turned off their television sets. Additional millions of voters were exposed to lead stories about these results the following morning in newspapers and on television news programs.

The Impact of the Debate

Ascertaining the long-term impact of the debate is a more difficult matter than asking viewers, "Who won?" In fact, the leading advisers to Carter and Reagan came to opposite conclusions on this matter. Reagan's advisers almost unanimously agree with Jim Baker's assessment that the debate "put a lock on it for us."[48] Richard Wirthlin, who had argued against entering the debate, said in March 1981 that "I think that the debate was one of— if not the major—conditioning event that established the foundation for the landslide." According to Wirthlin, Reagan "came off as a man of good humor, a man of reason, a man who could be trusted." Reagan's closing speech was critical, in Wirthlin's view, in focusing the attention of the electorate on Carter's record. This two-fold accomplishment of the debate, along with Reagan's massive last-week media blitz and his superior organization, all "folded together in the closing days of the campaign with tremendous impact."[49] Wirthlin supports this argument with polling data that show a steady shift to Reagan between Tuesday, October 28, the day of the debate, and Tuesday, November 4, election day. "Our studies show that we had a six-point lead on Wednesday, seven points by Thursday, nine by Friday, and ten by Saturday."[50]

Patrick Caddell, Carter's pollster, disputes both Wirthlin's data and his conclusions.[51] Caddell's polls showed that just prior to the debate, on October 24–26, Carter had a one-point lead. Immediately following the debate, on October 29–30, Reagan had opened a five-point lead. But, by Saturday, November 1, Carter was back even. The next day, Reagan jumped to a five-point lead, which doubled to a ten-point edge on Monday. Caddell notes that most of the public nationwide polls also agreed that on the final weekend the race was essentially even. Caddell admits that the debate hurt Carter temporarily, but argues that by the weekend Carter had regained any ground lost because of the debate. The trigger for Reagan's landslide, he contends, was the media's coverage of the Iranian hostage situation in the final two days of the campaign: the media focus on the possible return of the fifty-three American hostages turned the election into a referendum on the Carter administration. Carter's advisers wanted the voters to go into the voting booth thinking about what the future would be like under Carter and under Reagan. The news from Iran riveted the voters' thoughts to the present, particularly to the record of the Carter administration. In Caddell's view, this effect of the Iranian situation had far more impact than Reagan's media and organizational advantage, and more impact than the presidential debate.

Caddell's is definitely a minority view. Most analysts would agree with the assessment the President-elect shared with me the day following the election: "The debate with President Carter was, in my view, a critical element in our success in the election."[52]

NOTES

1. "The 1980 Presidential Debates: Behind the Scenes," booklet published by the League of Women Voters Education Fund, 1981, p. 5; interview, Ruth Hinerfeld, July 1, 1981.

2. Interview, Stuart Eizenstat, October 6, 1981.

3. Interview, James Baker, March 9, 1981.

4. Interview, David Gergen, March 10, 1981.

5. Memorandum, Myles Martel to James Baker, September 9, 1980.

6. Interview, Richard Wirthlin, March 10, 1981.

7. Interview, Robert Walker, July 9, 1981.

8. Interview with Robert Walker; interview, Mitchell Rogovin, July 2, 1981.

9. *Washington Post,* September 19, 1980, p. 9.

10. See the *Washington Post,* February 28, 1980, p. 1. According to Wirthlin's polling data, reported in this article, Reagan was named winner of the League's February 20, 1980 Manchester, New Hampshire Presidential Primary Forum by 33% of the voters surveyed. George Bush garnered 17%, John Anderson 14%, and Howard Baker 12%. Coverage of the League's Midwest Forum, held in Chicago on March 13, 1980, indicates that Anderson had difficulty selling himself as he drew heavy attacks from Reagan, Bush, and Philip Crane. See the *New York Times,* March 14, 1980, p. 16, and the *Philadelphia Bulletin,* March 14, 1980, p. B4. Reagan, upon hearing Anderson state in the Illinois forum that he would not automatically support the Republican Party's nominee, took command of the opportunity by dramatically turning to Anderson to ask: "John, you wouldn't really find Teddy Kennedy preferable to me, would you?"

11. Memorandum, Richard B. Wirthlin and Richard S. Beal to Governor Reagan, William Casey, and James Baker, September 12, 1980.

12. The term "pass through" was contained in a strategy memo prepared for the debate by David Stockman.

13. Interview with Mitchell Rogovin.

14. Interview with James Baker.

15. On several occasions I attempted unsuccessfully to arrange an interview with John Anderson to discuss his debate preparation and strategy.

16. Throughout the book, except as otherwise noted, the debate quotations are from transcripts prepared by me or my research assistants from audio or video recordings. The best published transcripts are found in: *The Great Debates: Kennedy vs. Nixon, 1960,* ed. Sidney Kraus (Bloomington, Indiana: Indiana University Press, 1962), pp. 348–430; Lloyd Bitzer and Theodore Rueter, *Carter vs. Ford: The Counterfeit Debates of 1976* (Madison, Wisconsin: The University of Wisconsin Press, 1980), pp. 253–391.

17. *Wall Street Journal,* September 17, 1980, p. 8.

18. *Washington Star,* September 23, 1980.

19. Interview with James Baker.

20. Interview with Richard Wirthlin.

21. Reagan's campaign strategy is discussed by Richard Wirthlin in "Face Off: A Conversation with the Presidents' Pollsters Patrick Caddell and Richard Wirthlin," *Public Opinion* 3 (December 1980/January 1981), pp. 6–9.

22. Jack W. Germond and Jules Witcover, *Blue Smoke and Mirrors* (New York: Viking, 1981), pp. 270–271.

23. Interview with James Baker.

24. Germond and Witcover, *Blue Smoke and Mirrors,* p. 269.

25. Interview with Richard Wirthlin.

26. Ibid.

27. Interview with James Baker.

28. Memorandum, Patrick H. Caddell to Carter campaign staff, October 21, 1980. This memorandum can be found in Elizabeth Drew, *Portrait of an Election: The 1980 Presidential Campaign* (New York: Simon & Schuster, 1981), pp. 410–439. All page references to the memorandum in these footnotes refer to the Drew book; for this note, see pp. 410–411.

29. Ibid., p. 411.

30. "Face Off: A Conversation with the Presidents' Pollsters," p. 11.

31. Memorandum, Richard B. Wirthlin, Richard Beal, and Myles Martel to Reagan campaign staff, October 21, 1980.

32. Ibid.

33. Memorandum, James Baker and Myles Martel to Governor Reagan, October 24, 1980.

34. Memorandum, Samuel Popkin to Patrick Caddell, October 18, 1980.

35. Ibid.

36. Memorandum, Caddell, October 21, 1980, p. 427.

37. Ibid.

38. Ibid., p. 434.

39. Memorandum, Baker and Martel, October 24, 1980.

40. Interview with Stuart Eizenstat. For a fascinating discussion of President Carter's debate preparation, see Hamilton Jordan, "The Campaign Carter Couldn't Win," *Life* (January 1981), pp. 91–100.

41. Interview, Samuel Popkin, July 8, 1981.

42. Interview with James Baker; memorandum, Caddell, October 21, 1980, p. 429; "Hanna Criticizes Candidates' Interference in Debate Set-up," *Broadcasting* (February 16, 1981), pp. 76–78.

43. *Washington Post,* October 30, 1980, p. A4.

44. "Face Off: A Conversation with the Presidents' Pollsters," p. 11.

45. Interview with Samuel Popkin.

46. See Frederick T. Steeper, "Public Response to Gerald Ford's Statements on Eastern Europe in the Second Debate," *The Presidential Debates: Media, Electoral, and Policy Perspectives,* eds. George F. Bishop, Robert G. Meadow, and Marilyn Jackson-Beeck (New York: Praeger, 1978), pp. 81–101.

47. Memorandum, Caddell, October 21, 1980, pp. 436–437.

48. Interview with James Baker.

49. Interview with Richard Wirthlin.

50. Ibid.

51. "Face Off: A Conversation with the Presidents' Pollsters," pp. 63–64.

52. Letter, Ronald Reagan to Myles Martel, November 5, 1980.

2

The Debate Option

Only five hours before mounting the rostrum of the 1976 Republican National Convention in Kansas City to deliver his nomination acceptance speech, President Gerald Ford summoned to his hotel suite his chief of staff, Dick Cheney, and trusted political adviser, Jack Marsh. The President showed them a challenge to Jimmy Carter to debate that he had just written. After reading the four sentences, Cheney and Marsh looked up at Ford and expressed their unqualified approval.[1] Ford's decision to challenge Carter had not been easy to make; it had been carefully weighed throughout the late spring and summer as Ford's political destiny faced perhaps greater uncertainty than that of any incumbent president seeking his party's nomination. Would the decision to debate be too strong an admission that Carter was a formidable contender? Would Ford relinquish too many of the precious advantages of his incumbency by appearing face-to-face with a contender who less than one year earlier had been a virtual unknown on the American political scene?

Questions like these are frequently considered by candidates when deciding whether or not to debate. Sometimes the decision is extremely easy, requiring little consultation, anxiety, or conflict. At other times, it is just the opposite. The amount of attention given to the decision is frequently related to the expected closeness of the election; candidates and their advisers are more likely to invest greater energy in making the decision in a close race than in an election where the contestants are separated by a wide margin. The decision is, indeed, a calculated political judgment, rooted in the potential of the debates to gain votes for the candidate, or to prevent their loss. Considerations of the public good that debating might serve are, at best, peripheral, although the candidate's public statements might suggest otherwise.

The relevant factors in candidates' calculations about debate participation differ significantly at higher and lower levels of American politics. Presidential debates occupy a unique position in American politics. Public interest and media coverage are intense, with debates generally being televised on all networks and viewership rivaling or exceeding that of the most popular sports extravaganzas. The political impact of the debates can be enormous—many analysts agree that the debates of 1960, 1976, and 1980 all played a critical role in the outcome of the elections.

Accordingly, in presidential elections, the decision whether or not to debate becomes a crucial decision in the entire campaign. The debate, because of its high visibility, plays proportionally a much greater role than it does at lower levels. Candidates will attempt to maintain as much flexibility as possible in committing themselves to a debate, with calculations about the desirability of a debate often changing rapidly as public opinion shifts throughout the campaign. Furthermore, presidential candidates will approach debates with considerable caution. Formats are likely to be highly structured and carefully negotiated to eliminate as much uncertainty as possible. The candidates will attempt to maximize their influence over the choice of panelists and moderators. Before both candidates agree to debate, long negotiations may be required on such items as the height of the lecterns, the presence of an audience, or the use of notes.

Debates at lower levels occur in dramatically different circumstances. Public interest in the debate, if not the campaign as a whole, is often low. Press coverage tends to be slight, and the debates are less likely to be televised. The decision to debate at this level is accordingly less crucial than at the presidential level. In some cases, electoral calculations may be overwhelmed by local customs that demand candidate confrontations (for example, the New England town meeting tradition) or by the candidate's desire to acknowledge and provide access to powerful community groups. Consequently, the decision to debate may be simple at this level—"candidates for mayor of Smithville *always* appear before the Chamber of Commerce."

The effective audience at lower levels is seldom the entire electorate, but instead, discrete groups within the community. In televised debates, the viewing audience is likely to be small and to consist mainly of the more politically involved segments of the community. Nontelevised debates are often sponsored by business and professional groups, where the candidates predictably address their concerns. Consequently, proposed debates at lower levels often are evaluated not so much for their potential to sway a mass electorate as for their impact on the candidate's image among relevant elite groups.

This chapter provides an analysis of the principal rationales for and against debating. It also discusses unique aspects of the decision to debate in primary elections and in elections with more than two candidates.

THE RATIONALES

"If you're ahead in the polls, don't debate"

This is one of the more frequently voiced axioms about campaign debates. One might point to the 1946 Voorhis-Nixon debates in support—a situation where Voorhis, a five-term incumbent with a substantial lead, debated Nixon, a political novice, and lost the election by a wide margin. However, even if there were concrete evidence that Nixon had won as a direct result of the five debates, which there is not, one should be wary about citing such precedents. For one thing, there are precedents that support the opposite conclusion—for example, John F. Kennedy's decision to debate Lyndon Johnson at the 1960 Democratic National Convention regardless of his solid lead, a decision vividly described by Kennedy's campaign manager, Larry O'Brien:

> Early in the convention week, Kennedy and I were driving across Los Angeles from a meeting with one state's delegation in one hotel to a meeting with another delegation in another hotel. It gave us a little time to talk and his thoughts returned to a challenge that Lyndon Johnson had issued to him the previous day. . . . We had first regarded the invitation as a Johnson ploy that we had best ignore. We were ahead, so why take any chances? But as we drove through the seemingly endless gilt and glitter of Los Angeles, Kennedy reconsidered. "I'm going to do it, Larry," he told me, "I'm sure as hell not afraid of Lyndon. It could be fun." I wasn't enthusiastic, but I accepted his challenge without further comment.[2]

Kennedy clearly outpointed Johnson, even in the eyes of the Texas delegation, and thereby enhanced his lead. Thus, despite the widespread popularity of the "don't debate if you're ahead in the polls" axiom, it (and, presumably, its implication that you *should* debate if you're behind) should not be taken as an absolute. The decision to debate is rarely straightforward.

For example, what does "ahead in the polls" mean? Integral to the definition of "ahead in the polls" is the quality of the lead. Is it, in the vernacular of the pollsters, "hard" or "soft," i.e., how susceptible is it to change? A candidate may be strong one week and not want to debate, and be on a sharp decline the next and have quite a different attitude. In fact, one of the major reasons for Carter's decision to debate Ford was the softness of his lead. While 20 to 30 percent more voters favored Carter than favored Ford at the height of the campaign, their reasons for supporting him were not strongly rooted and were, as a consequence, considered susceptible to the persuasive appeals of Ford's campaign. Similarly, in 1980, the softness of Ronald Reagan's lead over Carter was an important factor in his decision to debate. Reagan's advisers feared that doubts about his "mad bomber" image might cause marginal Reagan supporters to switch to Carter in the final weeks of the campaign. Therefore, most supported a debate, regarding it as a prime opportunity for Reagan to diminish lingering doubts about himself and thereby harden his lead.

Leuthold and Valentine contend that a leading candidate actually has a unique advantage in a debate.[3] Research has shown that most viewers tend to perceive their favored candidate as the debate "winner."[4] The leading candidate, then, unless he is clearly outperformed, normally will reinforce the preferences of more supporters than will his opponent and perhaps turn some of his "soft" support into "hard" support.

The validity of the polling process itself must also be considered. In close elections, polls can often be wrong. The Gallup Poll of 1948 that predicted Dewey's victory over Truman is a familiar example. More recently, in the fall of 1979, a survey in Iowa showed incumbent Democratic Senator Dick Clark leading Republican Roger Jepsen by an apparently safe margin, yet Jepsen won. Other polls conducted during the same period failed to predict the defeats of veteran Senators Edward Brooke (R., Mass.) and Thomas McIntyre (D., N.H.).

The decision to debate or not must also be from the vantage point of the candidate who wants to increase his lead—to win big. This was a major reason why incumbent Senator Joseph Clark, a former mayor of Philadelphia and frontrunner in the 1962 Senate race, agreed to debate his lesser-known opponent, Republican James Van Zandt. The "big win" offers the candidate several potential advantages, mainly enhanced strength within his party, a stronger mandate for his positions and programs, a greater tendency to be regarded as a prime candidate for even higher office, and increased potential to gain financial support.

While it has been generally, and probably correctly, assumed that most candidates who trail in an election campaign would welcome a debate as an opportunity to narrow the opponent's lead, there are compelling circumstances when such a candidate may not wish to debate. For instance, he may feel unprepared, possibly accompanied by the recognition that his opponent will probably project a better image. Therefore, pride and protection of the candidate's political future become significant factors in deciding whether or not to debate.

"Debates cannot be won; they can only be lost"

This advice, obviously pertinent only to frontrunners or to candidates in a tight race, is a consequence of the potentially devastating effect of "gaffes" in political debates. A gaffe is an ill-advised statement that can call into question a candidate's intellect, knowledge, ability, or sense of propriety or decency. Prior to the 1976 presidential debate, for example, Jimmy Carter had made a series of campaign gaffes, notably his comments about "ethnic purity" and his openness in discussing too graphically with *Playboy* magazine his views on sex. In the debate, however, it was Gerald Ford who committed a major gaffe in stating that Eastern Europe was not dominated by the Soviet Union. A similar series of events unfolded in 1980, when Ronald Reagan began his campaign by calling the Vietnam conflict a "noble cause," questioning the theory of evolution, and naming trees as a larger source of pollution than motor vehicles. Reagan's tendency toward gaffes was, therefore, a major concern for his advisers, who feared that such a mistake in a debate could seriously damage his campaign. But, ironically, while Reagan avoided any serious misstatements in his two debates, Carter committed the famous

"Amy" gaffe. Indeed, the dangers posed by gaffes are normally far greater before televised audiences than before live ones, since the sheer size of the television audience can draw increased attention to them.

The occasional occurrence of gaffes does not mean that a conservative, risk–averse debating strategy is appropriate or that debates cannot be "won." There are circumstances where debate participation might be considered inadvisable, especially when a frontrunner has a secure lead and the public and media will not exert pressure that might erode it significantly. But once a candidate decides to debate, regardless of his standing in the polls, he has not *ipso facto* invited a "no win" contest. He can "win" the debate if he is strategically and tactically prepared to do so. Moreover, the goal of avoiding mistakes to prevent losing may be his biggest mistake; in his zeal to minimize risks such as overspecificity, misstatements, or mistreating his opponent, he may project himself as too cautious or too conciliatory.

The outcomes of debates are at least partial reflections of the candidates' approach to them—their rationales for debating, including particularly the risk they assume and the quality of their preparation. For a candidate to "lose" a debate, his opponent must do something right to contribute to a "win," and for a candidate to "win," his opponent must do something wrong to contribute to a "loss." Thus, while Nixon is often referred to as having "lost" the first 1960 encounter with Kennedy because of his less than aggressive, almost conciliatory manner, and poor television image, Kennedy also "won" it because he projected the opposite qualities and, in doing so, diminished pervasive negative impressions about his youth and inexperience. And not only did Gerald Ford, the expected victor, "lose" his foreign policy debate in 1976, but Jimmy Carter also "won" it for several reasons, among them his ability to appear more informed on foreign policy than many viewers had expected, and his skill in highlighting Ford's famous Eastern Europe gaffe.

Finally, "winning" or "losing" a political debate is not like winning or losing a basketball game (or an election). The "game" goes on, the outcome is still to be decided—and there is no evidence that shows what effect debates have on elections. Often, in fact, both the winning and the losing candidate (in the election) argue that debates benefited them—and they may have. In fact, one might say that "debates can be principally won, principally lost, or be of equal advantage to all participants."

The "no win" assumption gains much of its impetus from the news media's tendency to force viewers to evaluate debates in win/lose terms. Particularly in presidential and senatorial races, the media conduct and publicize polls and interviews with politicians, academics (often including college debate coaches), and the general public to determine "who won." In 1976, for example, a Philadelphia television station asked viewers to call their verdict in to a special number while their television screens showed the station's tally board throughout the post-debate coverage. Referring to the media's treatment of the 1976 presidential debates, David O. Sears and Steven H. Chaffee, after reviewing three dozen studies, comment:

> Instead of their . . . content, news reports of the debates were preoccupied with *"who won"* and generally with the competitive, horse–race aspect. For example, 17 percent of newspaper space and 10 percent of TV news time dealt with the question of which candidate had won a debate. An additional 41 percent and 42 percent, respectively, of each medium's coverage was given over to statements about the performances of the candidates, the personalities and competence levels they projected, and the impact the debate would have on their campaigns. *Newsweek* spent one–third of its debate space, and *Time* one–fifth, on preparation, style, studio, and rules. In short, the media covered the debates much as they did any other campaign event, by focusing more on the "hoopla," media–event aspects of them as a vehicle for transmitting the candidates' positions on the issues. In this sense the media coverage did not address the self–reported needs of the voters.[5]

Given this media focus on win/lose perceptions, audience expectations are a critical factor to consider in the decision to debate. If an audience expects that a candidate will not do well in a debate and he does in fact perform competently, he may be credited with a "win" for that reason alone. In the first 1960 debate, John Kennedy not only outperformed Richard Nixon, but (as noted above) the strength of his performance was at least partially rooted in his ability to overcome expectations, based on his youth and relative inexperience, that he would be no match for the Vice President. In 1976 Jimmy Carter was expected to win the first domestic policy debate by attacking Gerald Ford's record, but when Ford acquitted himself well, he was credited with the win. Conversely, Carter, who was not expected to do well in the foreign policy debate, was helped by this audience expectation and by media attention to Ford's East European gaffe. In 1980 the attempts by the Carter camp to portray Reagan as irresponsible and dangerous were effectively countered by the genial personality Reagan projected during the debate. Thus, the harsh attacks on Reagan early in the campaign to some extent created public expectations that were easy for Reagan to confound. Late in the campaign Carter's advisers realized this and attempted to shift the focus of Carter's attack from Reagan's "dangerousness" to his "evasiveness,"[6] but by then the expectations had been set and Reagan was positioned to do well in the debate.

The candidate and his advisers may have cause for concern in contemplating whether the candidate will fare well in such a media-dominated environment. But they should also keep two potentially significant considerations in mind: first, there is little evidence to suggest that debate viewers are necessarily influenced by the win/lose coverage per se, although general coverage such as that given to Ford's Eastern European gaffe can be influential;[7] second, such win/loss coverage is more common in high level campaigns than in low level campaigns.

"If you're an incumbent, don't debate"

The incumbent has available to him throughout his term of office numerous opportunities to conduct an unofficial as well as an official campaign. Newsletters, computerized mailings, extensive media exposure, financing from interest groups, support by political action committees (PACS), meetings with constituents, inexpensive production costs for prepackaged radio and television messages, district offices (sometimes including a mobile office), and a sizeable staff are some of the major weapons in his campaign arsenal. A president, governor, or mayor of a large city also has the authority to request briefings and other forms of support from many of the officials serving under him.[8] On the surface, then, it would appear sheer folly for an incumbent to risk debate—to create audiences for an opponent, to dilute the status of incumbency by sharing a platform, and to offer up a record in office to attack.

Nevertheless, the 1980 Congressional Debate Survey indicates that the conventional wisdom must be questioned. In comparing races involving incumbents and those with open seats, the survey reveals much less difference in the extent of debating than would be expected (see Tables 2.1 and 2.2). Table 2.1 indicates that there are indeed fewer debates when an incumbent is in the race, but the difference is not striking. Moreover, this difference is largely created by long-term incumbents. Table 2.2 shows that when House incumbents have served four terms or fewer, the level of debating is almost identical to that in open-seat races. Only when a House incumbent has been in office for five or more terms is there a noticeable decline in the level of debating, from approximately 75 percent to 38 percent. Generalizations about Senate races are more difficult due to the small sample size, but it does appear that there was no significant decline in debating for at least first-term incumbents.

Why do House and Senate incumbents debate with such frequency, when it has long been a commonplace of political scientists that incumbency is a

TABLE 2.1   Was There a Debate?

House			
	Yes	*No*	*Percentage Debating*
Open Seat	17	6	74
Incumbent in race	29	17	63

Senate			
	Yes	*No*	*Percentage Debating*
Open Seat	6	2	75
Incumbent in race	16	10	62

TABLE 2.2 Was There a Debate?

House

Terms in Office	Yes	No	Percentage Debating
Open Seat	17	6	74
1 term incumbent	10	3	77
2 term incumbent	7	2	78
3 or 4 term incumbent	6	2	75
5 or more terms	6	10	38

Senate

Terms in Office	Yes	No	Percentage Debating
Open Seat	6	2	75
1 term incumbent	7	3	70
2 term incumbent	4	2	67
3 term incumbent	3	2	60
4 or more terms	2	3	40

decided advantage in congressional elections?[9] Why don't more incumbents avoid debates, keep a low profile, and count on their built-in advantages to carry the day? First, it must be recognized that an incumbent's visibility is not always an advantage. As Thomas Mann states, in a recent study of congressional elections:

> Incumbents have available numerous resources with which to present themselves in a favorable light to their constituents. *In the absence of other communication about the incumbent,* this generalized favorable image can have decisive electoral effects. But publicly perceived candidate images can also reflect the political dialogue in the district. Charges of impropriety, insensitivity, incompetency, or ineffectiveness, if plausible and forcefully made in the context of an attractive alternative, can override the incumbent's advantages in communication.[10] (emphasis added)

For those candidates with a blemished record and an attractive, well-financed opponent, the visibility of the incumbent can be a double-edged sword. Much more than in the past, an incumbent is on his own: the decline of party voting by the electorate has meant that incumbents now must win or lose reelection largely on their own, not by riding presidential coattails or national trends. An incumbent facing the possibility of a debate cannot automatically assume that his status requires him to avoid a debate; he must consider the specifics of his own contest. If his opponent has been unable to raise any serious issue challenges or otherwise induce a shift in public attitudes, it may be wise for an incumbent to avoid a debate and rely on his built-in advantages. But if the challenger has found a weakness and is beginning to generate public support, the incumbent must consider a debate as one means of defusing his opponent's charges and promoting his own accomplishments.

Mann believes that the electoral success of incumbent congressmen will decline significantly in the near future, as more races fall into this second, competitive category. In his view, the incumbency advantage is on the decline in American politics. He contends that challengers are just beginning to realize the full potential of modern campaign techniques, and that there will be an increase in the number of sophisticated, well-financed challenges to formerly "safe" incumbents.[11] This trend may be strengthened by the growing influence of single-issue interest groups and political action committees (PACS) that are able to generate substantial campaign funds and are often willing to target a congressman for defeat because of a few relatively obscure votes. The 1980 Senate elections, in which such groups apparently contributed to the defeat of several prominent incumbents, may be a harbinger of a significant change in American politics. If Mann is correct, and a trend toward more competitive congressional elections does develop, the pressures on formerly "safe" incumbents to debate will probably increase.

Presidents already feel these pressures to debate, as evidenced by the events of 1960, 1976, and 1980. When Vice President Nixon agreed in 1960 to debate John Kennedy, he confronted the strategic difficulties inherent when the number two man in an administration runs for the number one spot in the next. With few exceptions, the number two man in office has been a figurehead whose role in fashioning the policies and programs of his administration has been, at best, minimal. In deciding to debate, this candidate often finds himself torn in two directions. On the one hand, his need to identify with the incumbent administration may be crucial to maintaining the image of an experienced administrator. But on the other, he may also find himself forced to defend policies and programs that he disagrees with. In fact, any attempt to repudiate the administration's record could invite serious political liabilities: He could be perceived by voters as ineffectual—for not having brought about better programs and policies—or as too political—for having changed his position on an issue more for personal gain—or he could lose important support from the president or governor or from persons in organizations strongly identified with them. Richard Nixon, as vice president, was, therefore, prudent in defending the generally popular Eisenhower administration during his debates with John F. Kennedy. And Vice President Hubert Humphrey, apparently not anxious to defend Lyndon Johnson's unpopular Vietnam policy before 100 million viewers, may have been equally prudent in not pressing for debates with Nixon in 1968.

The conventional wisdom is that Nixon's decision to debate cost him the election, and it may well have—but not, I believe, merely because a debate took place: something had to happen to make Kennedy "win" and Nixon "lose," as discussed earlier. The basis for Nixon's decision to debate was, in fact, quite sound. His "credits" included the successful debates against Voorhis in 1946, the effective "Checkers" speech of 1952, the famous "kitchen debate" against Khruschev at the Moscow Trade Fair in 1959, and an impressive three-and-a-half-hour performance on David Susskind's "Open End" show. He also did not expect Kennedy to do well, in part because he thought his acceptance speech was "way over people's heads." Explaining his decision in his *Memoirs,* he states:

> An incumbent seldom agrees willingly to debate his challenger. . . . But there was no way that I could refuse to debate without having Kennedy and the media turn my refusal into a central campaign issue. The question we faced was not whether to debate, but how to arrange the debates so as to give Kennedy the least possible advantage.[12]

Perhaps the best objective explanation of Nixon's motivations comes from a Brookings Institution study of the 1960 election:

> That Nixon could gain something from the debates, he could have gained in no other way—access to millions of Democrats and independents—should have been an incentive to him. As a candidate of the nation's minority, this was a chance not likely to be foregone.[13]

In 1976 President Gerald Ford, not succumbing to blind faith in the power of incumbency, not only debated, but also challenged Jimmy Carter to debate. Ford and his advisers reasoned in part that the additional exposure provided by the debate would force Carter to become more specific on the issues, thereby bridging the "intelligence gap" between him and Carter and diminishing Carter's media campaign. The prestige of the presidency, the seemingly limitless research avenues at Ford's disposal, his ability to command the media's attention, and his expectation that he would be giving Carter presidential status by allowing him to appear with him, were outstripped by the public's less than favorable perceptions of his competence.[14] Ford's reasons for offering the challenge, and Carter's (in violation of the "don't debate if you're ahead in the polls" axiom) for accepting, are worth examining.

Challenging Jimmy Carter to debate had been a closely held strategy option throughout Ford's spring and summer campaign. As early as June 11, Michael Duval and Foster Chanock of the White House staff, had issued a memorandum advocating a "no campaign" strategy (now known as the "Rose Garden" strategy) that included a series of four nationally televised debates.[15] The memorandum proposed that Ford announce in late August or early September that he would not campaign actively for the presidency; doing so would, in effect, make the debates a surrogate campaign devoid of hoopla and confined instead to substance. Duval and Chanock were especially sensitive to Ford's declining popularity, attributed in large part to his pardon of Richard Nixon shortly after Ford became president, and to his growing image of being more a political campaigner than a president.

At least six important problems in addition to Ford's declining popularity faced Ford's campaign when the "no campaign strategy" was proposed:

1. Ronald Reagan continued to be a formidable candidate.
2. Ford had no experience in national campaigning.
3. Registered Democrats outnumbered Republicans by more than two to one: 43 percent to 21 percent.
4. Under the new campaign laws, spending had to be equal, despite the Republican Party's general ability to raise more money than the Democratic Party could.
5. The GOP convention would be held late, and since the Party was seriously divided by the Ford-Reagan contest, reconciliation would be difficult in the limited time available before the election.
6. Ford could not court interest groups by promising new programs, for that would seriously contradict his "bite-the-bullet" theme.[16]

Most members of Ford's inner circle were confident of his ability as a debater and reasonably assured that he would project himself as competent and intelligent, thereby refuting widespread perceptions to the contrary. Their confidence was rooted in Ford's twenty-six-year experience as a congressman (including his debating experience on the House floor and during campaigns), his two years as president, and his impressive performance at a budget briefing earlier that year. In addition, his competitive nature and favorable television image were expected to reinforce those experiences.[17]

Ford's advisers discounted the traditional arguments against participation in presidential debates. They claimed that Ford's appointed succession to Nixon's presidency did not offer him the protection ordinarily due an elected incumbent. To the argument that debating would put Carter on an equal plane with the President, Ford's advisers pointed to Carter's formidable lead in the polls: While Carter would indeed be given exposure, he would also be forced to become more specific on the issues.

One of the more intriguing questions to emerge from studying the 1976 presidential debates is why Carter, with such a formidable lead over Ford, wanted to debate. Gerald Rafshoon, Carter's media adviser and representative during the format negotiations, told me:

> We considered them [the debates] important because we were suffering from the fallacy that Jimmy Carter was wishy-washy on the issues or fuzzy on the issues because there was a lot of negative advertising going on about Jimmy Carter. And we knew that if we got him toe-to-toe with President Ford for an hour-and-a-half, three times, that it would put that thing to rest. People would see him on a par with the President of the United States, discussing issues and knowing as much as—and perhaps more than—the President. There was still a feeling that Carter wasn't that well known and I think it [the debate process] worked for us. We were very anxious to debate.[18]

Another reason for debating could not have escaped the notice of either Ford's or Carter's strategists: each candidate faced an electorate with the largest percentage of undecided and independent voters in American history.

Carter's advisers drew a parallel between the proposed Carter–Ford debate and the 1960 Kennedy–Nixon debates. One lesson they had learned from 1960 was that a debate tends to be an advantage to a challenger, who needs to reassure the voters about himself. In 1960, in the words of a Carter strategy memorandum, "Kennedy's advantage and gain from debates was largely because he was less well known than Nixon and his supporters were much less certain of him. Now, in 1976, Gerald Ford is giving Jimmy Carter some of the best exposure a challenger could possibly get."[19]

Carter's aides were especially eager to have him debate because they thought there was little chance of losing a significant number of voters even if he "lost" the debate to Ford. They contended that in 1960 "the major effect of the debates was by far to reinforce voter choices, to crystallize their convictions and to firm up their support," and they expected that the same would be true in 1976.[20] There would have to be a massive disparity between the two candidates in order to convert many voters. As long as Carter could be reasonably competitive with Ford, therefore, his advisers believed that the debate would be a low-risk opportunity.

This analysis, while comforting to Carter in 1976, was surely not so pleasing in 1980 when Carter was the incumbent and Reagan the challenger seeking to reassure his supporters. Carter's key advisers, in fact, acknowledged that by agreeing to debate, he would be entering a situation where the odds were against him.[21] Nevertheless, for the second consecutive presidential election, an incumbent agreed to meet his opponent in a campaign debate.

Are Carter's advisers right: Are presidential debates an inherent disadvantage to an incumbent president? It is at least an interesting coincidence that the challenger in 1960, 1976, and 1980 in each case went on to win the election. There are reasons to believe that it may be more than a coincidence. A presidential debate not only presents the lesser-known challenger on an equal plane with the President, thus sharing some of the majesty of the office, but also gives him a splendid opportunity to blame the incumbent for any or all of the ills of the nation for the past four years.

It has been argued that incumbents are likely to be even more vulnerable in the future. No president, no matter how competent, will quickly solve the seemingly intractable problems of the 1980s—inflation, unemployment, economic decline, energy costs, etc. Moreover, an increasingly aggressive and critical news media will be sure to give full coverage to what they perceive to be his policy failures. At least partially because of these factors, since 1968 one incumbent president has declined to run for reelection and two others have been repudiated by the voters; and, beginning with President Nixon, three consecutive presidents have experienced particularly low standings in the polls.[22] If these high levels of public dissatisfaction with presidential performance become a normal part of American politics, challengers should indeed be able to score heavily by focusing the debate on the salient negatives of the incumbent's record.

Does this mean that incumbent presidents are unlikely to debate in the future? The answer is not clear. At a 1977 conference on presidential debates, political scientist Evron Kirkpatrick argued that the 1960 and 1976 debates arose from unusual circumstances, and that future presidential debates are unlikely.[23] But Charls Walker, cochairman of the 1976 Debates Steering Committee, predicted that "there will be debates much more frequently than not."[24] In his view, because of the growth in public dissatisfaction with presidential leadership, future incumbents will not be able to pursue a passive "Rose Garden" strategy, but rather will have to launch a vigorous campaign to regain their earlier popularity. In these circumstances, Walker contends, debates are likely to occur. If Walker's notion proves correct, American presidents may find themselves in an unenviable position: The same forces that lead them to debate will make them vulnerable targets for their challengers.

An incumbent who decides to debate faces an additional burden: He must be prepared to exercise much greater restraint than his opponent in expressing opinions or in providing information, for an inadvertent pronouncement can be quickly interpreted as policy. Incumbents who choose to debate are ordinarily mindful of such risks. Gerald Ford summed up this predicament in his autobiography, *A Time to Heal:*

> How ironic it was, I thought, that his [Carter's] limited experience in government could turn out to be an advantage for him. I had been in Washington for nearly 28 years, had made thousands of decisions on national issues, all on the record. Carter had never had to make a hard decision on a national issue, so he could be more strident in his accusations and challenges.[25]

An incumbent president's debate decision leads to a related issue: might a misstatement by him in the heat of debate endanger national security or weaken relations with another nation? In 1963 the American Political Science Association appointed a Commission on Presidential Debates that reached the following conclusion:

> Extraordinary situations may be created by the exigencies of the world situation and the international position of the United States. In *some* of these situations it may be contrary to our national interest for the President to engage in debates. The Cuban invasion and the missile crisis are recent examples. It is possible to imagine even more perilous situations.[26]

However, the inadvisability of debating during a crisis must be distinguished from the more popular contention that an incumbent president should *never* debate because he may make a misstatement that might jeopardize national security or relations with another country. In 1976, when Gerald Ford debated Jimmy Carter, it is doubtful that he resolved the argument that an incumbent president should not debate because of the risk issue. In fact, his celebrated "gaffe" regarding Eastern Europe will probably add weight to the issue, despite its apparently negligible impact on the United States' relations with Eastern European nations.

The resolution of the "risk" issue hinges on answers to two questions: To what extent does the debate format increase or decrease such risks? To what extent are candidates prone to such risks, regardless of format? First, a debate format similar to that used in 1960 and 1976, characterized by timed alternating responses by the candidates to panelist questions, is probably not as conducive to a dangerous slip as a less structured setting where emotions may not be as constrained. Second, by the time the president debates, he has engaged in so many press conferences and question-and-answer sessions that he should be less prone to make a dangerous slip. In fact, some of the persons interviewed for the oral history phase of this research argue that presidential press conferences may be even more risky than debates; in such settings, they explain, the president is continually on the spot with no breaks, fielding questions from numerous competing reporters—some friendly, some hostile.

One tactic frequently suggested as a means for the president to avoid the "risk" is for him to "wrap himself in the flag" and say, "for reasons of national security I cannot comment on this matter." This approach has three major implications: (1) the president may emphasize his incumbency by demonstrating that he has privileged information and is discreet in handling it; (2) he may be perceived as taking unnecessary advantage of his position—using it to avoid discussing a less than sensitive issue or to communicate the opponent's lack of discretion in raising it; or (3) his unwillingness to comment may actually shed light on the issue. Still another alternative, raised during the 1964 campaign, involves videotaping a presidential debate behind closed doors and then editing it to eliminate any "risk" statements. This approach is questionable: it is unlikely that both candidates would agree to what should be excised; it may be difficult to keep the sensitive information confidential since so many technicians and other persons anxious to publicize it may be privy to it; and public interest and confidence in such a debate may be diminished.

A final consideration related to incumbency is the power of an incumbent president to move or shape events. While a president cannot cause events to fall precisely into place, he can influence their timing, and may be apt to do so when he is running for reelection. An incumbent, therefore, may not need the visibility afforded by a debate if he can improve his popularity by making a well-timed and popular decision. Under such circumstances, of course, a debate may be even more important to a challenger as a means of generating media coverage to counter the events orchestrated by his opponent.

The clearest example of this situation was the possibility in 1980 that President Carter might secure the release, shortly before the election, of the 52 American hostages being held by Iranian militants. Early in the campaign, Reagan's advisers had developed contingency plans to deal with what they called the "October Surprise." Ultimately, they agreed to debate Carter in part to assure that Reagan would not be crowded off the front page by the news from Iran in the critical final days of the campaign.[27] Had Carter been able to secure the release of the American hostages prior to November 4, he might not have needed a debate and might have won the election.

One of the more unusual reasons for an incumbent's decision to debate surfaced during a campaign in which I was recently involved. The incumbent, enjoying at least a 20-point lead in the polls, wanted, for the sheer experience, to meet his opponent in a debate with limited media exposure. He had never debated before and acknowledged the potential significance of becoming a skillful debater in a career marked by political promise.

Another unusual rationale—this one for an incumbent's decision not to debate—evolved in another recent campaign in which I also served as an adviser. The incumbent governor, who held a solid 22-point lead over his opponent, was unwilling to debate, not only because he was an incumbent or ahead in the polls but also because he was apparently concerned whether or not he could counter effectively his opponent's demagogic style. And compounding this concern was the fear among the governor's advisers that his opponent's demagogy could, in fact, cause him to lose his composure.

"Refusing to debate may generate damaging negative publicity"

Although a candidate may be leading by a reasonably safe margin, he may not want to risk jeopardizing his reputation for openness by refusing to debate, a risk that is especially strong if the organization that issues the invitation to debate has considerable community influence (for example, the Chamber of Commerce, Rotary Club, League of Women Voters), or is an influential newspaper or radio or television station. The pressure to debate is increased, of course, if there is strong public interest. Nixon chose to debate Kennedy partially because he feared negative publicity if he refused, and Carter was similarly motivated in deciding to debate both Ford and Reagan.

The 1980 Congressional Debate Survey found that public expectations of a debate have now spread to the level of congressional elections. Several respondents in the 1980 CDS said that a debate was "never desirable," yet they debated. One congressional incumbent explained: "No choice. It would have been politically undesirable to refuse the League of Women Voters' sponsored debate." Another reported that there would be "more damage from refusing [a debate] than from doing it badly." One challenger reported that debates were "not a part of the campaign plan. They were done to placate those sponsoring them," and another said that his campaign "always wanted to debate the incumbent. [The incumbent] managed to avoid debating for several weeks—until senior citizens' groups, the League of Women Voters, etc., set up debates and he had to show up."

Although it is impossible to measure precisely the extent to which fear of negative publicity influenced candidates' decisions to debate, judging from the twenty House incumbent debaters who responded to the 1980 CDS, this fear apparently was a major factor for a significant number of House incumbents in 1980. For the six respondents who reported that they entered the debate with enthusiasm and the six who said that the debate was considered unimportant in the campaign, fear of negative publicity was not an important influence on the decision to debate. Asked to rate on a *one* to *five* scale the relative importance of various factors in their decision to debate, with *one* indicating that the factor was unimportant and *five* indicating that it was crucial to the decision, these twelve respondents gave this an item average score of 1.75. But for the four incumbents who entered the debate with reluctance and the four whose staff was divided on the advisability of a debate, the fear of negative publicity was a major motivator. The average score of these eight respondents on the scale reported above was 4.25. This finding helps explain one puzzling fact uncovered in the incumbent study: many representatives reported having unfavorable attitudes toward a campaign debate, yet still agreed to debate. Apparently these candidates, although preferring to avoid a debate, felt that they could not afford to refuse a debate invitation from influential local groups.

For reasons not uncovered by the CDS, senatorial candidates were not as susceptible to these pressures to debate: there were few reluctant senatorial debaters. One explanation for this may be that in the smaller, more homogeneous House districts, there is likely to be a clearly recognizable local leadership group that both candidates are eager to please, while in the statewide arena of senatorial campaigns fewer groups occupy this privileged position.

Negative publicity attending a candidate's decision must be carefully analyzed. A candidate feeling pressure to debate from the media or from the public, as explained earlier, should not be forced into a debate he is not prepared for. The negative publicity caused by a poor performance may be more damaging than that caused by a continued refusal to debate. Furthermore, a delayed decision to debate may ironically aggravate rather than attenuate the image problems caused by the earlier refusal; that is, the debate may give the media and the opposition a high-visibility platform from which to chide the candidate for his grudging acceptance. In weighing these factors, a candidate must therefore consider how much of an issue his continued refusal to debate would be. If he has refused to debate throughout the campaign without creating a major image problem, he may be able to hold out for the duration without excessive cost. Moreover, a late concession to debate after a long period of avoidance may communicate to the media and public a sense of desperation. Thus, at some point, it may be too late to change his position even if he wanted to.

The candidate's pollster can often investigate the significance of his refusal. Specifically, if the candidate is being hurt by his refusal, his pollster can attempt to determine whether a reversal of his position would neutralize much of the voters' dissatisfaction, or whether his earlier reluctance to debate would still be held against him. He may find that there would be little payoff in debating once he has been perceived as being reluctant to debate.

Professor Robert Scott argues that a candidate who is perceived as avoiding a debate can create negative expectations that color the public's perception of his performance if he later does agree to debate. The image of "unfairness" acquired prior to the debate may cause viewers to be more critical of his conduct in the debate. Scott contends that viewers of the Reagan-Carter debate held such a bias against Carter due to his refusal to join Reagan and Anderson in the first debate, and hence were predisposed to find Reagan the "winner" of the second one.[28]

"Televised debates favor the candidate with the better image"

No notion about televised campaign debates has been more enduring than this one, prompted largely by John F. Kennedy's ability to project a more favorable image than Richard Nixon during the first 1960 debate. Three broad image factors often involved in the candidate's debate decision are physical attractiveness, speaking or debating ability, and personality. The candidate who possesses any or all of these qualities is more likely to debate than one who doesn't.

The 1979 Philadelphia mayoral race between Democratic frontrunner William Green and Republican David Marston is a good example of image discrepancies between candidates. Green projected an unusually handsome image, in dramatic contrast to Marston's boyish, slouched appearance. Marston, however, while acknowledging Green's good looks, felt that he had the intelligence and forensic skills to outpoint him in debate. Physical attractiveness also figured prominently in Edward Kennedy's decision to debate Edward McCormack in the 1962 Massachusetts Senate race. As a Kennedy adviser reasoned:

> What has Kennedy got going for him? That he looks like his brother. That he looks like a Kennedy. That he talks like a Kennedy. That he's got vigor, that he's an excellent and articulate person, and he makes a very strong presentation. And Eddie McCormack, although very capable, has got kind of a bad smile, unfortunately, and a little bit of lisp . . . and doesn't come through quite as well on television as he does in person.[29]

Interestingly, McCormack's advisers seemed confident that Kennedy's well-known short temper could be ignited during the debates, thereby diminishing any potential gains from his physical attractiveness and articulateness:

> . . . Ed McCormack can light Mr. Kennedy's extremely short fuse. I think this is a guy who could blow it on television. Ted Kennedy could be angered to the point where he could make a public display of his very famous temper. . . . This would be highly injurious and accrue to our benefit.[30]

Another dramatic example of physical attractiveness possibly making a difference in a televised debate occurred in the 1964 California Senate race between Pierre Salinger and former actor-dancer George Murphy:

In the Salinger-Murphy debate Salinger hoped to demonstrate to 3.5 million Californians that Murphy did not know enough to be a Senator. Murphy, however, was more interested in appearances—in looking like a senator than in talking like one. Salinger looked pudgy, self-indulgent, irritable, and shady, but Murphy smiled, radiated, and portrayed an image of sincerity and courtliness. Instead of responding to Salinger's arguments, Murphy (like Kennedy in 1960) reiterated the points he had made throughout the campaign. Salinger . . . complained, "I guess this just shows the futility of trying to come to grips with anyone as slippery as my opponent."[31]

Three studies conducted in nonpolitical, nonmedia contexts support the view that physical attractiveness is important in debates. Haiman (1949) found that physical attractiveness is correlated significantly with persuasive effectiveness.[32] Aronson and Mills (1965) discovered that a speaker's stated intent to influence audience opinion was more effective if the speaker was physically attractive.[33] Widgery (1974) concluded that the sex of *receiver* and attractiveness of *source* influence at least initial credibility perception and that females are more prone than males to make positive judgments of the source's credibility.[34]

An essential aspect of the candidate's assessment of his image is its impact in the most important medium of a debate. Is he better before a live audience than before a television or radio audience? Specifically, is he inclined to indulge in forceful verbal and nonverbal behavior that may be, as Marshall McLuhan, the reknowned media authority, has said, too "hot" for the "cool" medium of television? Such judgments are often exceedingly difficult to make for the candidate who has had little experience with television or radio. And, as was pointed out by Thompson (1967), after reviewing the accumulated research of nearly four decades: ". . . delivery affects comprehension and persuasiveness significantly."[35] It is no wonder that in 1976 Jimmy Carter was unwilling to agree to debate until he was certain that Ronald Reagan (whose delivery on and off television by most standards is masterful) would not receive the Republican nomination.[36]

The extent to which a candidate who is unattractive or speaks poorly can change his image during a televised debate is probably limited, although improvement is possible. Dress, grooming, make-up, camera angles, lighting, speech training, and lectern size and placement may be somewhat beneficial, although the piercing eye of the television camera is more likely to present an authentic than a created image. This is especially true when the candidates are not tied to carefully orchestrated scripts. Hahn and Gonchar comment: "A candidate's stand on issues is easier to 'manage' than the [physical] image he projects, primarily because image contains a nonverbal element that eludes complete control."[37] Anderson, who defines an image as "an orientation [by the receiver] toward the candidate containing varied perceptual expectations" addresses the issue even more pointedly:

. . . Any public figure can control to an extent such factors as appearance and speech content, [but] he cannot directly control image formation.[38]

Personality is a related and serious concern of televised debate participants. While media advisers can slim a candidate down, make sure he is rested, and use make-up to cover minor flaws, little can be done to make a stiffer candidate less formal or promote a sense of humor where none exists. In no recent election was personality more crucial than in 1980. Reagan's television personality was so warm and humane that Carter could not make his anti-Reagan charges believable. Carter's particular debate skills, such as an extraordinary ability to remember facts and statistics, paled beside Reagan's ability to present himself as a genuinely warm and concerned person—regardless of what he was or wasn't saying. Similarly, Anderson, a more articulate and forceful speaker than either Carter or Reagan, could not overcome Reagan's natural affability and charm. Next to Reagan, Anderson appeared too intense.

This ability to project an appealing personality allowed Reagan to attain important campaign goals in each debate. The debate with Anderson occurred just as the focus of Reagan's campaign was changing from the solidification of his Republican and conservative base to the broadening of his appeal to moderates and independents.[39] To do this, Reagan had to counter the impression that he was inflexible and perhaps irresponsible, and it is widely believed within the Reagan camp that the personal image he projected in the first debate did much to dispel this impression.[40] In the second debate, Reagan's major goal was to reassure his potential supporters that he was trustworthy. His ability to deflect Carter's attacks with smiles and good humor were crucial to his success; had Reagan projected anger and defensiveness, Carter's attacks would have done far more damage.

THE DEBATE CONTEXT

The decision to debate cannot be considered in a vacuum. A political debate occurs under specific ground rules, before a definable audience, and within a general political climate. These contextual factors can affect critically the advisability of a debate.

A format that allows close interrogation by panelists and significant refutation by the opponent maximizes the risk to the participants. A risk-averse candidate thus may be more willing to debate if the format avoids follow-up questions and extended periods of rebuttal and surrebuttal. The candidate must also consider the likely attitude of the panelists; a candidate who expects a hostile reception is normally less likely to agree to debate unless, of course, hostility tends to bring out the best in him.

A debate that will be televised only locally, or not televised at all, may present both less risk and less opportunity than one broadcast throughout the entire constituency. More limited media coverage has not only the obvious effect of reducing the number of viewers, but also narrows the number of different constituencies that can or must be appealed to. This point is illustrated by the 1978 New York gubernatorial campaign, where Hugh Carey and Perry Duryea participated in one debate televised by a Buffalo affiliate, another televised by an Albany affiliate, several televised by metropolitan New York City stations, and a debate carried statewide on public television. The Buffalo, Albany, and New York City debates allowed the candidates to target messages to different regional audiences; the statewide telecast, however, required the candidates to craft a strategy to appeal to all the various constituencies in the state, and thus presented far more potential for a major strategic or tactical mistake by the candidates. Thus, a candidate who prefers a minor role for debates, or one who prefers to direct messages to a discrete segment of the electorate, may shy away from a widely televised debate, but perhaps accept one with more limited media coverage.

Finally, the appeal of a debate can be greatly affected by the general political climate during the election campaign. Many Republican House members expressed to me their reluctance to debate in 1982 because of the widespread unpopularity of President Reagan's economic policies. On the one hand, they did not want to be forced to defend them; on the other, they did not want to engender the ire of their Republican colleagues, including the White House itself, by criticizing the party line.

THIRD OR NON-MAJOR PARTY CANDIDATES

The presence of third party and independent candidates confuses dramatically the decision to debate. For the non-major party candidates, the decision is usually not difficult: they are nearly always eager to debate their major party rivals, for the debate promises them stature and needed exposure. The major party candidates, however, are noticeably reluctant to enter a debate that will include third party candidates.

Friedenberg discusses one reason for this reluctance—the tendency of third party candidates to inject into a debate issues that major party candidates would prefer to avoid.[41] Third party candidates typically have little chance to win an election and are more likely than the candidates of the two major parties to use an ideological or issue-specific appeal. Accordingly, third party candidates may use a debate as a forum to stimulate issue discussion. A second difficulty is that one of the major party candidates may believe that his own electoral coalition would be more susceptible to the third party's appeals than would his opponent's. Such a candidate would probably attempt to deny the third party the increased exposure and status of a debate, while the other major party rival might well champion the inclusion of the minor party candidate. This is precisely what occurred in 1980, when all three camps agreed that Anderson would draw more votes from Carter than from Reagan. Reagan, therefore, had an interest in promoting Anderson's candidacy and his inclusion in the debate, while Carter refused to participate in a three-man forum.

There are, however, several factors working in favor of third party inclusion. If the third party candidate has gained a degree of public credibility, a major party candidate may find it difficult to oppose his participation publicly. Such a position could create the perception that the major party candidate is "afraid" of his opponent and is being "unfair" to him. Again, 1980 is a case in point. Carter's advisers knew that the media would be critical of his refusal to meet Anderson, but calculated that it was preferable to accept this temporary criticism, with the election still six weeks away, than to risk giving Anderson's campaign a major boost.[42] Reagan and his spokesmen, of course, attempted to maximize the damage to Carter by playing on the theme of Carter's unfairness.

This kind of rhetoric from the Reagan camp made it difficult for him to deny Anderson a two-man debate after Carter officially withdrew from the scheduled three-man affair. The decision to debate was by no means taken for granted, for there were drawbacks to debating, primarily the possibility of a Reagan gaffe and the risk that Reagan would diminish the stature of his own campaign by agreeing to debate a candidate who clearly had no chance of winning the election. Ranged against these factors, however, were these considerations: a debate would boost Anderson's candidacy (primarily at Carter's expense), it would create an embarrassing situation for Carter, and it would give Reagan much-needed exposure.[43] Reagan, therefore, agreed to meet Anderson alone.

A final consideration that may lead one or both of the major party candidates to favor the inclusion of a minor party candidate is the dilution of won/lost perceptions that typify debates. In a two-man debate, the "horse-race" element is at its height. The format pits two candidates in direct competition, and post-debate analysis inevitably focuses on the question of "Who won?" With three (or more) participants, the impression of direct confrontation is reduced, and it becomes more difficult for the general public and the news media to determine an unequivocal "winner." A candidate who is not aiming at a "knock-out" victory over his opponent, but is mainly concerned with performing "respectably," may, therefore, welcome a third party participant as a buffer between himself and his main opponent.

The presence of a buffer has four major implications on the format and therefore on the interaction of the candidates. First, to accommodate the additional participant, either the number of questions to be asked or the response time has to be reduced, assuming the length of the debate is not increased. This is advantageous to a candidate who doubts his ability to develop extended replies on a variety of subjects. Second, the reduced speaking time in the three-way debate decreases the possibility of an embarrassing gaffe. Third, the number of rebuttals and surrebuttals might also be reduced due to the difficulty of arranging an extended three-way give-and-take discussion, thus reducing the amount of direct candidate interaction. Fourth, a candidate's major opponent may be forced to fight a battle on two fronts rather than concentrating his efforts on drawing a contrast between the two main rivals.

All of these factors were significant in Ronald Reagan's calculations in 1980. When the League of Women Voters Education Fund proposed a three-man debate, Reagan had a comfortable lead over Carter. He, therefore, wanted to use a debate to present himself as a responsible, "presidential" alternative to Carter, not necessarily to "defeat" Carter in argument. Additionally, Reagan and his advisers respected Carter's debating skill and command of detail, and feared that Carter might be able to score heavily against Reagan by comparing his own in-depth knowledge with Reagan's more general positions. Thus, Reagan's camp wanted Anderson in the debate to reduce the likelihood of the debate turning into a showcase for Carter's mastery of detail *versus* Reagan's vagueness, to reduce the chances of a Reagan gaffe, and to add a target for Carter's attacks.

PRIMARY VERSUS GENERAL ELECTIONS

It is difficult for presidential candidates not to participate in primary debates, regardless of their preferences or their analysis of the political situation. The recent tendency for presidential primaries to have large numbers of candidates (as many as seven in the 1976 Democratic and 1980 Republican forums), strongly encourages participation. Few candidates want to be distinguished as the "odd man out," to lose the opportunity to legitimate their candidacy by sharing the platform with other candidates, to endure the inevitable criticism of those who do appear, or to run the risk that local voters may perceive their failure to appear as a gesture of indifference or arrogance. A candidate's need for exposure in the presidential primaries is also a persuasive reason for participating. Many candidates enter the presidential race with low public recognition figures. All candidates enter the race with a limited budget and a nearly unlimited desire for media coverage. Under the circumstances, few will want to pass up the exposure granted by a primary debate, especially if it is televised. It is doubtful that Jimmy Carter could have risen from a 2 percent recognition factor to win the Democratic nomination without his performance in the 1976 candidate forums. Similarly, John Anderson's campaign might never have gotten off the ground in 1980 had he not distinguished himself in the Iowa Republican forum.

Ronald Reagan's refusal to participate in the 1980 Iowa Republican forum is a good illustration of the danger of nonparticipation. Reagan was clearly the best-known of the candidates and was, according to a survey by the *Des Moines Register* and *Tribune,* the choice of 50 percent of Iowa Republicans.[44] He was sure enough of his position that he spent only 41 hours campaigning in Iowa prior to the state caucus vote, and apparently felt that he had no need for additional exposure in a primary debate.[45] Reagan's public justification for not debating: he felt that primary debates would unnecessarily divide the party, a reflection of the "Eleventh Commandment" of the California Republican party that Republicans should not criticize each other. Whatever his motivation, the consequences of the decision were disastrous. The *Register* and *Tribune* survey found that his standing fell from 50 percent to 29 percent immediately following the debate.[46] Eventually, he placed second to George Bush in the caucus voting, a reversal that must be attributed in part to his nonappearance at the Republican forum.

The incentives to debate in the presidential primaries, of course, apply far less to incumbent presidents than they do to other candidates. Presidents do not have to rely on primary debates to garner media coverage for themselves. Nor do presidents have as much to fear from voter backlash for a refusal to participate: an incumbent president can usually find an acceptable reason for his failure to debate, as Jimmy Carter did in 1980 (the crises in Iran and Afghanistan) when he decided that a debate with Edward Kennedy would not be in his political best interest. For other candidates, though, no matter how well-known, how well-financed, or how favored they are, the experience of Ronald Reagan in the 1980 Iowa primary should serve as a warning that ducking primary debates can be dangerous.

COMMENT

The decision to debate is tied not to the candidate's deep-seated desire to expound on the issues or to serve the public or to any other idealistic—or altruistic—motive. It is predicated on one major consideration: can the debate enhance his image? Can it promote his attractiveness as a candidate? All other criteria are, at best, secondary or, at worst, naïve.

Professors and political pundits from the safety of their desks may repeat the few maxims that encapsulate the conventional wisdom about whether or not a candidate should debate. But the candidate's world is too complex to be summed up by simple rules like "incumbents shouldn't debate" or "if you are behind, debate." His decision must take into account a variety of possible impinging factors: media coverage, issue vulnerability, format implications, the political climate, public expectations, etc.

If candidates have lost their faith in the wisdom of the ages, can they at least draw consolation from modern technology and the new prophet, the public opinion pollster? Perhaps some, but not much. The pollster can indeed tell the candidate where he stands now, but he cannot tell him what he most wants to know—whether his image will be stronger on election day if he accepts or rejects the debate challenge. No one can predict how a candidate will respond to the pressures of a debate, or how the voters will react to his performance.

NOTES

1. Interview, Richard Cheney, November 18, 1977.
2. Lawrence F. O'Brien, *No Final Victories* (New York: Ballantine, 1974), p. 83.
3. David A. Leuthold and David C. Valentine, "How Reagan 'Won' the Cleveland Debate: Audience Predispositions and Presidential 'Winners'," *Speaker and Gavel* 18 (Winter 1981), pp. 60–66.
4. Elihu Katz and Jacob Feldman, "The Debates in the Light of Research: A Survey of Surveys," In *The Great Debates, Kennedy vs. Nixon, 1960,* ed. Sidney Kraus (Bloomington, Indiana: Indiana University Press, 1962), pp. 206–207; Hans Sebald, "Limitations of Communication: Mechanisms of Image Maintenance in the Form of Selective Perception, Selective Memory, and Selective Distortion," *Journal of Communication* 12 (September, 1962), pp. 142–149; David O. Sears and Steven H. Chaffee, "Uses and Effects of the 1976 Debates: An Overview of Empirical Studies," in *The Great Debates: Carter vs. Ford, 1976,* ed. Sidney Kraus (Bloomington, Indiana: Indiana University Press, 1979), pp. 237–239.
5. Sears and Chaffee, "Uses and Effects of the 1976 Debates," pp. 229–230.
6. Memorandum, Patrick H. Caddell to Carter campaign staff, October 21, 1980, in Elizabeth Drew, *Portrait of an Election: The 1980 Presidential Campaign* (New York: Simon & Schuster, 1981), p. 427.
7. Kurt Lang and Gladys Engle Lang, "Reactions of Viewers," in Kraus, *The Great Debates: Nixon vs. Kennedy, 1960,* pp. 313–330; Land and Lang, "Intermediate and Mediated Responses: First Debate," in Kraus, *The Great Debates: Carter vs. Ford, 1976,* pp. 298–313.
8. A primary consideration related to assessing the advantages of incumbency is the extent to which the incumbent can command television and radio exposure. The president has the greatest opportunity to do so with governors, mayors of large cities, and senators generally following him at a considerable distance. Ordinarily, congressmen have to compete for such exposure, for thirty-two of the fifty states have three or more representatives (and far fewer television stations). This problem is especially pronounced for congressmen in metropolitan districts. New York is the most striking example, with at least forty congressional districts within range of its major television stations.
9. Milton C. Cummings, author of *Congressmen and the Electorate* (New York: The Free Press, 1966), pp. 68–75, analyzes data from each presidential election year since 1920, compared the victory ratio of incumbent candidates and non-incumbent candidates when the district presidential vote was held constant for partisan loyalties. He found that incumbents are far more likely to win than challengers in districts with similar presidential voting. Donald Stokes and Warren E. Miller in "Party Government and the Salience of Congress," *Public Opinion Quarterly,* 26 (Winter, 1962), pp. 531–546, conclude that incumbents are not only more frequently recognized by their constituents and non-incumbents, but that voters are more prone to vote for a candidate whose name they recognize. Charles O. Jones in "The Role of the Campaign in Congressional Politics," in M. Kent Jennings and L. Harmon Zeigler, eds., *The Electoral Process* (Englewood Cliffs, N.J.: Prentice-Hall, 1966), concludes after studying four congressional elections that the rate of election loss for incumbents is lower than the rate for same party non-incumbents who seek to replace a retiring congressman. Thus, the probability of the incumbent's party losing his seat upon his retirement

is a serious concern. Offering a less traditional viewpoint, Robert S. Erikson in "The Advantage of Inconsistency in Congressional Elections," *Policy,* 3 (1976), pp. 395–405, claims that on the average only about two percent of the vote can be attributed to the incumbency advantage, acknowledging that in close elections this percentage can, of course, make the difference. He contends that while "being an incumbent may increase a candidate's share of the vote, it is the candidates with the greatest electoral appeal [which is, of course, in part a function of incumbency] who have the best chance of becoming incumbents."

10. Thomas E. Mann, *Unsafe at Any Margin* (Washington, D.C.: American Enterprise Institute, 1978), p. 73.

11. Ibid., pp. 9, 106, 107.

12. Richard Nixon, *Memoirs* (New York: Grosset & Dunlap, 1978), p. 217.

13. *The Presidential Election and Transition, 1960–1961* (Washington, D.C.: The Brookings Institution, 1961), p. 2.

14. Interview, Michael Duval, debate coordinator for President Ford, December 20, 1979; Interview with Richard Cheney.

15. Memorandum, Michael Duval and Foster Channock to Ford campaign staff, June 11, 1976. Excerpts from this memorandum can be found in Martin Schram, *Running for President 1976: The Carter Campaign* (New York: Stein & Day, 1977), pp. 253–268.

16. Memorandum, Duval and Channock, June 11, 1976; interview with Michael Duval.

17. Interview, Gerald Ford, March 24, 1978; interview with Richard Cheney; see also Richard Cheney, "The 1976 Presidential Debates: A Republican Perspective," in *The Past and Future of Presidential Debates,* ed. Austin Ranney (Washington, D.C.: American Enterprise Institute, 1979), pp. 110–120.

18. Interview, Gerald Rafshoon, March 9, 1978.

19. Memorandum, Samuel Popkin to Carter campaign staff, August 30, 1976.

20. Ibid.

21. Memorandum, Caddell, October 21, 1980, p. 410–412.

22. President Nixon's approval rating in the Gallup Poll reached a low of 24%; Presidents Ford and Carter scored 37% and 28%, respectively. By way of contrast, Presidents Roosevelt, Eisenhower, and Kennedy at their weakest still received positive ratings from approximately half the electorate. See the American Institute of Public Opinion, *The Gallup Poll: Public Opinion 1979* (Wilmington, DE: Scholarly Resources Inc., 1980), p. 179.

23. Evron Kirkpatrick, "Presidential Campaign 'Debates': What Can We Learn from 1960?," in Ranney, *The Past and Future of Presidential Debates,* pp. 3–13, 51–53.

24. Ranney, *The Past and Future of Presidential Debates,* p. 51.

25. Gerald Ford, *A Time to Heal* (New York: Harper & Row, 1979), p. 414.

26. American Political Science Association, *Report of the Commission on Presidential Campaign Debates* (Washington, D.C., 1964), p. 2.

27. Interview, James Baker, March 9, 1981; interview, Richard Wirthlin, March 10, 1981.

28. Robert Scott, "You Cannot Not Debate: The Debate Over the 1980 Presidential Debates," *Speaker and Gavel* 18 (Winter, 1981), pp. 28–33.

29. Murray Levin, *Kennedy Campaigning: The System and Style as Practiced by Senator Edward Kennedy* (Boston: Beacon Press, 1966), p. 223.

30. Ibid, p. 222.

31. Dan Nimmo, *The Political Persuaders: The Techniques of Modern Election Campaigns* (Englewood Cliffs, New Jersey: Prentice-Hall, 1970), p. 160.

32. Franklyn S. Haiman, "An Experimental Study of the Effects of Ethos in Public Speaking," *Speech Monographs* 16 (September, 1949), pp. 190–202.

33. Elliot Aronson and Judson Mills, "Opinion Change as a Function of the Communicator's Attractiveness and Desire to Influence," *Journal of Personality and Social Psychology* 1 (1965), pp. 173–177.

34. Robin Noel Widgery, "Sex of Receiver and Physical Attractiveness of Source as Determinants of Initial Credibility Perception," *Western Speech* 38 (Winter, 1974), pp. 13–17.

35. Wayne N. Thompson, *Quantitative Research in Public Address and Communication* (New York: Random House, 1967), pp. 123–129.

36. *Washington Post,* October 24, 1976, p. 1; interview, Barry Jagoda, December 16, 1977.

37. Dan F. Hahn and Ruth M. Gonchar, "Political Myth: The Image and the Issue," *Today's Speech* 20 (Summer, 1972, pp. 57–65.

38. Robert O. Anderson, "The Characterization Model for Rhetorical Criticism of Political Image Campaigns," *Western Speech* 37 (Summer, 1973), pp. 75–86.

39. Interview with Richard Wirthlin.

40. Interview with Richard Wirthlin; interview with James Baker.

41. Robert V. Friedenberg, " 'Selfish Interests,' or the Prerequisites for Political Debate: An Analysis of the 1980 Presidential Debate and its Implications for Future Campaigns," *Journal of the American Forensic Association* 18 (Fall, 1981), pp. 92–94.

42. *Philadelphia Bulletin,* September 14, 1980, pp. 1, 8.

43. Memorandum, Myles Martel to James Baker, September 9, 1980. See also Myles Martel, "Debate Preparations in the Reagan Camp: An Insider's View," *Speaker and Gavel* 18 (Winter, 1981), pp. 39–41.

44. Interview, James Gannon, February 3, 1978; Jack W. Germond and James Witcover, *Blue Smoke and Mirrors* (New York: Viking, 1981), p. 111.

45. Germond and Witcover, *Blue Smoke and Mirrors,* pp. 110–115.

46. Ibid., p. 114.

3

Goals and Strategies

Debate goalsetting and strategy selection are two of the more complicated concerns facing the candidate and his advisers. What should the candidate seek to accomplish during the debates and how can he best map out a strategy to translate those goals into fruitful political realities? What are his own and his opponent's strengths and weaknesses as he, his advisers, and the public perceive them, and which should be emphasized during the debate? Which audiences should be targeted by the strategy? Is the strategy, once defined, compatible with the overall campaign strategy, including the candidate's image? These manifestly complex and crucial concerns are the focal points of this chapter, which is divided into two parts: goalsetting and strategy selection.

GOALSETTING

The Value of Debates to the Campaign

The candidate's assessment of the value of debates to his campaign largely determines the extent to which he bothers to define specific debate goals and, in turn, pinpoint strategies and tactics. Several factors can govern such an assessment: the results of previous debates he has participated in or knows about, his standing in the polls and need for additional exposure, whether the debates are being held during an important stage of the campaign, the nature and amount of media coverage given to the debates, and public interest in the election. Among the potentially crucial factors that lie beyond the candidate's direct control are: how many voters will watch a debate or series of debates, which debate in the series will draw the greatest viewership, which segment of voters will be watching, what reporters will cover the debates and how, and what excerpts will be televised or broadcast (regardless of whether or not the debate is carried live).

A noteworthy example of a candidate's failure to estimate the potential value of a campaign debate, and act accordingly, occurred on the vice presidential level in 1976. Robert Dole, Gerald Ford's running mate, derogated the value of his debate with Walter Mondale almost from the moment it was arranged, claiming at least half seriously that it would compete unsuccessfully with Friday night high school football. But he was surprised to discover shortly after the debate that nearly fifty million viewers watched him and Mondale grapple in a contest that some political analysts argue helped win Carter and Mondale the election. [1]

Compatibility of Debates to Campaign Goals and Strategies

Debate goals and strategies often reflect those established for the campaign in general. When they are not compatible, the candidate may be reacting to developments in the campaign or the campaign may be disorganized. Two examples of incompatibility between campaign strategy and debate occurred during the 1960 presidential debates and the 1978 Pennsylvania gubernatorial debates. One of Nixon's major strategies during the 1960 campaign was to emphasize the value of his eight-year vice presidential experience over Kennedy's eight-year tenure in the Senate. However, this strategy could not be controlled in the face of both the panelists' hard questioning of him and Kennedy's pointed refutations buttressed by the skillful "selling" of his own credentials. Similarly, in 1978, Democrat Pete Flaherty's campaign commercials and literature touted his effectiveness as Mayor of Pittsburgh, a major strategy adroitly combatted during two televised debates by Republican challenger Dick Thornburgh who, for his own part, remained virtually immune from attacks on his experience because he had never held elective office.

General and Specific Goals

The candidate's image orientation lies at the heart of the goalsetting process. He wants either to outperform his opponent, or, when facing an especially formidable one, to at least hold his own—to make a respectable showing that will help him to maintain, if not increase, his support. But the sophistication with which candidates produce specific goals beyond these generalized ones varies considerably. In high level, heavily-financed campaigns involving potentially decisive debates, specific goals designated for targeted audience segments are, naturally, more likely to be well formulated than in lower level campaigns.

If the debate will not be televised, the main goals are generally to reinforce the attitudes of supporters in attendance and, often more important, to impress journalists. Since live audiences are ordinarily highly polarized, it may be ill-advised to appeal at great length to the uncommitted or to the opposition, unless the press in attendance can report the appeals to an audience of at least equal importance. The setting of goals for a televised or broadcast debate is likely to be more complex. Hubert Humphrey failed to take this into account during the 1960 West Virginia primary debate with John F. Kennedy.

As a result, he appealed to Americans in general more than he did to West Virginians. Kennedy did not forget who would actually be voting, thereby pinpointing the most important audience to which to appeal. A win in the primary was a much stronger message to send to Americans in general than some quickly forgotten rhetoric.

The debate in Des Moines preceding the 1980 Iowa Republican caucus is a more recent example of the complexity of the goalsetting process. Initially, the debate was to be televised live by all three major networks during Saturday evening prime time. However, when the Democratic primary debate scheduled for two days later was cancelled, live coverage of the Republican debate was also canceled by the three networks, although public television did carry it and CBS televised a full taped replay the following morning, a Sunday, at 7:00 A.M. (EST). Had the original schedule been kept, the six primary contenders would have needed to appeal simultaneously to Iowans and to American viewers in general. But, since the revised schedule meant that relatively few Americans outside of Iowa would watch the debate, most of the candidates sensibly focused their arguments and appeals on issues pertinent to Iowans, e.g., grain exports.

Defining which segment of an audience should be targeted can be extremely complex. Should a candidate be more concerned with reinforcing existing support, winning the uncommitted, or converting the opposition? General campaign strategy dictates that supporters should not be taken for granted; not only might they defect, but more likely, they might not vote at all. This dictum has great currency for debates as well, but the extent to which it is stressed depends on the nature of the candidate's base of support and, of course, on his position in the campaign. If the candidate is leading his opponent by a reasonably safe margin, his major goal is generally to reassure his supporters or, at least, to avoid doing anything that might jeopardize their support. George Bush adopted this strategy for the 1980 Iowa caucus, which he won. Reassured by his victory, Bush used the same strategy six weeks later in the first New Hampshire debate, expecting that he would either defeat Reagan in the state's primary or lose by a small margin. But Reagan soundly defeated him, his more than two-to-one margin attributed in part to Bush's relatively lackluster debate performance. Thus, the strategy of caution through the ostensibly risk-free approach of reassuring existing supporters can invite serious risks, including defeat.

If the candidate faces a decidedly uphill climb, he must also woo the uncommitted, and possibly the weakly committed opposition, both of which, according to limited research, are more likely to be influenced by debates than are strong partisan opponents.[2] To accomplish these goals, the candidate may need to risk losing weakly committed supporters or creating nonvoters. In such instances, the candidate has to calculate (often somewhat blindly) whether the sacrifice of some supporters might not attract a greater number of his new audience. In so doing, he must not only understand his own support base—how large and solid it is and why—but the nature of the uncommitted and the weakly committed opposition as well. Do they constitute a potentially decisive audience? To what extent are they likely to attend, watch, or listen to debates? To what extent are they likely to vote? Are they more or less likely to vote than a segment of the candidate's supporters? What issues and image factors are most likely to influence them? What party do they generally vote for? What affiliations other than party might be pertinent, e.g., religious, ethnic, union, professional? How, specifically, do they perceive the candidates? In high level, well financed campaigns these questions are addressed mainly by the candidate's pollsters. In low level campaigns, candidates often form their own polling apparatus (sometimes with national party guidance); but the sophistication of their methodology and interpretations tends to be low.

John Anderson faced many of these questions in setting his goals and strategies for the 1980 presidential debate with Ronald Reagan. Anderson's minimal goal in the campaign, and by extension in the debate, was to maintain a support level of at least 5 percent, which was the qualifying standard set by the Federal Election Commission for receiving federal campaign funds. To many observers, there was little doubt that Anderson would attain this goal: his standing in the polls was 15 percent and rising, and the increased exposure and respectability conferred upon him by the debate was expected to boost his campaign even further. However, Anderson's maximal goal, winning the election, was problematic to say the least. In the short run, he needed to inspire and mobilize his dedicated supporters to increase campaign contributions dramatically to pay for an October media campaign. In the long run, he had to convert massive numbers of Carter and Reagan voters. He had to do this, moreover, without abandoning "the Anderson difference," i.e., the perception of him as a principled, "uncommon" politician that was the basis of his appeal to his original coalition. Taking all these factors into account, Anderson decided that his debate goal must be to distinguish himself clearly from both Reagan and Carter, and to do so on the basis of principled, issue-oriented stands, not on personal attacks.

Addressing the issue of goals for presidential debates, political scientist Nelson Polsby counsels a Republican candidate (whose party is significantly outnumbered by the Democrats) to "conduct himself in a way that does not polarize sentiment but appeals to a bi-partisan audience . . . ," and cautions his Democratic counterparts against debating at all, "since their chances of converting Republicans are in general far less than the chances that Democrats will defect."[3] The conduct of the candidates in the three presidential debates since 1960 has largely reflected this advice.

The soundness of Richard Nixon's goals for the 1960 presidential debates has often been questioned. Clearly, however, one of the principal reasons that he accepted the networks' invitation to debate was to gain access to Kennedy's Democratic support base, which outnumbered his own by approximately a five to three margin. Although he was severely criticized for his "me too" strategy in the first and most important debate, he had to court the uncommitted and the weakly committed Democrats; relying solely on his own support base would have been woefully inadequate. Thus, Nixon did define his goals well; his difficulty lay principally in his manner of implementing them, a point that will be developed later.

In 1976 Jimmy Carter's goals, according to key advisers Stephen Lesher, Patrick Caddell, and Gerald Rafshoon, were "to shore up perceived weaknesses among likely supporters rather than to expand support."[4] Carter's advisers, knowing that he held an eighteen-point lead over Ford entering the first debate, told him to approach the debates as a forum "for reassuring doubters, removing questions about competence and experience" rather than as an opportunity to convert the opposition.[5] Correspondingly, Ford's goal was to erode Carter's lead by stressing the value of his experience, and hence his competence, in contrast with Carter, who had never held national office.

In 1980 Ronald Reagan found himself in a position similar to Jimmy Carter's four years earlier. In fact, one of Reagan's predebate memos closely parallels the Carter memo quoted in the previous paragraph: "The Governor has built a coalition large enough to win the presidential election, and hence, we want to use this debate to reinforce our base and motivate them [sic] to turn out on election day."[6] Carter faced a more difficult task than Reagan in 1980. First, he had to improve his position among his own supporters, many of whom had no great enthusiasm for him and looked on him mainly as the lesser of two evils. Second, and more difficult, he had to strip Reagan of much of his independent and disaffected Democratic support. As noted previously, Carter's advisers believed that debates rarely converted voters, but they thought that the 1980 debate was potentially an exception to the rule, for it was occurring in an election "populated by two unpopular candidates," "marked with great volatility," and containing many "soft, undecided, and minor candidate voters."[7]

Image Goals

As candidates and their advisers contemplate goals, strategies, and tactics, they are, as explained in Chapter 1, significantly and sensibly concerned with the candidate's ability to project a favorable image. Candidates often rely heavily on their pollsters in defining their image goals, since they possess the most sophisticated basis for gleaning information necessary for this most important phase of the debate process. Pollsters often read off to the interviewee carefully constructed forced choice items regarding both the candidate and his opponent such as "strong . . . weak," "compassionate . . . uncaring," and "intelligent . . . dull," and open-ended questions that, once interpreted, can help the candidate form an image profile of himself and of his opponent. The profile clarifies not only how the sample as a whole regards him, but is normally broken down into numerous demographic categories which can be cross-referenced, e.g., sex, age, race income, education, party affiliation, marital status, voting intention, etc. For instance, the candidate can determine how he is perceived by married 25–30-year-old, middle-class, Republican females who wish to vote for his opponent. Once the candidate determines which voters he should appeal to, he selects from that polling information significant perceptions that should be reinforced or minimized within both the campaign and the debates.

In 1960 Nixon sought particularly to project competence and strength through both the general election and the debates; Kennedy, while also attempting to project competence, wanted as well to dissipate widespread perceptions that he lacked the maturity required for the presidency. In 1976 Ford's major image goals were to demonstrate that he was informed, intelligent, and competent, and to overcome the perception that he was a bumbler (a perception cultivated by the media), while Carter wanted mainly to demonstrate competence (which included grasp of the issues) and compassion.

In 1980 both sides agreed that affecting public perceptions of Reagan's image would be the most important aspect of the Carter-Reagan debate, and, in fact, of the entire campaign. Reagan believed that if he could project a "presidential" image, and show himself to be sensible and safe, he would win the election; therefore, he gave image strategy his highest debate priority. A pre-debate strategy memorandum makes this point clearly:

> The major debate task turns on enhancing Ronald Reagan's perceived trustworthiness. Simply, if more voters believe he is more worthy of their trust after the debate than they did before, his vote support will expand and strengthen. This can only be accomplished if the debate focuses (on the net) on Carter's incompetence and Reagan's compassion.[8]

After four years in office, Carter's own image was relatively set; he was given credit for being an honest and decent man, but doubts about his competence were widespread. Knowing that there was little that he could do in one debate to change perceptions of himself, he concentrated on attempting to mold the more malleable public perception of Ronald Reagan.

CREATING A STRATEGY

Two interrelated types of strategies are used to attain the candidate's image goals: relational and substance. Relational strategies pertain to the dominant mode of conduct or interaction between the candidates, panelists, moderator, and the audience. Substance strategies define the issues or content areas on which the candidate should focus.

Relational Strategies

Five broad relational strategies are available to the candidate: attack, defend, sell, ignore, and "me too . . . me better." *Attack* means that a candidate's arguments are offensively directed at his opponent's positions, party, character, or campaign. *Defend* is a candidate's response strategy after being attacked by his opponent. *Sell* is the candidate's presentation of credentials that are not clearly related to attack or defense. *Ignore* involves debating on the candidate's own terms, paying little or no heed to his opponent's arguments. *"Me too . . . me better,"* in effect a combination attack/sell strategy, is generally employed against a frontrunner or any candidate who has espoused a popular idea with which the opponent would be ill-advised to disagree. Thus, the candidate identifies with the idea ("me too") but explains that, if elected, he could relate to it more effectively ("me better").

The major factor influencing the choice of a relational strategy is the status of the candidates. Are the debaters both incumbents, or is only one or neither an incumbent? Generally, a non-incumbent, especially when he is behind, is more *attack*-oriented and the incumbent is more *sell*-oriented. When two non-incumbents are involved, a common strategy is for the candidate of the "out" party to attempt to associate his opponent with the alleged weaknesses of the incumbent administration, while the candidate under attack either dissociates himself from or defends it. Nixon and Humphrey, both vice presidents seeking the presidency, could not afford to dissociate themselves from Eisenhower and Johnson even if they had wanted to, since they needed their support. However, even candidates of the same party as an incumbent administration frequently dissociate themselves from it if the administration's image is considered a campaign liability. In fact, at this writing, shortly before the 1982 Congressional elections, one of the more frequent strategic concerns voiced by my clients, all House and Senate Republicans, is their uneasiness in identifying with President Reagan's austere economic policies and their realistic fear that their opponents will attempt to expose this vulnerability through debate.

The candidate's standing in the polls is another significant factor in choosing a relational strategy. Although incumbents are generally frontrunners, they do not always enjoy this position. They must be prepared to take risks— to attack more freely than they otherwise might—and, generally, to defend and sell with no less vigor. This approach is especially advisable if the challenger has a good chance to score big with weak, uncommitted opponents and supporters—hardly an unusual prospect.

Attacking

Under most circumstances, it is advisable for a challenger to attack an incumbent, especially if the challenger is behind by a sizable margin. The attack strategy is necessary to undermine the status afforded by incumbency, which consistently produces favorable attitudes among voters regardless of the incumbent's actual performance. To demonstrate crucial differences between the incumbent's actions in office and the voters' attitudes, it is necessary to attack, especially if he can be thrown on the defensive.[9] An incumbent frontrunner, on the other hand, in many cases does not need even to call attention to his challenger, much less attack him, for he can gain reelection merely by reminding voters of his identity.[10] If, however, his support is in any way endangered, he should probably at least refute his challenger and possibly counterattack. Thus, a candidate attacks not only when he is a challenger, but when he feels that he can lose support by not attacking. That is, if he is too sell-oriented and does not attack his opponent's positions enough, he might project either arrogance or softness.

In 1976 the attack element of Carter's debate plan focused on Ford's economic record. But Carter's advisers expected that Ford would hit hard at Carter's record as governor of Georgia, so they had to prepare a defensive strategy as well. Finally, Carter planned to use the area of foreign affairs to sell himself. A pre-debate memorandum stated that Carter should introduce foreign affairs issues not to attack Ford but to "expand perceptions of Governor Carter's competence by drawing out and fleshing out his background and experience."[11] Ford's principal strategy to erode Carter's lead was to use attack to force him to be more specific on the issues. As Dick Cheney, Ford's chief of staff, stated: "As long as the public perceived Governor Carter as holding views very close to their own, our prospects of winning in November were slim indeed."[12]

The complexity of the choices involved in determining relational strategies can also be seen in Ronald Reagan's two 1980 debates. The strategic question facing Reagan in the first debate was how does one relate to a debate opponent who is not a serious contender? The decision in the Reagan camp was to adopt a "pass through" strategy (a variation of the *ignore* strategy), which is a combination of ignore and attack: in effect, to debate Carter through Anderson, who would serve merely as a foil. That is, Reagan would ignore his actual debate opponent: he would direct little of his fire at Anderson's positions, and would refuse to enter into a lengthy defense when Anderson attacked unless the attack was potentially damaging. Instead, his main focus would be on his absent rival, Jimmy Carter, and in particular on the Carter record. In so doing, Reagan would try to sell himself as a moderate, responsible candidate.

Anderson's basic strategic challenge was to present himself as a viable alternative for voters dissatisfied with the Carter record, but also unsure about Reagan, which was clearly a sizable portion of the electorate. Public opinion polls showed that disaffected Carter supporters were the most likely source of increased Anderson support; however, trying to convert these voters by an aggressive attack on Carter involved some difficulties, especially in light of Carter's absence from the debate. An attack on the absent President might be seen as unfair, and would also lend credence to charges from the Carter camp that the debate was merely a partisan forum for two Republicans. Anderson, therefore, needed to direct at least some of his fire at Reagan. Prior to the debate, in fact, Anderson intimated that he would launch an all-out attack on Reagan to distinguish himself as a clear alternative. However, the actual intensity of Anderson's attack fell far short of what he had promised. Instead, he largely contented himself with contrasting his own issue positions with Reagan's, rather than raising questions about Reagan's competence or responsibility. Anderson's strategy thus mixed a strong element of "selling" with attack. Despite this well-crafted strategy, the debate must have been frustrating for Anderson. The man he most needed to attack had secured a degree of immunity by declining to participate, and the man available for attack ignored Anderson's charges while he pursued his own debate goals.

In the second debate, Reagan faced two important strategic questions: How could he attack Carter without reinforcing the public perception that he was overly aggressive, and how could he best defend against Carter's charges that his issue positions were extreme and simplistic? For the attack option, Reagan's advisers made two basic recommendations: first, Reagan's attack should focus on domestic policy, not foreign affairs, thus minimizing the chance of reviving his "mad bomber" image problems; second, he should allow Carter to set the attack tone of the debate, i.e., he should carefully modulate the intensity of his attacks so that they are no more aggressive than the attacks Carter is launching at him. Reagan's defense strategy was based on the idea that he must not *appear* defensive and thus imply some validity to Carter's charges. Reagan was advised to respond to Carter's attacks with a smile and good humor, thus diminishing the impact of the attack. He was also instructed to project a sense of righteous indignation when attacked, as if to say that Carter is leveling charges that are misleading and that have been refuted many times before. Reagan's line (which he created himself), "There you go again," embodied this strategy perfectly. Finally, Reagan's advisers thought it important that he "sell" his record as governor of California. Emphasizing his experience and his success as governor of the nation's largest state would counteract Carter's charges that his policies were based on an outdated and simplistic ideology. Specifically, Reagan could argue that the same ideas that worked in California would work at the national level.

Jimmy Carter's dominant strategy was heavily weighted towards attack. His advisers realized that it would be difficult to sell his policy accomplishments: in foreign affairs, the Camp David accord was overshadowed by the more recent Iranian and Afghanistan crises, while at home, the economy had worsened significantly. The sell strategy was, therefore, restricted mainly to Carter's personal characteristics—he was a man of compassion, of vision; a man who could be trusted to act thoughtfully and moderately. Wanting him to spend as little time on the defense as possible, Carter's advisers recommended that he minimize past failures by emphasizing two themes—"I have learned much in my first term," and "Some of my decisions were not popular, but they were right"—and then quickly counterpunch by attacking Reagan's positions.[13] The purpose of the attacks would not be to try to pin Reagan down on specifics, but to emphasize the vagueness and evasiveness of his answers.

Attack strategies are often implemented in a more aggressive manner in debates for lower level political office than in presidential debates. In presidential debates, an incumbent wants to be perceived as statesmanlike, not as a partisan in-fighter. A challenger is restrained in his attacks by the need to appear respectful toward the President and, of course, by his desire to project a "presidential" image of his own.

Strategic calculations actually encourage a more confrontational style in many lower level campaigns. Many candidates will enter the campaign with a decided advantage, whether based on party registration, incumbency status, or a combination of the two. The classic campaign advice under these conditions is to downplay issue appeals and entrust one's election to party identification, superior visibility, and whatever record of constituent service an incumbent can point to. A candidate in these circumstances would hope for a relatively noneventful debate. For the opponent, however, a major "breakthrough" is necessary if he is to win, and debates are often used to accomplish this. A candidate who is trailing badly has considerable incentive to raise emotional issues, escalate the rhetoric of the debate, and try to pressure his opponent into a serious mistake. The leading candidate, faced with such an attack, may find himself being drawn into precisely the kind of divisive and highly charged confrontation that he had hoped to avoid.

Finally, the nature of the issues and a lack of rhetorical sophistication may contribute to a more frequent occurrence of debate "fireworks" at lower political levels. Especially in local government and state legislative campaigns, the issues are likely to be ones with immediate and clearly-seen consequences: Where will the high school be built? How will the zoning laws be changed? Which neighborhood will be redeveloped? Will an offending land-fill be shut down? What is to be done about pornographic book stores? Emotional responses by both the audience and the participants are more likely on issues like these than on the remote and complex issues of public policy discussed in presidential debates. In fact, a candidate with limited debating skill may quickly, and perhaps unintentionally, escalate the emotional level of a debate in these circumstances by being unable to modulate his attacks.

The 1980 Congressional Debate Survey suggests that challengers in Senate and House campaigns differed in their use of an attack strategy. Senate challengers reported that "Attack the opponent's record" was the most important of the specific strategies in the debate. On a one to five scale of importance, "Attack the opponent's record" was given the highest possible score (5) by six of the nine challengers, and had an average score of 4.55. Among House challengers this same item was given the highest score by less than half of the twenty-one respondents, and ranked in average importance below the item "Display candidate's knowledge and competence" (a "sell" strategy). These results may reflect the fact that Senate incumbents, more than their House counterparts, are forced to take visible stands on policy issues and thus are more open to attack by their opponents.

Defending and selling

Defending and selling are popular as dominant strategies when the candidate has a hard lead, has a reasonable chance of capturing a lead, does not want to risk creating a backlash, or, of course, when the opponent is not particularly vulnerable to attack. Defending becomes especially important when a potentially decisive issue position or action has been attacked. A dramatic example of a defensive posture made imperative by a strong attack is shown in the following exchange between Republican presidential contenders Philip Crane and John Anderson during the 1980 Midwest Forum:

CRANE: John, I want to be up front with you, John, because you've done something most recently that I cannot support, and I cannot imagine any Republicans supporting it, if you want to know the truth.

We have not had a shot at that United States Senate, a realistic chance, in a quarter of a century or more. Now, you signed a fundraising letter for such progressive members of that Senate as George McGovern, Frank Church, John Culver, Birch Bayh, some of the most vulnerable people—I'm not talking about the issue, John—

ANDERSON: Will you yield?

CRANE: Yes, I'll be happy to as soon as I finish.

It's not the issue, John. It's a question of a Republican signing a fund-raising letter to try and keep those prominent, in my judgment, most ultra and extreme left-wing Democrats in the United States Senate, and you had a primary contest that I stayed out of last time, John. I didn't get involved in that race. It was a conservative challenging you. You had everyone from Jack Kemp to Jerry Ford come in there to campaign for you. The Republican Party has faithfully supported you for 20 years. And I think that is an ingratitude, John, it's an ingratitude that is sufficient that you forfeited the expectation of any support from Republicans.

ANDERSON: Will you yield?

CRANE: You know, honest men can disagree, and I have respected you, John, throughout the years even though I disagree with you. But keep in mind— you know [Senator] Don Riegle [D., Mich.] never voted with us. And your support for the GOP majority last year was 9 percent. . . .

ANDERSON: That's not so. But the letter was not a fundraising letter for George McGovern, for Frank Church, for any of these other people. What it was was a letter designed to raise funds for an organization which is supporting the principle of freedom of choice. And in the text of that letter it was pointed out that good men of both parties, and the names of two Republicans were mentioned in that letter, good men in both parties are being threatened with exorcism. They are to be exorcised from the political realm. They are to be driven out of political life simply because of the stand that they have taken on a single issue.

I happen to believe, Phil, that in the times that we live today, dangerous and critical as they are, that single issue politics is very divisive. . . .

And that letter, any fair reading of the text of that letter will indicate that it is designed to raise funds for the organization not for those individuals who are mentioned in the text of the letter. And I just have to insist on a correct interpretation.[14]

Selling is generally most appropriate when the candidate's credentials are not known, have been questioned or, of course, when a defensive or attacking strategy appears ill-advised. A good example of the skillful execution of the sell strategy was presented by Ronald Reagan during a debate in which he and other candidates were asked how they could relate effectively with a Democratic Congress:

> Well, for eight years I was the Governor of the most popular state in the United States. And that state, when I became Governor, was as bankrupt as the Federal Government is today. And I had a majority of Democrats, hostile Democrats, in both houses of the legislature.

> And yet we secured the welfare reforms, we secured—well, we took the state away from bankruptcy. I succeeded in giving back to the taxpayers over the eight years $5,700,000,000 in tax rebates and tax credits. Our bonds got a triple "A" rating, the reform of welfare cut a 40,000 increase in the welfare load to an 8,000 a month decrease. And it was all done with a Democratic legislature.

> And what Phil Crane said about communication, when I was faced with the opposition to all of those things, and I was, Democratic legislature—when you tell a Democratic legislature you want to give back an $850,000,000 surplus to the people, that's like getting between the hog and the bucket. You get buffetted about a bit.

> But I took my case over their heads to the people. And I told the people what it was we were trying to do. And I learned there that it isn't necessary to make the legislature see the light, just make them feel the heat.[15]

The 1980 Congressional Debate Survey suggests that both Senate and House incumbents placed their strategic emphasis on a "sell" strategy. Table 3.1 displays the average scores on a one to five scale for four strategies of incumbent debaters.

Among House incumbents, selling the candidate's competence is clearly the highest ranked item. Defending one's record and selling one's personality are rated equally and are of lesser importance. Attacking the opponent is of little concern. The Senate picture is somewhat different; defending one's record is ranked noticeably lower than in the House. The small sample size

TABLE 3.1   Incumbents

Strategy	Average Score	
	House	*Senate*
Display candidate's appealing personality	3.45	3.33
Display candidate's knowledge and competence	4.23	4.33
Attack opponent's record	1.95	2.17
Defend own record	3.43	2.50
	(n = 22)	(n = 6)

prohibits placing too much emphasis on this measure, but this low score may illustrate a point made earlier, that senators may find their record to be more vulnerable than do representatives and therefore may prefer to avoid a debate focused on defending their record.

Ignoring

Ignoring the opponent is an especially popular strategy when the format does not involve either cross-examination or counter-rebuttals, two features that make it difficult for candidates to avoid each other. Ordinarily, the frontrunner (especially an incumbent) is likely to ignore his opponent, although a challenger trailing the frontrunner by a narrow margin may want to employ this strategy either to promote the impression that he is the frontrunner or to avoid the risks of engagement. In other circumstances, opponents are ignored if they are so similar that attacking them would be fruitless or counterproductive, so far behind that referring to them may give credence to their positions and candidacy, or when an attack may introduce a tough issue to "win" or one that might conflict with more important points to be made.

Ignoring is probably easier to execute in multi-candidate debates than in one-on-one debates. The usually tight time constraints frequently restrict interaction, so that the potential backlash against a candidate who ignores his opponent (which may be perceived as arrogance) is effectively reduced. Such a pattern of interaction was obvious throughout the 1979 Philadelphia mayoralty debates, featuring William Green (D.) and David Marston (R.), who virtually ignored Lucien Blackwell (Consumer Party). This strategy was facilitated by the placement of the candidates' lecterns during their final televised debate. Marston's lectern stood stage left, Green's stage center, and Blackwell's stage right. Blackwell was, therefore, in essence, off to one side.

A common variation of the ignore strategy is the "above the battle" strategy. Here the candidate separates himself noticeably from the fray, using his response opportunities mainly to sell his positions and, on occasion, to refer lightheartedly to the tempest brewing amongst the other participants. Multi-candidate encounters are particularly conducive to this strategy, effectively executed by Ronald Reagan in 1980 in the New Hampshire and Illinois Forums.

"Me too . . . me better"

It may seem that the goal in a political debate is to differentiate oneself as much as possible from his opponents—to attack them doggedly as long as backlash can be prevented or to sell or defend one's credentials and positions as persuasively as possible. This impression is not altogether accurate. In campaigns where the candidates' more important positions are not particularly polarized and where the frontrunner is well respected, the trailing candidate, rather than disadvantageously polarizing sentiments, might want to employ a "me too . . . me better" strategy. By identifying himself, at least to an extent with the frontrunner's goals or policies, he can perhaps persuade weak partisans and noncommitted voters that he is better qualified to carry them out. In the first 1960 presidential debate, Richard Nixon chose such a strategy because he did not want to polarize sentiments. But, not only did he have difficulty proving the "me better" component, he overemphasized the "me too":

> (*Nixon's first words in the debate*): Mr. Smith, Senator Kennedy. The things that Senator Kennedy has said many of us can agree with.
> . . .
> And I subscribe completely to the spirit that Senator Kennedy has expressed tonight, the spirit that the United States should move ahead.
> . . .
> Here again, may I indicate that Senator Kennedy and I are not in disagreement as to the aims.
> . . .
> I agree with Senator Kennedy completely on that score.

Substance Strategies

In developing the substance strategy, i.e., the definition of the content area(s) on which the candidate focuses an attack, defend, or sell strategy, several factors should be considered. Among these are the candidate's and opponent's experience, character, issue positions, actions in office, party positions or record, and campaign practices. Where the strategic focus should be placed depends mainly on the candidates' potential or demonstrated strength in any of these substance categories in relation to his opponent's weakness. As mentioned earlier, if a candidate is not well-known, his major campaign goal is to sell himself—to place his credentials before the public; this takes precedence over issues.

During the 1976 campaign, Jimmy Carter's most frequently displayed credential was that he was not part of the corrupt, inefficient, Washington scene—that he was, instead, an effective administrator who had demonstrated as Governor of Georgia that he could make government work. Gerald Ford, trailing Carter, attacked these credentials during the first debate:

> . . . the Bureau of Census—we checked it just yesterday—indicates that in the four years that Governor Carter was governor of the state of Georgia, expenditures by the government went up over 50 percent. Employees of the government in Georgia during his term in office went up over 25 percent; and the figures also show that the bonded indebtedness of the state of Georgia during his governorship went up over 20 percent.

It is less common for members of a minority party either to attack the majority party or to promote their own party affiliation during a general campaign debate, since the minority party candidate must rely on support (and votes) from the "other" party to win. Thus, Republicans, who are frequently outnumbered, normally reserve their anti-party attacks for meetings of Republicans. Democrats, on the other hand, are prone both to tout their party identification and to attack Republicans at will. A major violation of the traditional Republican restraint took place during the 1976 vice presidential debate, when Robert Dole blamed the Democratic party for all of the wars of the twentieth century, a tactic that succeeded mainly in bringing his opponent, Walter Mondale, into his best debating form.

General campaign debates involving non-incumbents with little or no political experience often feature attacks on or defenses of the incumbent administration, since most other strategic options are generally less fertile. One of the better examples of this strategy occurred during the televised 1978 New Jersey Senate race debates between Democrat Bill Bradley and Republican Jeff Bell. Although this was a high level election, neither candidate had held political office. As a consequence, each sold or defended his own party positions and philosophy and refuted the other's in a reasonably spirited and informed exchange.

Alternatively, open-seat debates may focus on the personal qualities of the candidates, as is suggested by the 1980 Congressional Debate Survey. Candidates in open-seat races tend to be less well-known than incumbents, and do not have an incumbent's record to serve as a debate focus. The result, as shown in Table 3.2 is that open-seat candidates place a far greater emphasis on selling their credentials than on either attacking their opponent or defending their own record. These races thus seem to have a high potential for "personality" appeals as opposed to "issue" appeals. To the extent that an open-seat debate does focus on issues, the subject, for the reasons given above, will tend to be general political principles rather than specific past votes and positions.

Attacking an opponent's campaign methods, or selling or defending one's own, is seldom an important debate strategy, although it has been used skillfully in numerous instances. One of the more noteworthy examples occurred during the 1980 Iowa Republican primary debate when John Connally attacked Ronald Reagan's unwillingness to debate while also raising doubts about his positions on the major issues. After being asked how he and Reagan

TABLE 3.2   Open Seat Candidates

	Average Score	
Strategy	*House*	*Senate*
Display candidate's appealing personality	4.46	3.20
Display candidate's knowledge and competence	4.32	4.40
Attack opponent's record	2.76	2.40
Defend own record	2.44	2.20
	(n = 25)	(n = 5)

differed, Connally said after a rhetorically pregnant moment of reflection: "I can't answer that question. I wish Governor Reagan were here—Oh, how I wish he was here. I don't know how he stands on the issues."[16]

Congressional debates often provide an interesting contrast of substance strategies, with incumbents typically emphasizing their record of constituent service and challengers attempting to focus on policy issues. Most Congressmen assign a significant portion of their staff to constituent service, and thus can boast of a long list of benefits conferred on their district.[17] Their opponents, of course, are usually in no position to claim similar virtues. An appeal based on constituent service has the additional advantage of being relatively nondivisive, an important consideration given the mixed audience of congressional debates, especially when televised. Issue appeals, in contrast, risk alienating one portion of the audience in order to attract another. The incentives are thus strong for incumbents to minimize discussion of issue positions in campaign debates.

Of course, this rule is not without exceptions. Candidates with a weak record of constituent service or candidates who feel that they have staked out an especially popular position on an issue may choose to highlight issues in a debate. But the predominant election strategy for congressional incumbents is to minimize the impact of issues and depend on the incumbent's superior visibility and record of service to the district.[18] For the challenger, of course, arousing the voters over a sensitive issue is often the most effective way of overcoming the various advantages enjoyed by an incumbent. In these circumstances, the key to success in a debate will often lie in controlling the substantive focus of the discussion.[19]

PRIMARY DEBATE STRATEGIES

Debates in primary elections present unique strategic challenges for political candidates. The uniqueness arises from three factors: the undefined nature of issues in a primary election, the frequent occurrence of multi-candidate debates, and the constraints imposed by membership in the same party.

Issues are often more difficult to define and focus on in a primary debate than in the general election debate. The candidates, as members of the same party appealing to the same constituency, often have very similar positions. How many Democrats could have explained in 1976 how Morris Udall, Frank Church, and Birch Bayh differed on the issues? How many Republicans in 1980 could have differentiated among the positions of Ronald Reagan, John Connally, George Bush, and Philip Crane? (Senator Paul Laxalt, handed a copy of an unidentified speech by George Bush, the supposed "moderate" in the race, guessed that it was made by Philip Crane, the supposed "pure conservative.") Those issue differences that do exist are often difficult to transmit to the viewer in a multi-candidate race, in which each candidate must compete with other candidates attempting to focus attention on their own interests. Under these circumstances, it is unlikely that primary debates will result in a clear clash of issue positions in the way that general election debates occasionally do. It should be noted, however, that as the primary season wears on, the issues tend to acquire definition and the potential for issue clash increases. Some candidates will drop out of the race, and thus eliminate some of the "noise" in the campaign. Over time, certain issue appeals of the remaining candidates will prove to be more effective than others, and will gradually begin to dominate the primary campaign.

The multi-candidate format of the primary debate has several important consequences. It makes it difficult for a single candidate to focus the debate on a particular topic. Unless a topic has been defined clearly prior to the debate, multi-candidate debates will tend to shift rapidly across a variety of topics, as each candidate raises the points called for by his own strategy. It is also difficult to decide who one's opponent is in multi-candidate debates. Should less-favored candidates gang up on the favorite and attempt to bring him back to the pack, or does this strategy only result in improving the prospects for the number two man with little positive pay-off for the also-rans? Alternatively, should a candidate focus his attack on the candidate who is just in front of him in line, and attempt to move up by eliminating his rivals one by one?

Membership in a common party imposes a strategic constraint that does not exist in general elections: primary candidates must not be overly abrasive in their debate performance. Opponents in a primary debate are often colleagues, or even friends. Candidates also must be careful not to offend potential supporters in the party organization who may be supporting another candidate in the primary, but whose aid might become important in the general election. In addition, candidates must be aware that the candidate they are debating today may be their running-mate tomorrow. George Bush's characterization of Ronald Reagan's economic plan as "voodoo economics" may have won him some points in the primary, but it was repeatedly used against him by the Democrats in the general election (and hardly endeared him to many Republicans).

These factors combine to create difficult strategic problems for candidates in primary elections. The need to avoid abrasiveness plus the lack of one clear opponent mitigate against an aggressive "attack" strategy. The limited amount of time available in a multi-candidate forum, the competition from other candidates, and the frequent ideological similarity of rivals make it difficult for a candidate to adopt a strategy of "selling" the viewer on his issue positions.

Perhaps the most certain conclusion that can be drawn about primary debate strategies is that candidates will attempt to establish their uniqueness, i.e., to distinguish themselves from their fellow contestants. This uniqueness may be based on issue positions or personality, or most likely, of course, on some combination of the two. This was the recipe for Jimmy Carter's success in the 1976 candidate forums. In addition to being an "outsider," someone unassociated with "the mess in Washington," he also presented himself as the most conservative of the major candidates (George Wallace excepted). While the positions of the liberal candidates seemed to offer little ground for choice among them, Carter stood apart as someone clearly different. The combined vote of those attracted to this fresh personality and those looking for a more conservative candidate was enough to win the nomination for a man who started out with a 2-percent recognition factor. John Anderson tried to pursue a similar strategy in the Republican primary forums of 1980. "The Anderson Difference," as his slogan had it, consisted of an attempt to present himself as a candidate willing to adopt the right position regardless of its political popularity. Anderson took this to the extent of supporting President Carter's grain embargo in a forum in Iowa, and calling for gun control before a group of New Hampshire gun owners. Although Anderson was not as successful as Carter, he clearly became a force to be reckoned with throughout the primary campaign.

COMMENT

Goalsetting and strategy selection for political campaign debates are complex processes involving few, if any, absolute principles; hence the contingent nature of the foregoing discussion. The candidate and his advisers must, in the absence of absolutes, gather and study every available piece of authoritative information regarding their opponent's and their own positions, speaking skills, public regard, support base, and campaign momentum. From a careful analysis of this information, goals and strategy are born. Simultaneously, the candidate must decide the amount of risk he wants to take as he employs an attack, defend, sell, ignore, or "me too . . . me better" strategy, or a combination of any of these compatible with his campaign image. Since debates are highly unpredictable, the candidate must be strategically flexible. For example, if he is attacked more than he anticipates, should he defend or attack just as hard, or should he almost passively wait for the backlash generated by his opponent to take effect? While there is no definite answer to this question, a clearer sense of his strategic (and tactical) options can help him respond more effectively to the challenge.

Strategy is often perceived more as an obstacle to the public need for campaign information than as a debating necessity. And one of the major attacks leveled against the candidate's ostensibly overweening concern for strategy is the failure of debates to yield anything fresh or new. But should they? When Lincoln and Douglas met crowds as large as 20,000 seven times during the stormy 1858 Illinois Senate race, their audiences were not drawn by the expectation of something new; they wanted to enjoy the drama of conflict as they learned how the candidates stood in relation to one another on the most pressing issue of their day. And, 122 years later, when between 100 and 125 million Americans watched Reagan and Carter grapple, they wanted primarily to see how the candidates stood on the issues and to learn about their personalities. The absence of new information in debates is due not so much to the candidates' strategy consciousness as it is to their having followed closely each other's campaign. By the time they debate, each has generally treated on the campaign trail most of the important issues, including the opponent's positions. Political debate, therefore, rather than presenting an opportunity for the exposure of new issues, is mainly a forum for refining ones already raised.

One could now ask logically, "Doesn't strategy conflict with the refinement of issues?" Indeed it may. But understanding why the conflict occurs must go beyond simply blaming the candidates. They should be granted at least a reasonable opportunity to pursue a campaign strategy; in fact, failure to do so would be a sign of incompetence. Moreover, as we shall see, a candidate's lack of responsiveness could be as much the fault of poor questioning or a weak format as of an intent to evade the issues.

NOTES

1. Hal Bruno, journalist and panelist for the vice-presidential debate, now political director for ABC Television, told me in an interview on June 12, 1978 that he and many of his colleagues felt that Dole had injured the Republican ticket's chances by his debate performance. See also Jules Witcover, *Marathon: The Pursuit of the Presidency 1972–1976* (New York: Viking, 1977), pp. 612–616.

2. David O. Sears, Jonathan C. Freedman, and Edward F. O'Connor, "The Effects of Anticipated Debate and Commitment on the Polarization of Audience Opinion," *Public Opinion Quarterly* 28 (Summer 1964), pp. 615–627.

3. Nelson W. Polsby, "Debatable Thoughts on Presidential Debates," in *The Past and Future of Presidential Debates,* ed. Austin Ranney (Washington, D.C.: American Enterprise Institute, 1979), p. 184.

4. Stephan Lesher with Patrick Caddell and Gerald Rafshoon, "Did the Debates Help Jimmy Carter?," in Ranney, *The Past and Future of Presidential Debates,* p.137.

5. Memorandum, Samuel Popkin to Carter campaign staff, August 30, 1976. Popkin, a political scientist from the University of California at San Diego, worked closely with Patrick Caddell in the Carter campaign.

6. Memorandum, Richard B. Wirthlin, Richard Beal, and Myles Martel to Reagan campaign staff, October 21, 1980.

7. Memorandum, Patrick H. Caddell to Carter campaign staff, October 21, 1980, in Elizabeth Drew, *Portrait of an Election: The 1980 Presidential Campaign* (New York: Simon & Schuster, 1981), p. 410.

8. Memorandum, Wirthlin, Beal, and Martel, October 21, 1980.

9. James T. Kitchens and Betsey Stiteler, "Challenge to the 'Rule of Minimum Effect': A Case Study of the In Man-Out Man Strategy," *Southern Speech Communication Journal* 44 (Winter 1979), pp. 176–190. See also Joseph Napolitan, *The Election Game and How to Win It* (Garden City, New York: Doubleday, 1972), pp. 122–123; J. Larry Powell, "Strategies in a Statewide Secondary Education Race: A Case Study," *Georgia Speech Communication Journal* 6 (Fall 1974), pp. 19–30.

10. Ibid., p. 180.

11. Memorandum, Samuel Popkin, August 30, 1976.

12. Richard Cheney, "The 1976 Presidential Debates: A Republican Perspective," in Ranney, *The Past and Future of Presidential Debates,* p. 115.

13. Memorandum, Caddell, October 21, 1980, p. 422.

14. This quotation comes from a transcript of the debate prepared for the League of Women Voters.

15. Ibid.

16. "The Republican Presidential Debate," transcribed and printed by PTV Productions (Kent, Ohio, 1980), p. 11.

17. For a discussion of the importance of constituent service to Congressmen, see Morris P. Fiorina, *Congress: Keystone of the Washington Establishment* (New Haven: Yale University Press, 1977) and David B. Mayhew, *Congress: The Electoral Connection* (New Haven: Yale University Press, 1974).

18. Richard F. Fenno, Jr., *Home Style: House Members in Their Districts* (Boston: Little Brown, 1978); Thomas E. Mann, *Unsafe at Any Margin* (Washington, D.C.: American Enterprise Institute, 1978).

19. For a similar argument see Mann, *Unsafe at Any Margin,* pp. 74–79.

4

Tactics

Although debates have been criticized with some justification as nothing but showcases for highly programmed candidates engaged in displays of differences often more symbolic than real, they are obviously less managed than some other major forms of political communication: television and radio commercials, for example. Debates involve a real element of unpredictability for the candidate, and especially in a close race, this can be risky. No matter how well articulated the strategy or how well briefed the candidate, something unfortunate could happen: a gaffe, a weak response to an important question, a dramatic memory failure, a surprise issue, disproportionate attention to a minor issue, a self-defeating flash of temper, an awkward relationship with the television cameras, etc. However, preparation of a tactical plan can improve the candidate's ability to cope with or to avoid such factors.

This chapter is devoted to exploring the major considerations involved in selecting relational and substance tactics to implement the strategy already adopted. Relational tactics refer to those behaviors intended to influence the audience's perception of the candidate's personality. These tactics can be directed toward the opponent, the moderator or the panelists, or toward the audience itself. Substance tactics refer to the issue positions the candidate selects and his manner of couching them for maximum strategic advantage.

RELATIONAL TACTICS

Three interrelated categories embrace the relational choices available to candidates: physical, forensic, and tonal. Physical tactics refer to actual physical movements by the candidate. Forensic tactics refer to those argumentative behaviors or ploys that enable the candidate to project dramatically his mental agility or skillfully apply pressure to his opponent. Tonal tactics refer to the overall attitude or tone the candidate seeks to project or prevent through both his physical and vocal cues.

Physical Tactics

Stage tactics

Before the debate even begins, the candidate should make two tactical decisions that can affect significantly his command of the stage and the tone of
the debate: when to take the stage and whether or not he should shake
hands with his opponent. If the candidate decides to take the stage first, he
can project confidence—his readiness to do battle. At the same time, however,
he may be left anxiously and awkwardly waiting on stage, wondering when,
or even if, his opponent will show. The candidate who decides to come on
stage after his opponent can create an air of expectation which, upon his
arrival, heightens his command of the stage. Carter took the stage first during
the debates with Ford and Reagan, using the time to make notes. Reagan
deliberately took the stage after Carter to maximize command.

Strengthening Reagan's command of the stage was his decision to approach Carter at his lectern to shake his hand before taking his own position.
This decision is obviously easier to execute by the debater who shows up
last. Not only did the handshake project Reagan's command and friendliness,
but it caught Carter noticeably by surprise before at least 100 million viewers.

A handshake at the end of the debate can also be effective, although it
poses some risks. Specifically, it can appear phoney or wholly improper if
the battle between the two debaters was especially tense. If a handshake
nevertheless seems required, the candidate can, of course, certainly control
his friendliness.

Following the debate, a candidate may want to project the "good sport"
image by engaging his opponent in friendly conversation. In most instances,
this is inadvisable if television cameras are on or if photographers are present,
since a newsclip or photograph of the two in this pose might deemphasize
the polarity between them. However, there may be instances when a candidate
will want to deemphasize polarity to achieve closer identification with his
opponent, particularly if the opponent is more popular.

A final tactical consideration applies to who shows up on stage following
the debate and in what sequence. For instance, after the 1976 and 1980
presidential debates television cameras captured the candidates being greeted
by their wives and families. In 1980, Reagan's family was followed by a
procession of well known, prestigious advisers. Through such a tactical decision, the candidate can project such image traits as family loyalty, decency,
and, through the prestige of his advisers, competence.

Tactical eye contact

Eye contact is an important aspect of the candidate's physical image, especially
during televised debates where the audience has a closer view than do most
members of a live audience. Candidates use eye contact in a variety of ways.

Sometimes they do not look at their opponents when they are speaking for fear that their reaction to them might inadvertently communicate a perception inconsistent with their strategy. For example, a candidate would not want to project interest by looking at a candidate when his major strategy is to ignore him. This applies particularly to party candidates who often ostracize third party candidates by refusing to look at them. When a candidate does look at an opponent who is speaking, he often manifests dismay at what the opponent is saying. This can be risky, however, since it is easy to create an impression of disrespect.

Decisions about eye contact become difficult when a debate is televised from a studio where an audience is not present, or where the audience or panelists are blocked from the candidates' view. Even if there is no obstruction, given the stress of the situation, it is frequently impossible to understand an audience's or a panelist's reactions immediately—to interpret feedback. For example, although Gerald Ford was able to see panelist Max Frankel's reaction to his response to the Eastern European question in the second debate, he was apparently unable to interpret it. Some of Ford's advisers contend that had he realized its implication, he might not have committed the gaffe that may have contributed to his defeat.[1]

Whether or not advice about eye contact was given to Kennedy and Nixon in 1960 and Ford and Carter in 1976 is uncertain. Nevertheless, cameras did accentuate through reaction shots the candidates' eye and facial communication. Kennedy was generally seen listening intently to Nixon, a pose that may have projected maturity and confidence. Occasionally, Kennedy glanced quickly at Nixon and smiled in amused disagreement. These reactions were probably effective, largely because they *were* occasional. Nixon had eye contact problems throughout the debates; he often shifted his eyes dartingly and awkwardly toward Kennedy without turning to look at him directly. In 1976, Ford looked at Carter frequently, but seldom showed disagreement or ridicule. Carter, however, was caught a few times smiling in confident disagreement, a shot that probably appeared disrespectful to his detractors, but pleasingly strong to his supporters.

During preparations for the 1980 presidential debates, Carter received little if any advice about eye contact. This subject was, however, stressed during Reagan's preparations. He was advised to look at Carter when expressing righteous indignation and was told: "When Carter is speaking—especially when he is attacking you—look at him or take notes."[2] He was further counseled to avoid looking downward, a tendency he had during the debate with John Anderson, and which can suggest lack of confidence, indecisiveness, or lack of preparation.

Tactical notetaking can complement or serve as an effective alternative to tactical eye contact. Ford was counseled to take notes in his debate with Carter, not only when he needed to record a point he might forget, but also when he wanted to distract his audience when Carter was saying something with which he disagreed.[3]

While speaking, a candidate may occasionally look at or even point to his opponent to communicate his willingness to confront him. This tactic, while potentially effective, must be used cautiously by the candidate challenging a particularly popular contender. Otherwise, it may draw too much attention to itself—be too showy—especially if the candidate being pointed at calls his opponent on this behavior. John Anderson did just this against George Bush during the 1980 Illinois Republican primary debate: "George, you don't have to point your finger at me. Really, don't get so excited."

When candidates in televised debates are not looking at their opponents, at whom should they be looking? Should they look at the television camera, the live audience, the moderator, or the panelists? While there are no simple answers to these questions, the candidate's advisers often attempt to prevent or reduce the risk of misdirected eye contact by negotiating for the television cameras to be positioned so that the candidates will always be looking at a camera without seeming to. For example, they may arrange for at least one camera to be placed for the candidate to address the panelists and the television audiences simultaneously. This camera can also capture a front view wide reaction shot of both candidates. In addition, one or two sidestage cameras are often used to present a side view reaction shot of either or both candidates. This shot is normally closer and more dramatic than the wide front shot. During the 1980 presidential debates, a camera was designated for each candidate with color-coded Christmas tree lights to indicate clearly when it was on the air. This helped to lessen any confusion regarding which camera to look into.

The point to remember, however, regarding camera shots is that regardless of whatever influence the candidates' representatives may have concerning camera placement, lighting, or stage design, the director and cameramen are photojournalists and, therefore, exercise their own prerogatives regarding all shots. Nevertheless, the media advisers often confer in advance with the director to check the quality of all major shots. The head and shoulders closeup is the most frequently seen, the most potentially revealing, and therefore the most carefully scrutinized. According to Mark Goode, who served with Bill Carruthers as Ford's media adviser during the 1976 debates and as Reagan's in 1980, "on a head and shoulders closeup I want to see only the candidate, not a foreign object. If the eye wanders, the mind wanders."[4] If the shot is unsatisfactory during the check, the media adviser can request lighting adjustments or modifications in the set, e.g., straightening a wrinkle in the curtain, or moving a microphone or lectern. During one of the 1960 presidential debates, Kennedy's media adviser, Leonard Reinsch, visited the director's booth to protest the camerawork. Since then, director's booths have been off limits to candidates' media advisers during presidential debates.

Leaving the lectern

This tactic, employed more often before a live audience than in a televised debate (where the candidate's movements are more confined because of cameras and lighting), has three major purposes: first, to establish a close relationship with the audience; second, to contrast the candidate's extemporaneous skills with the opponent's rigidity; and third, to catch the opponent off-guard and perhaps force him to look foolish. I witnessed this tactic effectively used during a nontelevised congressional race debate in 1976 between incumbent Robert Edgar (D., Pa.) and challenger John Kenney (R., Pa.). Edgar, a minister with a well-deserved reputation for platform effectiveness, left his lectern at an appropriate point and moved closer to the audience, thereby bridging both the physical and psychological distance between them. Kenney's attempt to follow suit seemed awkward and self-conscious. The immediate result: he was told by audience members that they couldn't hear him, a reaction that caused him to return even more awkwardly to his original position.

Sitting versus standing

During the negotiations for the 1976 presidential debates, a lengthy, tense controversy developed between the Ford and Carter camps over whether the candidates should stand or sit. Carter's advisers insisted that he sit to reflect his informal style, while Ford's insisted that he remain standing, a position they regarded as presidential. The compromise between the two camps left both candidates standing but with access to stools adjusted to prevent the perception of differences in height between them in the sitting and standing positions. During the first debate, particularly during the twenty-seven-minute sound outage, Carter used his stool not only to relax but also to communicate his informal manner, while Ford determinedly stood throughout.

The sitting versus standing position may be preferable to a candidate for four major reasons: (1) to make the event appear to be more of a "discussion" than a "debate"; (2) to offset any impressions of equal status with his opponent which could be accentuated by a standing debate; (3) to reduce speech anxiety (including stiffness or lack of animation) which he is more prone to experience when on his feet; or (4) to deemphasize his lack of facility as a speaker or debater.

One technical problem posed by a seated debate is the opportunity to present opening and closing addresses naturally and compellingly. This problem is compounded by the fact that the speech manuscripts would be normally placed on the table flat and in open view of the audience, rather than on the slanted table of a lectern.

An allied concern is the extent to which the candidates should be physically separated from one another during the debate. Normally, if one candidate is much taller than the other, the shorter candidate's representatives vie for greater separation to prevent the live or the viewing audience from noting the contrasting heights. The height issue, in fact, was negotiated in preparation for the 1976 presidential debates. Since Jimmy Carter was approximately four inches shorter than Gerald Ford, the negotiators agreed to lecterns of various heights; specifically, each lectern was constructed to reach each candidate's belt buckle.

Closer lecterns, in addition, can accentuate both the perception of clash or conflict and the image that Candidate A can stand up to Candidate B. However, some campaign advisers prefer lecterns separated at a greater than normal distance, not only because they might want to deemphasize clash or equal stature but, as well, because they fear that if the candidate is too close to his opponent, he might be too prone to lose his composure—even to the point of initiating a fistfight.

One of the more dramatic instances in which the physical closeness of the candidates made a difference occurred in the 1982 Massachusetts governor's race debate between former governor Michael Dukakis (D.) and John Sears (R.). Sears, at least a foot taller than Dukakis, occupied a lectern immediately beside Dukakis, dwarfing him in a manner suggestive of the contrast struck between the tall, gaunt Abraham Lincoln and the short, rotund Stephen A. Douglas. The contrast between Sears and Dukakis was, in fact, accentuated when Dukakis would turn to lecture Sears, forcing the cameras to capture both candidates. Sears intelligently ignored Dukakis, as he prepared notes for his turn to respond.

Audience right or audience left?

Another issue related to the sitting versus standing question is whether the candidate should stand or sit to the audience's right or left. While no empirical study has addressed this issue, three interesting and conflicting hypotheses are worth considering: (1) in live, nontelevised debates, it makes little difference, since audience members will normally pay more attention to their candidate, regardless of where he is positioned; (2) in debates with a large, noncommitted audience, the speaker on the audience's right has the advantage, since most people are right-handed; (3) in debates with a large, noncommitted audience, the speaker on the audience's left has the dominant position, since we are trained to read from left to right.

To my knowledge this issue, normally resolved by a coin toss, has not become a thorny one in debate negotiations, nor should it, since most other issues are far more significant. One point, however, requires elaboration. The hypothesis advanced by some media advisers that the right side of the television screen is inherently more dominant than the left is of little significance, since cameramen present few shots of both candidates at once, relying instead almost exclusively on head and shoulders close-ups.

Dress

Normally, candidates for live or televised debates appear in well-pressed, attractive, but reasonably conservative business suits, complemented by white or telegenic blue shirts and coordinated ties. Republican candidates (particularly incumbents) sometimes round out this attire with a vest—traditionally associated with a more conservative political ideology. There are, however, occasions when one candidate attempts to gain an advantage by choosing a unique form of dress. During the 1976 California Senate race between incumbent John Tunney and S. I. Hayakawa, one of the thorniest issues raised during the debate negotiations was whether or not Hayakawa would be allowed to wear his Tam O'Shanter, his trademark. Tunney's team prevailed. During the 1978 Pennsylvania gubernatorial race, Democrat Pete Flaherty showed up for the first televised debate with Republican Dick Thornburgh in his shirt sleeves, a maneuver regarded as "tacky" and manipulative by many who watched it. During the 1979 Philadelphia mayoral race, Democrat Bill Green frequently debated while wearing half-glasses, an act that projected not only his confidence in winning (which he did), but also aloofness, if not arrogance.

The smile

There is little argument that the public is impressed by a candidate's ability to be confident and friendly—better known as "the nice guy image." Indeed, too serious a look can not only communicate a lack of confidence, but can as well transmit a contagious tension to the audience. The smile is a major means by which the candidate can simultaneously project confidence, control, "the nice guy image," and even superiority. During his first debate with Nixon, John F. Kennedy flashed a winning smile that contrasted markedly with Nixon's dour expression. In 1980, Reagan's engaging smile contrasted strongly with Anderson's taut, intellectual mien and with Carter's edgy, self-conscious appearance. The smile, however, as most any tactic, has its risks. It must not appear foolish or project ridicule; nor should it look like an arrogant smirk. For example, Jimmy Carter's smiles during his debates with Ford were regarded by many as forced and disrespectful to the President of the United States.

Press availability

The candidate's exposure to the press immediately following the debate has significant strategic and tactical implications. In fact, the media are often prone to give as much attention to this exercise as to the debate itself. Should the candidate claim victory, or humbly note that the voters should decide who won the debate, or choose some middle ground approach? Should he refute the opponent's last closing address or anything else said during the debate?

Claiming victory, while occasionally effective, is more likely to appear phoney and self-serving. Acting pleased nonverbally is another matter; specifically, if the opponent feels that he performed at least respectfully during the debate, his satisfaction with his performance should be no secret to his audience, including particularly the media.

Carrying the debate into the press interview can invite accusations of defensiveness if the candidate does not treat this event with consummate skill. I normally advise candidates to comport themselves during press availability as they did during the debate, unleashing attacks or refutation mainly in response to any damage noticeably inflicted upon them by their opponent. Of course, the challenging candidate who is trailing significantly in the polls may wish to take greater liberties in this regard.

Seldom is the press availability session conducted with the opponent present. Separate availabilities help prevent the debate from continuing beyond the structured exchange into an unstructured verbal—or even physical—confrontation. While separate availabilities protect both candidates, they are probably of particular benefit to candidates in a close race and to confident front-runners.

Forensic Tactics

Forensic tactics, as explained above, consist of the use of argumentative behavior or ploys to influence the audience's perception of the candidate's personality. The dividing line between forensic tactics and substance tactics (which will be discussed later) is not always clear. The essential distinction is that forensic tactics seek to shape the audience's perception of the candidate by controling the verbal interaction between the debaters, while substance tactics attempt to provide effective means for presenting the content of an argument.

Forewarning

A significant defensive tactic available to the candidate who feels that he can anticipate his opponent's attacks is to forewarn the audience of them—to preempt his opponent. Frequently, this tactic (called "innoculation" by persuasion theorists) involves refuting attacks made on the campaign trail, but not yet brought up in debate. The candidate who opts for this approach can be explicit or implicit. He can begin his argument with, "My opponent has said that I . . ." or simply state the argument without necessarily implying that he is refuting his opponent. Deciding which approach is best is not easy: the explicit approach can produce the appearance of defensiveness, or invite more clash over the issue than is intended, while the implicit may not be sufficiently strong to register the reaction sought.

Research has, to a limited extent, reinforced the advisability of forewarning. Sears et al. (1964) discovered that forewarning highly committed subjects of "forthcoming discrepant onesided propaganda" reduced its influence. The result, they reason, stemmed from the subjects' tendency to prepare their own arguments to fend off the anticipated "propaganda."[5] Research, however, has not yet considered the effectiveness of forewarning on weakly committed opponents. Nevertheless, since most candidates need to strengthen the resolve of their partisans, forewarning is generally advisable when a substantial number of them are included in an audience.

The shotgun blast

Few political debate tactics are more effective in throwing the opponent off balance than what I term "the shotgun blast," a forceful, concentrated, multifaceted denunciation of the candidate's character, record, positions, or campaign, containing references to several issues that cannot possibly be refuted within the response time alloted. The candidate who uses this tactic, rather than developing each element of his denunciation, shifts the burden of proof to his opponent. One of the more dramatic uses of this tactic occurred late in the 1972 Democratic presidential primary campaign when in a nationally televised debate Senator Hubert Humphrey (D., Minn.) hurled the following accusations at Senator George McGovern (D., S.D.):

> And I believe that Senator McGovern, while having a very catchy phrase where he says "Right from the Start with McGovern," or "McGovern Right from the Start"—that there are many times that you will find that it was not right from the start, but wrong from the start. We were both wrong on Vietnam [implying that both supported the Gulf of Tonkin resolution]. Senator McGovern is wrong on Israel. Senator McGovern has been wrong on unemployment compensation. Senator McGovern has been wrong on labor law, and on the three great issues here in California, on his massive, unrealistic, and I think rather outside welfare program. He's wrong. And on defense cuts, I believe they cut into the muscle and the very fiber of our national security.

McGovern, not to be thrown unduly on the defensive, the major risk in responding to such a tactic, fired at Humphrey a salvo of his own:

> Let me cite one quote, and I'm not going to belabor the record, but as late as October, 1967, several years after I had referred to Vietnam as the worst moral and political disaster in our history, Senator Humphrey was saying, "Viet Nam is our greatest adventure and a wonderful one it is."

Indeed, going on the attack right after being attacked is normally the ideal response unless the initial attack creates potential damage that requires a defend or sell response. If a defend or sell response is available, it must be selective, focusing only on where the damage has been the most serious; drawing too much attention to a less important problem can only accommodate the opponent's strategy.

The laundry list

The "laundry list" is a variation of the "shotgun blast," the major difference being that the debater, instead of leveling accusations, poses a concentrated series of difficult and often incriminating questions. The candidate to whom the list is being presented has available to him the same response options noted under the "shotgun blast," plus the opportunity to appeal to the audience's understanding by stating in effect: "Anyone can ask questions; not everyone can discuss complicated public policy questions intelligently."

Direct questions and challenges

The direct question and challenge is a most risk-prone tactic and is, therefore, unpopular. No presidential or vice presidential debate has included direct questions between the candidates, nor has more than a small percentage of debates on other levels. In fact, only 8 percent of the debates represented in the 1978 CDS involve this feature. If direct questioning is effective, it can pay enormous dividends, since it both enhances the electorate's perception of the candidate's strength, knowledge, and intelligence. Moreover, it can implicitly differentiate him from his opponent—particularly if the tone of the question suggests that the opponent could not answer it if he had to. But, not only can the direct question or challenge fail, it can also backfire; if the opponent anticipates it and responds skillfully, he can usually achieve an important gain that few, if any, other debate interactions provide.

Those candidates who do agree to direct examination normally attempt to select questions which will embarrass their opponent. This effect can be heightened by phrasing the question to contain a damning preamble often consisting of statistics, examples, the results of a study, or a quotation. Candidates, in fact, may be particularly anxious to ask the more damning questions as early as possible to throw the opponent off balance. Reinforcing this desire may be the expectation, accurate or not, that an early salvo may attract more viewers and even sustain viewership.

As a candidate prepares for direct examination, two caveats must be noted: first, he must assess the extent to which his opponent might "turn the tables" on him (see following discussion), reinforcing the axiom, "people who live in glass houses shouldn't throw stones"; second, the direct give and take, as implied above, is conducive to escalating emotions with all its attendant risks, including stridency, defensiveness, gaffes, and yes, even fist fights.

An additional implication of the direct question is that it can give more equal stature to both candidates. Specifically, in the absence of the panelists, the interaction of the candidates can cause the audience to compare them more closely, particularly since this format feature often results in more televised shots of both candidates at once than other format features.

In 1960 Kennedy confronted Nixon with a question that Nixon did not (and perhaps could not) answer: "You yourself said, Mr. Vice President, a month ago, that if we had provided the kind of economic aid five years ago that we are now providing, we might never have had Castro. Why didn't we?" At the end of the fourth debate, with no time remaining, Kennedy taunted Nixon: "and I challenge you tonight to deny that the administration has sent at least several missions to persuade Chiang Kai-Shek's withdrawal from these islands." Shortly before the final 1976 presidential debate, Gerald Ford was advised to relinquish the balance of his time to try to force Jimmy Carter to add to his answer to a question that he had ostensibly glided over. Mike Duval, his debate coordinator, disagreed:

> This isn't a bad idea, but obviously would work only if Carter did not expect it. The fact is that so many people have made this suggestion, [that] I am certain [that] Carter has been forewarned.

> Accordingly, I recommend that you do *not* use this ploy. Instead, we will provide you with a recommended response to Carter's refusal to answer the question.[6]

The most notable recent example of a direct question backfiring occured during the 1982 California Senate race debate between Democrat Jerry Brown and Republican Pete Wilson. During their televised debate on foreign policy, Brown tried to trap Wilson with an obscure question about the African nation, Namibia. Wilson, to Brown's apparent surprise, responded adroitly with a fluent, knowledgeable answer which reflected well on his grasp of international affairs and which drew widespread praise from the media.

Turning the tables

Turning the tables, a traditional debate tactic, has also been used effectively in political campaign debates. Basically, the tactic involves redirecting the essence of the opponent's attack back at him. The candidate who employs this tactic not only displays impressively his mental agility, but heightens the dramatic conflict of the debate as well.

During a 1952 Massachusetts Senate race, in a debate between Congressman John F. Kennedy (D.) and incumbent Henry Cabot Lodge (R.), each candidate cleverly turned the tables on the other. Directly following Lodge's opening remarks, which consisted of a general pillorying of the Democratic party, Kennedy deftly and forcefully challenged Lodge's accusation that previous Democratic administrations and Democratic controlled Congresses deserved the principal blame for not meeting the nation's needs, saying: "If we are to be held responsible for everything that went wrong, we must be credited with everything that went right."[7] Kennedy contended throughout the debate that the Republican party was divided. Lodge finally aroused the crowd to spontaneous laughter by saying: "I am looking forward to the day when Senator (John) Sparkman (D., Ala.) [Adlai Stevenson's vice presidential running-mate, a prototype anti-Civil Rights Dixiecrat] comes to Boston and Mr. Kennedy goes to meet him."[8] Kennedy later retorted in his own attempt to turn the tables, that Senator Richard M. Nixon (R., Calif.), Eisenhower's vice presidential running-mate, had also voted against civil rights legislation.

Another dramatic instance in which "turning the tables" was put to effective use occurred during the 1968 Oregon Senate race between Republican challenger Robert Packwood and four-term Democratic incumbent Wayne Morse. Throughout the campaign Morse's main "sell" strategy was his twenty-four-year seniority. In a debate held shortly before Election Day, Packwood revived a verbatim quote Morse had used fourteen years earlier:

> Never confuse seniority with ability because when you go to the mat ability will win every time. When you've got a chance to replace an incumbent U.S. Senator, even if he is a committee chairman, with a dynamic young legislative leader, take that opportunity.[9]

Flat denial

Flat denial is an exceedingly effective tactic in blunting an attack. This tactic involves the candidate flatly, forcefully, and succinctly denying the opponent's attacks in a line or two that may or may not be followed by an elaboration. In fact, a strong denial can make elaboration unnecessary. Flat denial was one of the major tactics in Ronald Reagan's debate repertoire, one that worked most effectively in his 1980 debate against Jimmy Carter:

> That is a misstatement, of course, of my position. . . .
>
> Well, that just isn't true. . . .
>
> There you go again.

Quotable and attack lines

A reasonably concise, compelling phrase standing by itself or used to introduce or to end a line of argument can have more impact than any other thing said during the debate. And its potential is especially pronounced when a television camera captures an excerpt for the nightly news—a strong possibility if the candidate has a "camera ready" repertoire of them. Quotable lines used in debate are ordinarily keyed to the candidate's major strategy—to attack, defend, or sell. Two good examples occurred during the 1980 Iowa Republican primary debate:

> If you're looking for a younger Ronald Reagan with experience, I'm here. [Robert Dole]
>
> I think the least qualified Republican in the race is infinitely superior to the alternatives. [Philip Crane]

The following examples are taken from the 1960, 1976, and 1980 presidential debates:

> KENNEDY: I don't think it's possible for Mr. Nixon to state the record in distortion of the facts with more precision than he just did.
>
> NIXON: Now, as far as his figures are concerned here tonight, he is again engaging in this, what I would call, a mirror game of "here-it-is-and-here-it-isn't."

CARTER: Mr. Kissinger has been the president of this country. Mr. Ford has shown an absence of leadership, and an absence of a grasp of what this country is and what it ought to be. That's got to be changed. And that's one of the major issues in this campaign of 1976.

FORD: Now, the Governor has also played a little fast and loose with the facts about vetoes.

CARTER: This is a heartless kind of approach to the working families of our country, which is typical of many Republican leaders in the past, but I think has been accentuated under Governor Reagan.

REAGAN: He [Carter] sees the solution to anything as another opportunity for a federal government program.

Highlighting evasiveness

A stereotypic and largely justifiable notion of political debates is that the debaters engage in a duel characterized by skillful evasiveness. Thus, the candidate who can project himself as nonevasive or as less evasive, without being too specific or sounding too much like a college debater, can increase his credibility and, as a consequence, the likelihood that he will "win" the debate. While the candidate can project his nonevasiveness by appearing candid, forthright, and comprehensive, he can also—and perhaps more effectively—project this quality by highlighting his opponent's evasiveness. Jimmy Carter was counseled to do just that in his 1980 debate with Ronald Reagan. In fact, Pat Caddell, Carter's pollster, considered one of the major strategies of the debate to be the need "to educate the audience about Reagan's elusiveness, capitalizing on the simplistic and rambling nature of the responses Reagan happens to give."[10] Caddell even recommended specific lines Carter could use:

Governor Reagan has not been specific. He has ducked that issue. Well, in the Oval Office you can't duck the issues. . . .

Well, I wish that issue were as simple as you make it sound. There is much more to it though.[11]

Caddell further advised that "the audience should be politely drawn into an amiable game in which each of Reagan's responses is watched closely to see if he ducks or doesn't understand another issue."[12]

Reagan, too, having reviewed videotaped excerpts of Carter's debate performances against Ford in 1976, was primed to be on the alert for Carter's evasiveness and to highlight it in a manner similar to that advised by Caddell. Reagan, leading off his rebuttal to Carter's response to a question Barbara Walters had posed regarding each candidate's proposed policy on terrorism, stated, "Barbara, you've asked that question twice. I think you ought to have one answer to it." Reagan's tactic backfired, however, when Walters later accused him of not being responsive to the same question.

Closing with a surprise

The debater designated to deliver the last closing address not only has an opportunity to project a strong or potentially effective last impression, as Kennedy and Reagan did in their crucial debates with Nixon and Carter, but, in addition, can use this address to "pull a surprise" on his opponent. Specifically, the debater can use this address to make a damning statement that can't be responded to. During the televised 1980 Pennsylvania senatorial race debate between Arlen Specter (R.) and Pete Flaherty (D.), Flaherty drew the closing position and used it to produce a seven-year-old newspaper editorial highly critical of Specter's role as Philadelphia's District Attorney. Specter, wary that Flaherty might use the surprise tactic in some form, was prepared to call a press conference following the debate to denounce it. However, he chose not to, since he did not consider the editorial to be particularly damaging and especially since he was pleased—and justifiably so—with his overall performance.

While the surprise might at first blush be considered a clever tactic, and one certainly within the ground rules of political campaign debates, it poses two major risks. First, a negative surprise ending may actually cause the candidate who uses it to be perceived as too negative—to the point of generating backlash in his opponent's favor. Second, it can be perceived as foul play—as sneaky—since the opponent had no opportunity to respond.

Tossing bouquets

In certain instances, it may be advisable for the candidate to compliment the opponent's conduct in office or during the campaign. This tactic has four major purposes: (1) to project the "tosser" as fairminded; (2) to diminish the impression that the candidate is too contentious; (3) to make it more difficult for the opponent to direct a strong attack; and (4) to diminish the object of the compliment as an issue for debate or as a criterion for the voter's choice. When, during the 1952 Massachusetts Senate race, John F. Kennedy applauded Henry Cabot Lodge's foreign policy record, he was not only enhancing the audience's perception of his fairmindedness, but he was, as well, pushing foreign policy aside as an issue, implying very indirectly that other issues in that race were more significant. Similarly, in the 1980 congressional race between Robert Edgar (D., Pa.) and Dennis Rochford (R.), Rochford complimented Edgar for his constituent service mainly as a means of keeping the issue off the debate agenda. An important variation of tossing bouquets is what I call the "bouquet with a thorn." A candidate might, for example, say: "I have to give my opponent credit for working hard while in office, but hard work is only as good as the results it produces."

The apology or confessional

The apology or confessional seems to be gaining favor as a debate tactic. The most notable example of a qualified apology was used by Jimmy Carter in the third 1976 presidential debate when he adroitly apologized for a controversial self-damaging interview recently published in *Playboy* in which he discussed far more openly and graphically than what generally seemed appropriate his views on sex. With eyes fixed on the TV camera and with all the sincerity at his command, he stated:

> I have to say that my campaign's been an open one. And the *Playboy* thing has been of great, very great concern to me. I don't know how to deal with it exactly. I agreed to give the interview to *Playboy*. Other people have done it who are notable—Governor Jerry Brown, Walter Cronkite, Albert Schweitzer, and Mr. Ford's own Secretary of Treasury, Mr. Simon, William Buckley, many other people. But they weren't running for President. And, in retrospect, from hindsight, I would not have given that interview had I to do it over again. If I should ever decide in the future to discuss my deep Christian beliefs and condemnation and sinfulness, I'll use another forum besides *Playboy*.

This apology, tooled largely by Charles Kirbo, one of Carter's more intimate advisers, was not actually responsive to the question being asked; rather, it was inserted as soon as Carter found an opening. Furthermore, as Carter sought to soften his culpability, he cleverly avoided mentioning that the *Playboy* interviews involving the other notables did not include their views on sex.

An example of a mildly qualified apology was used by John Anderson during the debate preceding the 1980 Iowa Republican caucus when seven presidential contenders were asked by Mary McGrory of the *Washington Star*, "Is there anything in your public career that you'd do differently if you had the chance?" While the candidates who addressed this question both before and after Anderson verbalized mainly in generalities, Anderson was disarmingly forthright.

> But I suppose as I look back over a career in the Congress and the thousands of votes that have been cast during that time, if I had one that I would change it would have been the vote that I cast in favor of the Gulf of Tonkin resolution in 1965, the vote that later was to be interpreted by Mr. Katzenbach [Attorney General and Undersecretary of State under President Lyndon Johnson] as a functional declaration of war, that led us down the road to Vietnam, with all the divisiveness that that brought.

Six weeks later, at the Manchester Republican Forum held shortly before the New Hampshire primary, Ronald Reagan used a far more qualified apology when in responding to an audience member's question he defended himself against a report that he had told an ethnic joke about Italians:

> I'm glad you asked that question because I don't think my apology was abject. It was sincere. I had not told the story the way it was reported by the reporter

who reported it. I do not go around telling ethnic jokes. I have been on the opposite side of that question, on the right side, long before there was anything called civil rights.

Very frankly, I was the victim of—in slang expression of the press—I was stiffed. I did not do it in the manner in which it was said. I did not tell that story to the press for that purpose. All I can do is say to those people who might have thought that there was an insult intended that they have my apology. I plead that I was the victim of something that was done.

The discussion happened to deal with humor and jokes to a few people of my own surrounding, not knowing anyone was overhearing. I said that here was one that had come along that had a new twist in the so-called ethnic joke. But you can rest assured that I don't tell them. I don't like them; and from now on I'm going to look over both shoulders, and I'm only going to tell stories about Irishmen because I'm Irish.

The apology gave Carter, Anderson, and Reagan an opportunity to show their human qualities by admitting error or poor judgment—contrasting themselves with the stereotypic politician who skillfully finds ways to mask his weakness. Indeed, there is within the human spirit a need to forgive—and even admire—the wrongdoer who confesses.

Timing tactics

The skillful tactician is sensitive to time. This sense includes the understanding that the crude impulse to speak as long as one can to increase his own and to reduce his opponent's exposure is often not the best approach to take. Indeed, tactical use of time in debate, by itself (regardless of content, personality, or any other factor) can influence electors both consciously and subconsciously. If, for instance, a candidate speaks excessively long, his opponent might try to highlight the candidate's prolixity and, in contrast, his own succinctness, with a strikingly shorter answer. A candidate might also offer an exceedingly short answer or none at all to call attention to what his opponent has said (perhaps at considerable length), to avoid a possible backlash, or to throw his opponent off balance by forcing him to speak sooner than he had expected.

Although lengthy answers create an impression of prolixity, they may also suggest knowledgeability and intelligence—traits integral to a selling strategy. The latter impression is especially likely if the opponent has been unable to sustain a response; thus, a well-informed candidate's negotiators often seek a format that provides for both specific topics and lengthy responses. For instance, during the 1976 debates, one of the major findings of the instant response analysis study conducted by Robert Teeter, Ford's pollster, was that the President fared particularly well when offering comprehensive, sustained responses. According to Dick Cheney, Ford's chief of staff:

The instant response analysis [conducted by Teeter] clearly demonstrated that the President had the greatest impact on those leaning toward Carter when he took the time to explain his position on an issue and his reasons for holding that view. The fairly lengthy answer moved 'Carter leaners' a significant distance toward a pro-Ford response, but brief answers did not provide sufficient explanations to overcome their bias. At the same time, the scores for the subgroup composed of 'Ford leaners' did not drop off even during a lengthy response. As a result, we altered our original beliefs that short, punchy answers were sometimes desirable and sought to emphasize lengthier answers in later debates.[13]

Repeating the question or commenting on the quality of the question to gain additional thinking time are two other fairly common tactics. Since a candidate's silent contemplation during a televised debate can be easily mistaken for his appearing stumped, stupid, or both, these tactics can serve as useful fillers to protect the candidate's image while he attempts to fashion a persuasive response.

One of the major timing decisions a candidate must make during a debate is how he can take the greatest advantage of the response opportunities available to him within a round of questioning. Does he, for instance, fire his strongest shots during his first response opportunity, or during the rebuttal or surrebuttal? Candidates probably approach this issue more by what comes to mind at the moment than by any preset plan. Nevertheless, it is not uncommon for a candidate to save his "best lines" for the last response opportunity within the round, thereby allowing him to end strong, especially since his arguments are more likely to stand unrefuted if they come at the end.

While there are very few hard and fast rules in political debates, one which has withstood well the tests of time is "honor thy time limits religiously." Any impact intended for remarks preceding the moderator's announcement of overtime is normally dwarfed by the impact of the announcement itself. Moreover, being the victim of an overtime announcement more than once in a debate can cultivate perceptions of both longwindedness and of taking undue advantage of the format.

During a Massachusetts Congressional debate between Margaret Heckler (R) and Barney Frank (D), both incumbents vying for the one seat resulting from their recently combined districts, Heckler was prone to going overtime. Frank, hardly known for subtlety, humored the audience during one of Heckler's more extended overtimes by taking a pretend nap.

"I pass"

Occasionally a candidate might choose to relinquish his response time with "I pass," or with "I have nothing to add" under the following circumstances: (1) when he sincerely feels that no more needs to be said—that all major points have been covered; (2) when the subject of the question pertains more to his opponent; or (3) in a related vein, when the question and the response incriminate the character of Candidate A and a response by Candidate B would be considered in bad taste. In this latter regard, the "I pass" can also allow the opponent to "stew in his own juices"; that is, by not responding, the candidate can, in effect, refocus the audience's attention on the negative perceptions cultivated by the opponent's previous response.

Tonal Tactics

The physical and forensic tactics discussed above comprise a repertoire of specific ploys or behaviors for creating desired perceptions of the candidate's personality. In addition, candidates need to control the general attitude or tone of their self-presentation so that it is consistent with their image goals. Tonal tactics address some of the perplexing problems candidates face in this regard. For example, how can a candidate appear strong and assertive without appearing combative or overbearing? How can he be responsive to his opponent's attacks, yet not be perceived as being defensive? How can he project assurance without projecting arrogance? This is the domain of tonal tactics.

Controlling backlash

A primary concern in debate is to avoid creating backlash; that is, an adverse audience reaction to a debater's behavior that results in a benefit to an opponent. Backlash can solidify the opposition, lose both uncommitted and weak supporters, and even reduce voter turnout. Backlash was a major concern in all of the presidential debates. In fact, backlash is probably the most serious risk a debater faces, particularly if the debate is televised.

The backlash issue has received considerable research attention. Stewart (1975)[14] found that any attack on a political opponent was regarded as mudslinging by at least a majority of the respondents. This result is even likelier when a low credibility source attacks a high credibility source on an issue with which the audience is identified. In such cases, the audience's opinion of the high credibility source (victim) becomes higher and that of the low credibility source (attacker) becomes lower. Cronen, relying on congruity theory[15] analyzed the effect of fallacy exposure and counterargument on backlash. (Fallacy exposure is an attack of the opponent's reasoning process, while counterargument simply justaposes arguments.) He concluded:

1. When meeting a weak opponent a public debater is better advised to use counterargument to enhance his likeability *if* he [the opponent] represents a point of view that is *contrary* to prevailing audience attitudes.
2. A public debater is best advised to use fallacy exposure when possible against a weaker opponent to enhance his likeability *if* he [the opponent] represents a point of view that is *consistent* with prevailing audience attitudes.[16]

Cronen's conclusions strongly imply that counterargument is less direct or personal and less capable of producing backlash than fallacy exposure. This may not always be true, however, since phrasing, tone, and nonverbal behavior are integral to whether or not backlash can be produced. The choice of counterargument versus fallacy exposure must be weighed in relation to the major relevant variables of the campaign, including: what the candidate is prepared to say; how prepared he is to exercise either fallacy exposure or counterargument; whether his style is slashing, statesmanlike, or something in between; the specific levels of commitment of both his supporters and opponents; and the predispositions of noncommitted voters.

Jeff Greenfield, in his primer for political candidates, advises that "it is generally bad form to attack first."[17] He argues that many viewers will regard an unprovoked attack as just standard political rhetoric, and that the opponent may even be able to capitalize on sympathy backlash. It is therefore preferable to allow the opponent to level the first attack, and then counterpunch. Even then, he suggests, attacks should be made quickly and casually as part of a longer and more positive statement, so that an opponent who attempts to respond will be perceived as overly defensive and carping.

Despite candidates' concern about producing backlash, they sometimes accept it willingly—even welcome it. A candidate may take a position that sacrifices potential support from one segment of the population to win or fortify that of another. And, as the backlash itself is witnessed and publicized, it can help to strengthen the support of the audience segment to which the appeal or argument is directed; that is, its members appreciate the sacrifice the candidate has ostensibly made in their behalf.

If a candidate is addressing both a live and a television audience, he may produce backlash in one and not the other. An example of this occurred during the 1962 Massachusetts Senate race debate between Edward Kennedy and Edward McCormack. McCormack's slashing attack of Kennedy's lack of political credentials other than the Kennedy name helped galvanize McCormack's supporters who watched him in person on the auditorium stage of his high school *alma mater;* but the people watching on television largely sympathized with Kennedy.[18]

Avoiding defensiveness

One of the more difficult persuasive challenges facing the candidate on the attack is to avoid appearing defensive. While attacking has the inherently positive psychological effect of implying that the candidate can perform better than his opponent, attacking too frequently or too stridently not only invites possible backlash, but also can suggest that the attacker is desperate. Righteous indignation is the happy medium between too much anger and too much defensiveness. By projecting this trait, or tone, the candidate appeals to the audience's sense of fair play. And in so doing, he also projects a strong image congruent with the audience's expectations of the personality traits required of the office. No better examples of this trait exist than Reagan's tone when he seized the microphone in Nashua during the 1980 New Hampshire primary and exclaimed, "I paid for this microphone!" or when, eight months later, with measured calmness, he said in his debate with Carter, "There you go again."

A candidate can also reduce the risk of appearing defensive by couching some of his attacks as self-sell arguments or by occasionally agreeing with his opponent in such a way that he doesn't concede too much. Verbalizing agreement was integral to Nixon's "me too . . . me better" strategy during the first debate with Kennedy, but it was probably overemphasized. Kennedy, who had won an earlier coin toss, began the debate with a seven-minute speech that, many have argued, made the difference in the election. Communicating confidence, maturity, and decisiveness through his aggressively earnest, rapid delivery accented by pleasing, well-tailored phrases, he laid out his thesis for the four debates:

> I should make it very clear that I do not think we're doing enough, that I am not satisfied as an American with the progress that we are making. This is a great country, but I think it could be a greater country; and this is a powerful country, but I think it could be a more powerful country.

He outlined the several areas requiring improvement, introducing each with "I'm not satisfied . . .," placed the blame squarely on Eisenhower's administration, and concluded by reaffirming his thesis: "I think it's time American started moving again." Nixon responded in what became one of the stronger examples of the "me, too" component of his strategy:

> The things that Senator Kennedy has said many of us can agree with. There is no question but that we cannot discuss our internal affairs in the United States without recognizing that they have a tremendous bearing on our international position. There is no question but that this nation cannot stand still; because we are in a deadly competition, a competition not only with the men in the Kremlin, but the men in Peking. We're ahead in this competition, as Senator Kennedy, I think, has implied. . . . And I subscribe completely to the spirit that Senator Kennedy has expressed tonight, the spirit that the United States should move ahead.

Reference tactics

Candidates are often uncertain about how to refer to their opponents, concerned that an improper reference might conflict with the tone which best complements their strategy, that it might communicate too much respect or, possibly, invite backlash. In fact, candidates who do not effectively resolve this issue sometimes hesitate awkwardly during debate when referring to opponents. The five most common forms of address and their major implications appear below:

1. *My Opponent.* The candidate who chooses this form helps establish a cold distance between himself and his opponent. Such distance may not be advisable if a challenger is involved in a nonpolarized campaign—if the

candidate must, to an extent, identify with a frontrunner. And it may be even less advisable if the opponent is so popular or holds such a powerful office that referring to him coldly could project disrespect.

2. *Mr., Mrs., Miss, Ms. (last name).* This form is, in most circumstances, safer than the preceding one, for such references connote simultaneously respect and distance. Ronald Reagan occasionally referred to Jimmy Carter this way with little fear of being perceived as disrespectful.

3. *The (title alone).* Candidates and their advisers often shy away from this form, feeling that it emphasizes the opponent's incumbency and thereby subordinates the challenger to him—even making him appear deferential. However, it may be effective if the incumbent is highly vulnerable to attack and the audience needs to be reminded that he is responsible for many of the problems cited. Whenever the form is used, it is important, particularly in presidential debates, that it is clear that the office *holder,* not the office, is being derogated.

4. *(Title plus last name).* The use of this form by a nonincumbent challenger may also emphasize his opponent's incumbency, but in a less cold manner than the previous form. Such an effect is not especially desirable unless, as mentioned earlier, the incumbent is particularly vulnerable. The form may, in addition, sound too deferential, although probably less so than reference to the opponent by title alone. When both candidates have titles, the candidate with the more prestigious one might, to emphasize his own superior credentials, refer to his opponent by title and name (or possibly by title alone). In 1960 Kennedy only occasionally referred to Nixon as Vice President Nixon, while Nixon rather consistently referred to Kennedy as Senator Kennedy. In 1976 Ford frequently referred to Carter as Governor Carter, while Carter only occasionally referred to Ford as President Ford. In 1980 Carter consistently referred to Reagan as Governor Reagan.

5. *(First name only).* First names are generally used to diminish the stature of an opponent, to establish the superiority of the candidate, or to suggest informality and warmth. This was Ronald Reagan's purpose when he referred to John Anderson as "John," (a decision made during his debate preparations). But first names cannot be used carelessly or backlash could result. For example, an incumbent president and his challenger would not be expected to refer to each other on a first name basis because it would appear disrespectful (particularly if the challenger chose this form), or too "palsy"—even to the point of diminishing the audience's perception of the polarity between the two.

There are several interesting strategic implications to how the candidate refers to himself. John F. Kennedy, Richard Nixon, and Jimmy Carter consistently used "I" when referring to actions they had taken, while Gerald Ford often used "we." The "I" can communicate the singularity of responsibility facing the presidential candidate—"the buck stops here" philosophy popularized by Truman. Moreover, it can convey strength by implying the candidate's instrumental role in fashioning the policies of his administration. However, if overused, it can communicate conceit, selfishness, and haughty insensitivity to the reality that few accomplishments in politics are made alone. The "we" is symbolic of the team player. It may imply the candidate's openness to advice and ability to work cooperatively with others, including the willingness to compromise; but it may also fail to communicate singularity of responsibility or strength. Thus, Ford might have been better advised to choose "I" more often than he did.

A less common practice is for the candidate to refer to himself by name. Lucien Blackwell, a minority party candidate in the 1979 Philadelphia mayoralty race, repeatedly did this in his five debates with William Green (D.) and David Marston (R.). While this form sounded unorthodox and was overdone, it helped to project Blackwell's sense of commitment and, of course, may have helped to increase his name identification.

Wit/humor

Wit can be a very effective and at the same time a very risky tactic in a political debate. On the positive side, it can project the candidate's deftness of mind and naturalness while creating rapport with the audience. Moreover, it can be used to attack an opponent without undue stridency. On the negative side, it can come off as flippant or caustic—as incongruous with the traits required for the office being sought.

In 1960 John F. Kennedy used his well-known wit to defend his presidential nomination when facing the Texas delegates who were considering the nomination of favorite son, Lyndon Johnson, the Senate's Majority Leader. Johnson opened the debate as chairman of the host delegation. He masked his acknowledged hostility toward Kennedy, introducing him as "a man of unusually high character" and "great intellect" and "a dedicated" and "devoted public citizen."[19] However, he coyly used innuendo to criticize Kennedy by referring to "some Senators" who had answered none of the quorum calls and had missed thirty-four of the voting roll calls during the round-the-clock debate on the civil rights bill held earlier that year. In his five-minute rebuttal, Kennedy took impressive command of the situation, putting his disarmingly pungent and effective wit on full display. Refuting Johnson's dig, Kennedy said that since Johnson had not identified the "some Senators," then "I assume he was talking about some other candidate, not me." He praised Johnson for his "wonderful record answering those quorum calls":

> So I come here today full of admiration for Senator Johnson, full of affection for him, strongly in support of him—for Majority Leader.[20]

Kennedy's wit was again displayed in one of the presidential debates when a panelist suggested that he apologize to Nixon and the Republican Party for some remarks of Harry Truman's:

> CHARLES VON FREMD: The Chairman of the Republican National Convention, Senator Thruston Morton, declared earlier this week that you owed Vice

Oregon Primary Debate, May 18, 1948. Harold Stassen addresses a national audience in the first broadcast debate ever held between presidential aspirants. Thomas Dewey (center, right table) is flanked by his issues advisors. *(Wide World Photo)*

John F. Kennedy makes a point in his first televised debate with Richard M. Nixon on September 26, 1960. Howard K. Smith, center, served as moderator. *(United Press International Photo)*

Two modern political gladiators have just made history, as their first presidential debate has ended. September 26, 1960. (*United Press International Photo*)

The last 1976 presidential debate is about to begin. October 22, 1976. *(White House Photo)*

Betty Ford writes a note while standing in for Jimmy Carter during an audiovisual check: "Dear Jimmy, May the better man win...and I know it's my husband." (*White House Photo*)

Ronald Reagan demanding the right for the four standing Republican presidential aspirants to be heard during the Nashua (N.H.) Primary Debate, February 23, 1980. Standing from left to right, candidates John Anderson, Howard Baker, Robert Dole, and Philip Crane. Seated: Jon Breen, moderator, and an upstaged George Bush, Reagan's scheduled debate opponent. (*Nashua Telegraph Photo*)

"There you go again." Reagan's famous deflecting line in the debate against Jimmy Carter.
October 28, 1980. *(League of Women Voters Photo)*

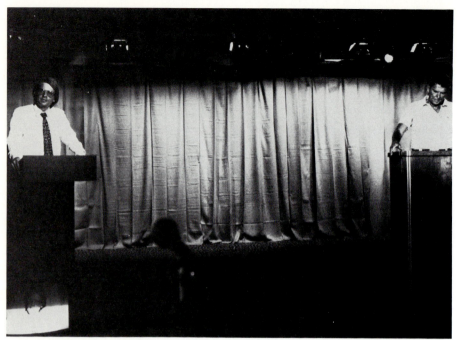

Ronald Reagan with David Stockman as John Anderson during a practice session on September 18, 1980. *(Photographed by Senator Howard Baker)*

Pete Wilson, Mayor of San Diego, pointing an accusing finger at California Governor Jerry Brown in one of their many encounters during the hotly contested 1982 Senate race. Wilson regarded the final two campaign debates as instrumental to his victory. *(Wide World Photo)*

LOST

Big-spending senator.
Believed hiding in Hyannis. Fearful of debating Ray Shamie, his 1982 election opponent. Known widely as "liberal" but now answers only to "progressive."

Allergic to reporters who ask trick questions, such as: "Why do you want to be President?"

CAUTION: To avoid irritating the senator, do not quote to him from his 1980 debate challenge to the previous president -- "I wonder how the Democratic party can nominate a Democratic nominee who refuses to debate his own record over the last four years. What's he afraid of? What in the world is he afraid of?"

$10,000
REWARD

To any person or non-partisan organization, not related to Edward M. Kennedy or his staff, who is able to get the senator to schedule a one-on-one debate with Ray Shamie for a statewide, prime-time audience. The debate must take place before the 1982 election.

This offer expires midnight, October 1, 1982
To apply to the senator for debate, call his campaign headquarters at 482-1982.

To apply for the reward, call RAY SHAMIE FOR U.S. SENATE headquarters at 969-9740. To be eligible a contestant must be a resident of Massachusetts. Or Roger Mudd.

Paid for by Ray Shamie for U.S. Senate

One of the cleverer gimmicks to entice a candidate to debate. Edward Kennedy was pressured by Ray Shamie's metadebate campaign to accept and turned in a lackluster performance to the pronounced benefit of the lesser known Shamie.

An Oval Office reunion including President Reagan, the author (center), and James Baker III, Chief of Staff and head of Reagan's Debate Task Force during the 1980 presidential campaign. *(White House Photo)*

President Nixon and the Republican Party a public apology for some strong charges made by former President Harry Truman, who bluntly suggested where the Vice President and the Republican Party could go. Do you feel that you owe the Vice President an apology?

KENNEDY: Well, I must say that Mr. Truman has his methods of expressing things. He has been in politics for fifty years. He has been President of the United States. They are not my style, but I really do not think there is anything that I can say to President Truman that is going to change his particular speaking manner. Perhaps Mrs. Truman can, but I do not think I can. I will just have to tell Mr. Morton that, if you'd pass that message on to him.

In sharp contrast to Kennedy's skillful and effective use of wit is Robert Dole's behavior in his debate with Walter Mondale. Undoubtedly, Dole's wit was far too caustic and flippant for many of the fifty million viewers.

I think tonight may be sort of a fun evening. It's a very important evening. It's a very historic evening. But I've known my counterpart for some time and we've been friends, and we'll be friends when this debate is over. And we'll be friends when the election is over and he'll still be in the Senate. . . .

Well, I've said, as I've traveled around the country, and mostly in jest, that as they say, "Why are you running for vice president?" I've said, "Well, it's indoor work and no heavy lifting.". . .

I know they [the Carter/Mondale Campaign] get great support, monetary support from George Meany. In fact, I've been suggesting that George Meany was probably Senator Mondale's makeup man. He may or may not have been. They did a good job. . . .

SUBSTANCE TACTICS

Substance tactics concern both the ideas a candidate decides to present in a debate and the means he uses to communicate these ideas. Both the ideas and the manner of their presentation should be in accord with the overall debate strategy. I shall first discuss how issues are selected and then describe the specific tactics for communicating them most effectively.

Issues

A major rationale for conducting debates is that they give voters more in-depth exposure to issues than other forms of campaign communication. While debates are normally more potentially informative than most other forms of campaign communication, there is uncertainty whether voters are, indeed, becoming more issue-oriented, as Nie, Verba, and Petrocik claim (1976)[21] or whether, as Margolis argues (1977)[22] this contention is based upon faulty research. Whatever the case, issues, defined as questions of public policy on which two or more candidates differ, pose for the candidate a host of tactical decisions. Chief among them: Which issues within the selected substance strategy areas should be introduced? Which issues raised by the opponent should be attacked? And, with what degree of specificity should they be introduced or attacked?

To understand the role of issues in a political debate, one must understand their role in the general campaign context. Professor Benjamin Page of the University of Chicago describes this nicely:

> Indeed, the most striking feature of candidates' rhetoric about policy is its extreme vagueness. The typical campaign speech says virtually nothing specific about policy alternatives; discussions of the issues are hidden away in little-publicized statements and position papers. Even the most extended discussions leave many questions unanswered. In short, policy stands are infrequent, inconspicuous, and unspecific.[23]

Debates, then, can pose a serious threat to the candidate who relishes the art of ambiguity and, conversely, can be a boon to that less common commodity, the issue-oriented candidate.

Although uncertainty surrounds the significance of issues and the issue-oriented voter, candidates rely heavily on issues as vehicles to build their images. Richard Wirthlin elaborates:

> Issues and the way the candidate addresses them can be the major vehicle to build or reinforce the image dimension. Thus, significant research will provide a campaign with information not only about which issues are salient, but also where the candidate and the opponent are perceived on the key issues. In this way, the campaign can focus on those issues that can best be developed to the candidate's advantage.[24]

Four major factors influence the selection of and emphasis on issues in campaign debates: vulnerability, strength, voter interest, and time. Naturally, if the candidate were vulnerable to attack on a particular issue, he would avoid raising it unless he could effectively preempt an expected attack or present a convincing defense. The candidate's vulnerability or strength on an issue can often be discerned from media accounts, mail, the candidate's formal and informal networks of advisers and informants, and from polls. Reasonably confident frontrunners, especially incumbents, often emphasize the three to five issues that they expect will help generate a favorable reaction, and determinedly avoid both raising others and refuting their opponents.' Being drawn in by an opponent's fire, they feel, promotes vulnerability and sacrifices crucial time needed to emphasize their priority issues. This thinking was significantly reflected in the advice given Reagan and Carter for their debate. Carter was advised to focus the debate as much as possible on nuclear proliferation, an issue that would draw attention to Reagan's major liability, the fear that he might be too prone to start a war. Reagan, naturally wanting to minimize his exposure to the war and peace issue, was advised to concentrate the weight of his attack on Carter's economic policy.

Although frequently important for the candidate's planning purposes, voter interest in issues is often subordinated to questions of vulnerability and strength. Particularly in lower level campaigns, candidates often engage in guesswork to assess voter interest in issues. However, candidates on higher levels benefit significantly from polls. In fact, polls even assess how an issue should be treated rhetorically; that is, what particular dimensions of the issues should be stressed. Indeed, the interest the electorate has in an issue can be far different from its capacity to be made interesting.

A candidate frequently concentrates on three to five major issues, but he must take pains to prevent any one issue from drawing too much attention to itself unless, of course, his position on it is extremely popular. However, avoiding the reputation of being a "one issue candidate" is not necessarily easy; a candidate may strive mightily to emphasize several issues almost equally, but nevertheless draw his opponent's or the media's attention to only one. This happened during the first third of the 1980 Illinois primary debate when John Anderson drew virtually uninterrupted fire from Bush, Crane, and Reagan for his heavily publicized proposal to reduce both gasoline consumption and social security taxes with a fifty cent tax on each gallon of gas.

The candidate's ability to establish issue priorities is crucial to his debating effectiveness. Not only must he determine what issues should be presented within the constraints of the format, but he must also determine how much time he should spend on each of them. This decision can be made tentatively before the debate begins, but must remain flexible in case of an opponent's attack, which may necessitate setting aside one or more important issues or developing them less fully than had been planned.

Once a candidate has established his issue positions and priorities, he has three major tactical options in deciding how to present his approaches to them: (1) as a way of alleviating or remedying a given problem or removing an obstacle that causes the problem; (2) as a way of treating a problem better than it is being treated; or (3) as a way of assuring the continued satisfaction of a need. Although the candidate's choice may vary from issue to issue, challengers are prone to choose the first two, which are inherently attack-oriented, while incumbents gravitate toward the third, which is a defensive or sell approach.

The extent to which a candidate should be specific or general in a debate once the criteria of vulnerability, strength, voter interest, and time have been assessed is both complicated and controversial. An important distinction must, of course, be made between the appearance and the reality of specificity. The candidate can give his audience the impression of specificity while he skillfully avoids revealing whether he is for or against a policy, whether his position is contingent or unqualified, or when and how the policy should be implemented (if he is for it).

There are three major reasons for a candidate to avoid specificity (whether or not he disguises his effort): (1) he may not know much about the issue in question; (2) specific commitments may be politically dangerous: public declarations of support or opposition have a binding effect that can impede the candidate's ability to negotiate; and (3) a specific approach to one issue may consume time that might better be spent on another issue. Traditionally, both the candidate facing an uphill fight and the frontrunner have gravitated toward generality: The trailing candidate has believed that generality is likely to alienate only opponents; the frontrunner, holding the same view, has commonly felt that electoral success involves keeping his name, credentials, and general appeals before the voters as he carefully avoids complicated issue analyses. In few debate settings, however, can a candidate rely on a steady diet of evasiveness. Although both supporters and opponents may react positively to a certain amount of evasiveness as an example of political skill, their tolerance is hardly unlimited.

Samovar (1962) conducted a revealing study regarding the relationship between ambiguity and party affiliation in the Kennedy-Nixon debates. He first asked twenty-five Purdue communication professors to classify twenty-four preselected passages from the Kennedy-Nixon debates into two categories, ambiguous or unequivocal. This method yielded only six passages which could be discretely placed in each category. He then played original tape recordings containing the twelve passages separately to thirty-five Republicans and thirty-five Democrats. His conclusion:

> Members of a political organization often found meaning in a message spoken by a speaker whose political affiliation was congruent with their own; when the source of the political message was incongruent with the listener's party, many listeners tended to report that the speaker failed to offer any information. When the speaker represented the *same* party as the listener there was an average of three (out of 20) responses that reported the speaker never gave his position. When the speaker represented a *different* political organization the average jumped to eleven responses.[25]

Froman, challenging traditional notions about issue tactics, argues (without empirical backing) that position issues rather than party symbols and broad generalizations (style issues) should be used with both potential supporters and opponents:

> And especially with opponents, broad generalizations about one's party being a party of peace, prosperity and clean government are likely to backfire, because they already perceive their own party in these terms. With opponents, it is necessary to stress position issues which might give them grounds for thinking that perhaps the candidate is an exception to the usually perceived party differences and hence the feeling of safety in supporting them.[26]

Potential supporters, Froman suggests, fall somewhere in between. The implication of Froman's argument for campaign debates is that specificity serves mainly the trailing candidate; secondarily, the one who leads by only a small margin; and, not particularly, one who holds a sizable hard lead.

A major Ford strategy throughout the three 1976 presidential debates was his use of relational and substance tactics to force Carter to make his stands more specific, since his major positions (according to Ford's pollster, Robert Teeter) were ambiguous enough to appeal to all segments of the electorate. Since Ford's positions and political philosophy were regarded by his advisers as well-known, he supposedly had few if any concerns about being too specific. A major tactic used by Carter during the second debate to protect his broad base of support was to avoid taking any foreign policy positions that could be labeled by Ford as liberal or conservative. "Hit him from the left and from the right," Carter's pollster, Pat Caddell, advised him.[27] Carter was further counseled to talk about human rights and then condemn Ford's handling of Chile; to talk about his inept handling of the SALT agreement and then highlight the world hunger problem. There was, therefore, something in Carter's attack strategy for nearly everyone.

Pseudo-issues and Pseudo-clash

The fake or pseudo-issue and pseudo-clash are two major substance tactics used by candidates to differentiate themselves from their opponents and to project desirable image traits. A pseudo-issue is a position taken by a candidate for selfish political gain which in reality is far less important than he implies— if not actually insignificant.[28] The classical "straw man" tactic is a popular species of the pseudo-issue. Here, as a diversionary measure, the candidate exaggerates the importance of the weaknesses within the minor arguments of his opponent's case, normally because he has difficulty assailing its strengths.

Pseudo-clash is a far more common commodity in political campaign debates and may, in fact, be one of their dominant features. This phenomenon involves projecting the impression that disagreement exists when it may not. For instance, a mayoral candidate asked to present his major proposals for improving police-community relations may suggest firing the police commissioner, establishing a police review board, and instituting a public relations program to boost the department image. His opponent may ignore these recommendations (thereby implying possible disagreement) and present his own. In reality, however, one or both candidates might approve of the other's proposal partially or wholly. The basis for the prevalence of pseudo-clash is probably clear from the foregoing discussion. It helps the candidate avoid attacking a popular proposal, defending an unpopular one, or creating backlash from perceived stridency or from polarizing the issues. Finally, pseudo-clash also allows a candidate to use his time and to be as specific or general as he pleases without being controlled by his opponent.

Appeals to special audiences

A major characteristic of political campaign communication is a candidate's inconsistent policy stands, a phenomenon rooted largely in his attempts to vary appeals for different audiences. However, a political debate, especially a televised one, is a great leveler; it makes such a practice difficult because a debater is exposed to many audiences simultaneously. Debaters do not abandon selective appeals. Rather, they generally proceed with greater caution and generality unless the debate is "off the record" before a special interest group. In effect, the normal appeal becomes so vague that almost anyone can accept it, or at least not reject it. A presidential candidate who might, for example, need to reinforce or woo the support of politically active Jewish voters by reaffirming his commitment to Israel's survival, might do so without discussing how he would actually carry it out. One can combine this kind of "commitment" with an attack on an opponent.

A prominent example of the skillful use of appeals occurred in a televised debate between John F. Kennedy and Hubert Humphrey during the 1960 West Virginia primary.[29] Throughout the debate Humphrey directed his appeals to the American people at large while Kennedy, in dramatic contrast, focused his appeals sharply and effectively on West Virginians as he identified with their promise, patriotism, and problems:

> Many of you who may be watching television in other parts of the country have been seeing a good deal of West Virginia through your television, and I wonder whether you realize what a varied state it is, and how unusual is its past, and how bright is its promise. . . .

> More men from West Virginia lost their lives in the Korean War than from any state in the union of its size. More West Virginians served in World War II than for any state of its size. I was in Hinton this morning, which is the home of the navigator who flew with my brother [Joseph] before he was killed.

He concluded by addressing the most important concerns facing his immediate audience:

> Last night I was in McDowell County. That county produces more coal than any county in the world. There are more people on relief in that county than in any county in the country. Now, why should there be 250,000 people living on a subsistence and below-subsistence distribution from the federal government who want to work—and 100,000 able-bodied men who want a job and can't find it, who have spent their lives in the coal mines, who have spent their lives underground working in thirty-five or forty inches and who want to get a job again, who want to work? That is the problem of West Virginia.

Jimmy Carter, without committing himself to any concrete action, was particularly effective in using appeals. During the 1976 debates he exposed Ford's less-than-vigilant response to the Arab boycott and his no more impressive policies on behalf of minorities. In 1980 he again demonstrated this skill in the debate with Reagan when he successfully appealed to Blacks, Hispanics, women, and Jews. In fact, these appeals probably owed some of their effectiveness to Reagan's tendency not to use them himself, despite the strongest advice that he do so.

Appeals to commonly held values

Persuasion theorists have long held that an audience's values are an integral part of the foundation upon which their attitudes are built. Values, according to social psychologist Milton Rokeach, act as life guides. He explains that values can be classified into two categories: terminal, the ultimate goals which motivate us; and instrumental, the guidelines which motivate our everyday behavior.[30] Values are not static; rather, they change gradually according to a person's condition and depend as well on sex, age, race and education. Any candidate who can genuinely and compellingly appeal to the more salient values can strengthen both his credibility in general by virtue of his own identification with the values and the acceptability of his positions as well, particularly if he skillfully links the values to them. An essential characteristic of any value to be appealed to in a debate is that it be applicable to all major segments of the audience. Thus, a candidate would support religion, not Lutheranism; ethnic pride, not Swedish pride.

Ritter and Gibson argue that while Carter was the master of "value images" during his debates with Ford, he became too focused on "reality images" during his debate with Reagan: He was too concerned with attacks on Reagan and a defense of his own record. The authors argue that this example illustrates a natural tendency for incumbents to be drawn into a discussion of "the details of governing and to neglect to address the hopes and aspirations of the electorate."[31] Indeed, Carter faced this problem, encumbered by a realization reinforced by his advisers that it would be extremely difficult for him to use credibly futuristic, value-oriented rhetoric. Moreover, since Carter used this type of rhetoric extensively during his campaign, particularly during his town meetings, Reagan was prepared to refer to it as diversionary if Carter also decided to rely on it during the debate.

Rhetorical questions

Rhetorical questions are used not only to stimulate audience involvement, but to control the issues of the debate without the necessity of developing the arguments the questions imply. John F. Kennedy used rhetorical questions effectively during the opening address of his first debate with Nixon:

> . . . I think the question before the American people is: Are we doing as much as we can do? Are we as strong as we should be? Are we as strong as we must be if we're going to maintain and hold out the hand of friendship to those who look to us for assistance, to those who look to us for survival? I should make it clear that I don't think we're doing enough, that I am not satisfied as an American with the progress that we're making.

In a strikingly similar fashion, Ronald Reagan, in his debate with Carter also used rhetorical questions to reinforce his major strategy, to keep the close of the debate focused as much as possible on the negative features of Carter's record:

Next Tuesday, all of you will go to the polls, and stand there in the polling place and make a decision. I think when you make that decision it might be well if you ask yourself, are you better off than you were four years ago? Is it easier for you to go and buy things in the stores than it was four years ago? Is there more or less unemployment in the country than there was four years ago? Is America as respected throughout the world as it was? Do you feel that our security is as safe, that we're as strong as we were four years ago?

"Man with the facts" tactic

A particularly common substance tactic is for the candidate to cite statistics and examples, sometimes to the point of excess. This tactic is used mainly by a candidate whose political experience and knowledge have been challenged or by one involved in a multicandidate debate who needs to distinguish himself from the others. Although the candidate's ability to refer freely to such evidence may enhance his image as one who is qualified to serve, this information may, of course, have been spoon-fed to him shortly before the debate. Kennedy used this tactic in the 1960 debates to diminish the alleged superiority of Nixon's vice presidential experience over his own as a senator.

In a 1968 debate Republican challenger Robert Packwood used this tactic adroitly against the Democratic incumbent, Senator Wayne Morse, while refuting the value of Morse's twenty-four-year seniority:

> When Senator Morse went to the Senate in 1944 we were third from the top of all states in the West when you compared what we got as opposed to what the federal government taxes. Today, in 1968, twenty-four years of Senator Morse later, we are last. Oregon gets $1.59; California, $1.63; Washington, $1.83; Idaho, $1.93; Nevada, $2.03; Utah, $2.86; Montana, $3.01; Arizona, $3.15; and Alaska, $7.33. We can't afford any more seniority.[32]

In 1976 Carter, according to one of his advisers, attempted to "spew out lots of facts as an indication of what a good grip he had on the difficult questions, especially economic questions."[33]

Complementing the "man with the facts tactic" is the candidate's use of credible source citations. John Anderson did this conspicuously during his debate with Reagan: "I recently saw a Princeton University study . . ." "The Harvard Business School study indicated . . ." By citing such sources, Anderson was stressing the rational character of his proposals and his determination to solve complex policy issues, a perception which may have contrasted markedly with what many viewers regarded as Reagan's simplistic, ideological—even radical—approach to issues.

A related use of the source citation is for the debater to refer to damning information contained in a report authorized by his opponent's administration. Reagan's briefing materials contained many such references drawn from reports prepared by the Carter administration, but he did not use any.

Visual aids

The use of objects during political debates can add spark to what often amounts to a dull exchange. Richard Nixon did so with great effect during his last debate with Jerry Voorhis in October 1946. Nixon opened by saying to Voorhis: "Congressman, I flatly challenge you to name one public bill of your authorship which passed both Houses of Congress during the last four years." When Voorhis' turn came for a reply, he referred to his instrumentality in establishing National Employ the Physically Handicapped Week. Thoroughly prepared, Nixon retorted, "It's merely a resolution," dramatically placing a copy of it in Voorhis' hands.[34]

During the 1960 West Virginia primary debate between John F. Kennedy and Hubert Humphrey, Kennedy produced a carton of powdered eggs to demonstrate the gravity of the poverty problem facing West Virginians. During a 1978 Illinois Senate race between incumbent Charles Percy (R.) and challenger Alex Seith (D.), Seith held up a dollar bill to emphasize its shrinking value and read verbatim an unfavorable characterization of Percy from his biography (which he held up to the television camera).

Another dramatic use of visual aids occurred during the 1982 Massachusetts Senate race debate between incumbent Edward M. Kennedy (D.) and Ray Shamie (R.) when Shamie effectively quoted and held up Kennedy's book (co-authored with Sen. Mark Hatfield) on nuclear disarmament to stress the irresponsibility of Kennedy's position. In this instance Shamie's use of the book made it transparent that he was not putting words in Kennedy's mouth regarding his position on the most important foreign policy issue of the campaign.

The use of such objects is not without risk. For this reason, advisers to frontrunners sometimes attempt during format negotiations to prevent them. A notable example of such a tactic backfiring occurred during a 1978 Pennsylvania Congressional race debate between Robert Edgar and Eugene "Sonny" Kane when Kane, emphasizing the purchase of American products, held up a picture of Edgar's Volvo. As many audience members were reacting to this tactic as a gimmicky cheap shot and, to an extent, as an unwarranted invasion of Edgar's privacy, Edgar cleverly retorted by offering anyone in the audience a ride home in his new Plymouth.

Illustrations, anecdotes, metaphors, analogies

One of the more frequent criticisms leveled at televised debates is that they are boring. While the degree to which they are or are not boring depends largely on the personalities and issues involved, television viewers are conditioned to expect more stimulation than what is characteristically offered by a debate.

All of the tactics herein discussed are capable of heightening audience attention. Illustrations, anecdotes, metaphors, and analogies are, however, especially suited to this purpose. Not only can they display the candidates' deftness of mind, compassion, or other qualities, but they can make the discourse of the debate more graphic as well; they can, in a sense, create word pictures in the viewer's mind that can facilitate both comprehension and believability.

In the Packwood-Morse debate of 1968, the year in which anti-Vietnam protest reached its climax, Packwood cleverly and graphically characterized the dissenters negatively as he acknowledged their right to dissent:

> What is my position on the right to dissent in this country? If we are talking about the people carrying pickets, the funny looking, barefooted, bearded, bead-wearing guys, they are not my cup of tea, but if they want to go up on the hill and raise turnips, if they want to come down here . . . and parade around like the rest of us have a right to do, that's their business.[35]

During the 1980 debates Reagan used two especially graphic references that simultaneously projected compassion and attacked Carter's effectiveness:

> Stand in the South Bronx, as I did, in the spot where Jimmy Carter made his promise that he was going to, with multi-billion dollar programs, refurbish the area that looks like bombed-out London in World War Two. I stood there and I met the people, and I heard them ask just for something that would give them hope. . . .

> We talk about the unemployment lines. If all of the unemployed today were in a single line, allowing two feet for each one of them, that line would reach from New York City to Los Angeles, California.

The difficult question

Potentially crucial to the candidate's ability to perform well during the debate is his ability to listen to a question, understand what it means, know what type of question it is, and remember its elements. He must also, of course, have been adequately briefed on the issues related to the question, and be able to answer it persuasively within the prescribed time limit in a manner compatible with his debate goals and strategies. This is a difficult task, but the skills necessary to accomplish it can be cultivated.

Listening to a question in a heated debate is not as simple as it may seem. As the question is being asked, the candidate may, for instance, be thinking about how he could have improved on an earlier response; about points unrelated to the question that he wants to make during the next response opportunity; about how well he is doing so far; and so forth. Compounding the difficulty may be the phrasing of the question itself. The panelist may be beclouding it with too much background information, or may be stating as part of the question an assumption or argument with which the candidate disagrees or a fact that he finds inconvenient. This may cause the candidate to tune the panelist out or to refute him internally while losing focus on the question itself. Any of these factors may be operating at once. And to make matters worse, a candidate may be loathe to ask for clarification, fearing that the rephrased question might be even more difficult to answer or that he may appear unintelligent to the audience.

Remembering the elements of the question can also be complicated, for the reasons just stated. Although taking notes might help candidates cope with this problem, they are often reluctant. This is either because: (1) they do not want to sacrifice eye contact with the panelist or audience; (2) they are fearful that such behavior might communicate lack of intelligence; (3) they are confident that they can remember the elements of the question; (4) or they may not want to "remember" all the elements because one or more might be difficult or awkward to answer—or actually unanswerable. The candidate who wants a portion of the question repeated faces two possible audience reactions: he may appear forgetful, possibly even unintelligent, or appear earnestly responsive. The latter reaction is more likely if the candidate's credibility is reasonably strong and if the question is lengthy, awkwardly phrased, or festooned with subquestions.

Crucial to the debater's effectiveness is his ability to handle questions which pose danger because of the manner in which they are phrased. These questions, called "banana peels" because of the candidate's potential to "slip" on them, fall into eleven categories. Listed below are examples of each and the major options a candidate has in responding to them, acknowledging, of course, that different circumstances might call for a response option more desirable than the ones presented here.

Type	Example	Major Options
1. Hostile	"How do you expect more liberal groups to support you with your rotten record on the environment?"	1. Point out hostility. 2. Show cool, nondefensive disagreement, taking exception to terms chosen. 3. Project righteous indignation, short of losing composure.
2. Speculative	"What do you expect union membership to be in this state in four years?"	1. Label question as speculative. 2. Generally, don't predict with any attempt to be precise; stick with optimistic generalities (if, of course, they apply).

Type	Example	Major Options
3. Hypothetical	"If interest rates drop to 12 or 13 percent within the next year, would you still propose raising the state sales tax?"	1. Point out hypothetical nature of question. 2. Refuse to answer because of phrasing. 3. Answer directly.
4. Picayune/ Overspecific	"What has been the percentage of growth of the Department of Transportation budget since 1978?"	1. Label question as overspecific. 2. If you don't know, say so. (Sometimes you may need to explain in a nondefensive manner why you don't know.)
5. Leading	"Why can't this state attract more industry with one of the best labor forces in the nation?" This question carries three assumptions: 1. The state is not attracting new industry as it should. 2. The state has one of the best labor forces in the nation. 3. The labor force should attract more industry.	1. If you agree or disagree with any of these assumptions, let it be known.
6. Value	"Which is a better choice for energy conservation, carpools or public transportation?"	1. Apply your definition of "better" without drawing attention to this term. 2. Point out the value term, define it and then answer the question. 3. Ask Questioner to define it and then respond.
7. Question Begging	"Isn't the main reason why we have so little	1. Point out politely that the question in es-

Type	Example	Major Options
	available energy because there are significant shortages of the types of energy we normally rely upon?"	sence argues in a circle—it answers itself without probing further.
8. Multifaceted	"How many workers are unemployed in this state? How has this level changed over the past four years? How does this state's unemployment compare with that of neighboring states'? What do you plan to do about the unemployment problem?	1. If each facet can be remembered and answering all won't cause harm (assuming there is ample time), then answer fully. 2. If harm can be caused by answering a remembered facet, it is probably best to "forget" it. 3. Don't hesitate to ask for a facet to be repeated if you are reasonably certain you forgot a "safe" one. 4. You may want to refer humorously to the number of questions asked. 5. If the questions cannot be realistically answered within the time allotted, say so, e.g., "perhaps it takes only a minute to ask all those questions, but it will take a lot more than that to answer them."
9. Vague, Unfocused	"What do you plan to do, if elected, to make this a better state in which to live?"	1. Define the question the way you wish—consistent with your persuasive goals. 2. Ask the questioner to clarify his focus.

Type	Example	Major Options
10. "Yes-No"	"Your campaign has been funded mainly by PAC contributions, yes or no?"	1. If "yes" or "no" is safe by itself, answer accordingly. 2. If risky, point out how the forced alternatives can interfere with a presentation of "the full truth." Then answer the question.
11. Nonquestion	"Unemployment is climbing; inflation is still spiraling; we are in a depression and ought to admit it."	1. Ask for a question, noting the nonquestion. 2. Respond to the nonquestion in whole or in part.

Nonresponsive insertions

One of the more obvious distinctions between traditional or classical debates and political campaign debates is the extent to which candidates are nonresponsive to the questions posed by the panelists. Since the relationship between panelists and candidates involves largely a polite, implicit struggle over who controls the issues agenda of the debate, the candidate must find openings within the debate—regardless of the format or of the questions—to insert arguments and evidence to reinforce his debate strategy. Waiting too long may result in a lost opportunity. John F. Kennedy, Jimmy Carter, and Ronald Reagan were encouraged to use and did use this tactic in their presidential debates. This tactic also appears no less frequently in many of the middle and lower level debates analyzed in this study.

The nonresponsive insertion can take on three forms: (1) it constitutes the entire response, regardless of the question; (2) it is presented at the beginning of the response opportunity, then followed by a more appropriate response to the question; or (3) it may follow the appropriate response. Normally the third one is executed without the candidate drawing the audience's attention to it, although a candidate occasionally asks for or states politely that he will use the remaining time to develop further an earlier response or to advance a new argument.

COMMENT

Indeed a political debate is fraught with countless behaviors springing from no fewer contingencies which may or may not impact on the candidate's performance. Because the interactions are complex and the stakes high, candidates are obliged to make the debate environment as risk-free as possible while benefiting from few, if any, absolute principles.

A mythology has developed that a candidate's detailed attention to tactical (and strategic) concerns results perforce in an unwarranted manipulation of the masses; anything done to improve the candidate's image, including his issue positions, is therefore a violation of the public interest.

This reasoning is simplistic. A candidate can phrase a position to make it more palatable without tampering with reality or with the electorate's rationality. He can attempt to catch his opponent unprepared or force him to make a damaging statement without being deceitful. He can apply the basics of relating to a television camera without deserving to be branded as "an actor." Candidates, therefore, should not be faulted for manifesting an image consciousness—for putting their best foot forward; to do so is integral to the human condition, particularly human competition. Candidates do deceive; there is no question about it. But strategic and tactical preparation and deception are not ipso facto equivalent.

NOTES

1. Interview, Michael Duval, debate coordinator for President Ford, December 20, 1977.
2. Memorandum, James Baker and Myles Martel to Governor Reagan, October 24, 1980.
3. Interview, William Carruthers, television advisor for President Ford during the campaign, March 25, 1978.
4. Interview, Mark Goode, July 8, 1982.
5. David O. Sears, Jonathan C. Freedman, and Edward F. O'Connor, "The Effects of Anticipated Debate and Commitment on the Polarization of Audience Opinion," *Public Opinion Quarterly* 28 (Summer 1964), pp. 615–627.
6. Memorandum, Michael Duval to President Ford, October 18, 1976.
7. From a tape recording of the Kennedy-Lodge debate supplied by the John F. Kennedy Library.
8. Ibid.
9. *Portland Oregonian,* October 26, 1968, p. 9.
10. Memorandum, Patrick Caddell to Carter campaign staff, October 21, 1980, in Elizabeth Drew, *Portrait of an Election: The 1980 Presidential Campaign* (New York: Simon & Schuster, 1981), p. 427.
11. Ibid.
12. Ibid.
13. Richard Cheney, "The 1976 Presidential Debates: A Republican Perspective," in *The Past and Future of Presidential Debates,* ed. Austin Ranney (Washington, D.C.: American Enterprise Institute, 1979), p. 122.
14. Charles J. Stewart, "Voter Perception of Mudslinging in Political Communication," *Central States Speech Journal* 26 (Winter 1975), pp. 279–286.

15. Congruity theory assumes that persons seek to maintain a state of balance or harmony between basic attitudes. The theory attempts to explain how a change in one attitude will lead to changes in other attitudes in order to reestablish this state of balance. For a discussion of congruity theory, see Charles E. Osgood and Percy Tannenbaum, "The Principle of Congruity in the Prediction of Attitude Change," *Psychological Review* 62 (1955), p. 43.

16. Vernon E. Cronen, "Responding to a Weaker Opponent: A Study of Likeability and Refutation in Public Debate," *Western Speech* 38 (Winter, 1974), p. 115.

17. Jeff Greenfield, *Playing to Win: An Insider's Guide to Politics* (New York: Simon & Schuster, 1980), p. 213.

18. James MacGregor Burns, *Edward Kennedy and the Camelot Legacy* (New York: Norton, 1976), p. 90.

19. *New York Times,* July 13, 1960, p. 18.

20. Ibid.

21. Norman H. Nie, Sidney Verba, and John R. Petrocik, *The Changing American Voter* (Cambridge, Massachusetts: Harvard University Press), 1976, pp. 156–174.

22. Michael Margolis, "From Confusion to Confusion: Issues and the American Voter (1956–1972)," *American Political Science Review* 71 (March, 1977), pp. 31–43.

23. Benjamin Page, *Choices and Echoes in Presidential Elections* (Chicago: University of Chicago Press, 1978), pp. 152–153.

24. Letter, Richard Wirthlin to Myles Martel, July 14, 1982.

25. Larry A. Samovar, "Ambiguity and Unequivocation in the Kennedy-Nixon Television Debates," *Quarterly Journal of Speech* 48 (October 1962), p. 279.

26. Lewis A. Froman, Jr., "A Realistic Approach to Campaign Strategies and Tactics," in *The Electoral Process,* eds. M. Kent Jennings and Harmon Ziegler (Englewood Cliffs, New Jersey: Prentice-Hall, 1966), pp. 8–9.

27. Stephan Lesher with Patrick Caddell and Gerald Rafshoon, "Did the Debates Help Jimmy Carter?," in Ranney, *The Past and Future of Presidential Debates,* p. 147.

28. During the second and third 1960 presidential debates, the subject of Quemoy and Matsu, the two islands off Mainland China, became because of a panelist's question the focal point of debate despite widespread perceptions that the islands were hardly a major issue on the public agenda. The substance of the exchange, therefore, was far less significant than its image implications; specifically, who was tougher on communism, Kennedy or Nixon?

29. A transcript of this debate is included in Goodwin F. Berquist Jr., *Speeches for Illustration and Example* (Chicago: Scott, Foresman, 1965), pp. 157–177. A tape recording of the debate is on file at the John F. Kennedy Library. For a discussion of the debate see Hermann G. Stelzner, "Humphrey and Kennedy Court West Virginia, May 3, 1960," *Southern Speech Journal* 37 (Fall 1971), pp. 21–33.

30. Milton Rokeach, "Change and Stability in American Value Systems, 1968–1971," *Public Opinion Quarterly* 38 (Summer 1974), p. 229.

31. Kurt Ritter and James Gibson, "The Quality of the 1980 Presidential Forums: A 'Revisionist' Position on Presidential Debates" (Paper delivered at the annual meeting of the Western Speech Communication Association, San Jose, California, February 14–17, 1981.)

32. *Portland Oregonian,* October 26, 1968, p. 8.

33. Lesher with Caddell and Rafshoon, "Did the Debates Help Jimmy Carter?," p. 147.

34. Nixon, *Memoirs,* p. 40.

35. *Portland Oregonian,* October 26, 1968, p. 8.

5

Formats

When Lincoln challenged Douglas to debate during the heated Illinois Senate campaign in 1858, the format of their seven historical encounters was resolved through a few simple letters exchanged between them within a week. Lincoln asked Douglas, "Will it be agreeable to you to make an arrangement for you and myself to divide time, and address the same audiences during the present canvas?"[1] Douglas replied:

> I will, in order to accommodate you as far as it is my power to do so, take the responsibility of making an arrangement with you for a discussion between us at one prominent point in each Congressional District in the State, except the second and sixth districts [Chicago and Springfield] where we have both spoken, and in each of which cases you had the concluding speech.[2]

No controversy surfaced regarding the format, which consisted of a sixty-minute opening speech, a ninety-minute reply, and a thirty-minute rejoinder. In fact, this format still draws praise for its capacity to promote a spontaneous, penetrating exchange about slavery, the most compelling issue of its day.

Today, however, the formats of campaign debates generate more criticism than almost any other aspect of the debate process. Journalists fault them because they favor the presentation of information already overused in the campaign. College debate coaches attack them for not having the essential features of true debates. And critics in general claim that they are designed to place emphasis on images more than on issues.

The most frequent specific indictments leveled at political campaign debate formats are: (1) they fail to focus on a specific proposition; (2) they depend unduly on panelists, usually journalists; and (3) they tend to prevent direct interaction (usually questioning) between the candidates. Whether changing any of these features would yield a more stimulating or enlightening exchange has not yet been established empirically. Such an assessment would, in fact, be difficult if not impossible to make; a researcher would be hard put to design a study that could separate format effects from the host of other variables affecting the electorate's response, e.g., stylistic factors (including delivery), credibility, and content. Indeed, portions of the ensuing discussion will suggest that traditional debate format features may be just as suspect—if not more so—than those features generally found in televised and broadcast campaign debates.

Formats have neither become standardized nor have they succumbed to the preferences of their critics. One major reason for this is that the personalities involved in each campaign are invariably different. Especially for potentially significant debates, formats are generally tailored to the debater's predilections; through negotiations with the sponsor, the candidate's representative vies for a design compatible with the candidate's goals and anticipated strategies that will permit him to maximize his strengths and minimize his weaknesses—to present a favorable image. For example, if a candidate is a poor speechmaker but reasonably competent in answering questions, his negotiators may arrange for a format without opening or closing addresses. A standard format, however, would clearly favor some candidates over others, and is therefore not only undesirable but potentially dangerous.

This chapter discusses four topics: (1) How are debate formats negotiated? (2) Should political debates have a specific proposition, a general topic, or be open-ended in content? (3) What is the proper role of the panel in political debate? (4) What are the strategic and tactical implications of typical debate formats?

THE NEGOTIATING PROCESS

The complexity of the format negotiation process varies significantly from campaign to campaign. At times it can be exceedingly simple, especially if the candidates are sincerely committed to debating, are reasonably confident of their speaking or debating skills, and do not plan to engage in broadcast or televised debates. At other times, it can be very complex, particularly when a candidate tries to force a breakdown in negotiations as a ploy to avoid debates, or if the debates are regarded as potentially critical to the election outcome.

The candidates' negotiators are generally press secretaries, campaign managers, or attorneys who are chosen because they are familiar with the campaign strategy, including the importance their candidate places on debates, and with his strengths, weaknesses, and preferences. Occasionally the negotiators are chosen for their negotiating skill, although relatively few have had prior experience negotiating formats.

Negotiators vary significantly in their understanding of the strategic and tactical implications of the format. Many, justifiably or unjustifiably confident in their candidate's capacity to perform, pay little heed to it. Those who do appreciate the implications of the format scrutinize each option to assess its potential to enhance or weaken their candidate's performance. Jimmy Carter's closest advisers discussed format issues with two college debate coaches before the 1976 presidential debates. Gerald Ford's, despite their intensive preparation for the debates, made no comparable effort.

Negotiations are almost always conducted in private. Public negotiations (including those restricted to reporters), by exposing a candidate's preference for certain format features, risk harming his campaign image. This risk applies particularly in presidential, senatorial, and gubernatorial races where negotiations are ordinarily more heavily publicized than in lower level races. Despite the privacy, it is not unusual for one camp (frequently the underdog's) to leak information intended to make the opponent look bad (e.g., his aversion to engaging in cross-examination). However, if a negotiator decides to leak information, he may be inviting serious problems; a leak can be taken as a sign of bad faith (which it probably is), creating a more difficult negotiating climate than had already existed. To protect against leaks, negotiators sometimes agree not to divulge anything themselves, and instead let the debate sponsor release a summary of the agreements reached.

Critics of campaign debate formats have advocated that negotiations be conducted in public, thereby placing pressure on the candidates' representatives to approve of format features possibly inimical to their candidates' legitimate interests.[3] This proposition makes sense only if one wishes to produce formats that favor some candidates over others. In any event, its advisability must be measured against the possibility that candidates who otherwise might debate would not.

A critical factor in the negotiating process is the extent to which the negotiator has the authority to make decisions for his candidate. In 1960, for instance, Nixon held tight control over his negotiators while Kennedy gave virtually free rein to his. In 1976, both Ford and Carter exercised fairly firm control over their negotiating teams. In 1980 Reagan's, Carter's, and Anderson's teams had considerable latitude. The amount of control possessed by the negotiators is not necessarily obvious from the outset. Vagueness about authority can lead a team with virtually free rein to trade costly and possibly revealing format features for what turn out to be only tentative commitments. And while the trades can sometimes be withdrawn when not approved, uncertainty regarding the negotiator's authority can complicate the process, reduce good faith, or lead to failure.

Candidate accessibility during the process is a related and potentially significant issue, especially when a candidate is controling the process himself. During the negotiations for the 1976 presidential debates, Carter, to the frustration of Ford's negotiators, was less accessible by telephone than Ford. And, quite naturally, Carter's negotiators probably savored the psychological advantage of testing the patience of Ford's team.

The amount of good faith the representatives bring to the bargaining table is not always evident either. Opponents' rationales for debating are often unclear and their calculated public pronouncements about debates are almost by definition unrevealing. Negotiators sometimes feign a strong desire for debates while deliberately complicating negotiations, aiming to pressure the opponent to back out and to expose him as "the bad guy." During the first round of negotiations for the 1960 and 1976 presidential debates, Kennedy's and Ford's negotiators were less than certain that their opponents intended to debate. Initially, they felt that the negotiations might be a charade to disguise Nixon's and Carter's unwillingness to participate. Kennedy's negotiators were particularly wary of Nixon's motives; since they very much wanted the debate, their basic negotiating strategy was to be as agreeable as reasonably possible—not to do anything that might allow him to back out. In 1980 Mitchell Rogovin, John Anderson's negotiator, took the same approach.[4]

It is not uncommon for the candidate's and sponsor's representatives to appear at the bargaining table with varied, even disparate, goals. For example, one negotiator may wish first to discuss how many debates will take place, while another contends that the topics should be agreed upon first, thereby resolving how many debates will take place. At the same time, the sponsor may be interested in establishing which, if any, of the debates should be televised. Competent chairing by a reasonably neutral party, generally the sponsor, can aid greatly in keeping such conflicts to a minimum.

However, the negotiating process is not always a pitched battle between the candidates' camps with the sponsor remaining neutral. In 1960 Kennedy's and Nixon's negotiators joined in a successful protest against the sponsoring networks, which insisted that print journalists be excluded from all panels. During negotiations for the 1978 Pennsylvania gubernatorial debates, Republican candidate Richard Thornburgh's representatives and the sponsoring League of Women Voters pressed for direct examination against the objections of Democrat Pete Flaherty's negotiators.

Generally, agreements about formats are final and not subject to change from debate to debate. This helps to control criticism and second-guessing. When agreements are subject to change or review, candidates and their aides can wage metadebates about the format openly, hoping either to decrease the importance of the actual debates by criticizing the formats, or to minimize a weak performance by blaming it on some format feature, e.g., lack of response time or poor questioning by panelists. And, quite naturally, such tactics frequently invite accusations of sour grapes by the opponent and the public alike.

PROPOSITIONS, TOPICS, OR OPEN-ENDED DEBATES

Propositions

A significant difference between political and traditional debates is that political debates seldom focus on propositions; that is, specific, debatable arguments. In fact, of the 181 congressmen and senators represented in the 1978 CDS, not one debated an explicit proposition. In traditional debate, a specific proposition helps the contestants to define the parameters of their case, avoid irrelevant excursions, and give the crucial issues a reasonably comprehensive hearing. It also provides judges with a focus that helps them to reach a well-reasoned decision. In political debates, a defined proposition is commonly regarded as restrictive and risk-prone. Candidates may be wary of placing too much weight on one specific issue, unable to disagree about a proposition of sufficient importance to the electorate to merit attention, fearful that a proposition will favor the opponent—particularly if he is an incumbent more familiar with the issue and with greater research facilities at his disposal— or concerned that such a focus might favor the better debater.

J. Jeffery Auer, a leading scholar of academic debate, contends that specific weaknesses in the Kennedy-Nixon debates resulted from the absence of defined propositions:

> But the contestants, Nixon and Kennedy, fencing with their quizmasters, were compelled to contrive facile answers to queries on an encyclopedic range of topics, with none of the rhetorical elements of unity and coherence to bind them together. These limitations were especially apparent, of course, in the middle two broadcasts; the first and the fourth presumably had some central focus.[5]

The absence of a defined proposition can indeed, promote facile responses often lacking in unity and coherence. But whether or not the electorate is thereby disadvantaged is open to question. I would argue that the electorate may be more likely to understand and retain information exchanged during a typical political debate than during one involving a proposition; for a large percentage of the electorate, the propositional debate might be too complex to follow.

Topics

The most popular means of giving focus to political debates is through the use of topics. The first and fourth 1960 presidential debates were devoted, respectively, to domestic policy and foreign affairs. The 1976 vice presidential debate covered foreign affairs, domestic matters, and general issues. In 1980 the Reagan-Anderson debate focused on defense and economic policy, while the Reagan-Carter debate was open-ended.

The use of topics is an effective compromise between propositional and open-ended formats. Topics provide focus without being unduly restrictive, thereby avoiding the worst features of the open-ended and propositional approaches. More important, responding to questions about agreed-upon topics is a relatively familiar situation for politicians and viewers. They do not feel threatened by the stringent demands that a traditional debate with a proposition would impose. Topics generally include a sufficient variety of sub-issues to interest a large audience, contribute to coherence, and allow both candidates and panelists to concentrate their efforts on a limited number of issues, thereby increasing the likelihood that the discussion will be of higher quality.

If not carefully selected, topics and subtopics can favor one candidate over another. In 1976 the League of Women Voters proposed that the first presidential debate focus on the role of the presidency. Ford's negotiators disapproved because they felt that this topic could call attention to Ford's identification with Watergate politics and his controversial pardon of Nixon. Interestingly, Carter's advisers also agreed privately that the topic posed risks to their campaign: "Every advantage of a sitting President is maximized in a debate which focuses directly on the awesome trust, the grave responsibility, the burden, etc., of the President."[6] In 1979 David Marston, Republican candidate for Mayor of Philadelphia and a well-known foe of political corruption, was opposed to crime as a topic largely because he did not want to be perceived as a one-issue candidate.[7]

The order in which topics are taken is another important matter. Lamenting over the sequence of topics chosen for the 1960 debates, Richard Nixon states:

> The most critical decision made at this time turned out to be the subject matter of the first and fourth debates. It was readily agreed that one should be devoted exclusively to domestic issues and the other to foreign policy. I believed that I would have a considerable advantage over Kennedy when the subject matter was foreign policy and consequently wanted that subject to be discussed on the program that would have the larger audience. But our public relations advisers disagreed on the key question: which of the debates would draw the bigger audience? My own view was that the first would be larger and that interest would go down as the novelty of the debates wore off. A majority of our group, however, thought that the audience would build up because of increased interest in the debates and in the campaign generally, and that the fourth debate would outdraw the first. I yielded to the majority and in this case their opinion proved to be wrong. We agreed that foreign policy would be discussed in the fourth debate and domestic policy in the first. When the debates were held, at least 20 million more people listened to and watched the first than any of the others, including the fourth and final appearance. I turned in my best performance before the smallest audience.[8]

During the format negotiations for the 1976 presidential debates, the sequence issue was no less significant. Carter expected the first debate to draw the largest audience; therefore, he insisted on leading off with domestic and economic affairs so that he could press Ford on the state of the economy and his record number of vetoes, rather than leading off with foreign policy and defense matters, Ford's presumed strengths.[9] Carter got his way in exchange for agreeing to ninety-minute rather than sixty-minute encounters. But ironically, Ford did better than Carter in the first debate, while Carter outperformed Ford in the second.

Clearly, candidates are normally well advised to lead off with their strength, even if the opponent shares that strength. Doing so not only can increase the likelihood of a quality performance, but can correspondingly prevent the seemingly insurmountable doldrums resulting from a weak performance. In addition, leading off with one's strength often provides valuable additional research time for the subject areas with which the candidate is less familiar. Finally, by the time the candidate debates the topic with which he is less familiar, he has at least cut his potential losses by having become a more experienced debater.

Open-Ended Formats

Because open-ended formats seldom provide coherent focus, they tend to promote a "joint interview" or "joint press conference" atmosphere, especially since they rarely include opening addresses. They are also considered to be more controllable by the candidates than topical formats. Jimmy Carter, for example, wary of Ford's government experience, wanted all of the 1976 presidential debates to be open-ended; this arrangement, he felt, would permit him to be less specific than would a topical format—to shift into another subject area if either the questioning or the clash between him and Ford became too difficult. In 1960 the middle two debates were open-ended; in 1976 the last was. According to the 1978 CDS, the more common practice is to use the open-ended format at the conclusion of a series—as a "net" to catch any major issues that have not been treated.

THE ROLE OF THE PANEL IN POLITICAL DEBATES

The use of panelists in campaign debates is the prime target of critics of campaign debate formats. Three major questions are raised: (1) should a panel of questioners be used at all; (2) if so, who should be eligible to serve and how should the panel be selected; and (3) what is the proper role of the panelist in a political debate?

A Panel, Direct Examination, or Both?

Panels are frequently criticized as obtrusive, self-serving and ineffectual. Typical panel formats, critics contend, are not sufficiently probing and, as a consequence, candidates are too protected by them. (Thus the epithets "pseudo-debates," "counterfeit debates," and "joint press conferences,").

Bitzer and Rueter contend that a panel format is inherently flawed, for it forces a candidate to choose between answering the questions put to him by the panel and debating his opponent. They argue that given the nature of most panelists' questions, a candidate who is strictly responsive to the question will rarely engage his opponent on significant campaign issues, while a candidate who is eager to respond to his opponent's statements can do so only by ignoring the questions he is asked. In their view, formats utilizing panels are "not suited to either debating or answering; and [their] shortcomings make adequate debate practically impossible."[10] Consequently, panels must be discarded entirely in favor of more direct candidate interaction.[11]

Panels do have their defenders. One positive aspect is that a panel format may be more attractive to prospective debaters than direct examination. As a substitute for the traditional debate format, panels not only create a "buffer zone" between the candidates but also make it unnecessary for the candidates to be expert debaters. The ten to fifteen questions typically asked during a two-party political debate on a variety of subjects (regardless of whether or not they are related to a designated topic) are ordinarily less formidable to the candidates than would be a debate focused on one or more propositions. Finally, panels also preclude the need for candidates or their advisers to be expert questioners.

It has also been argued that panels increase the likelihood that the candidate will have to contend with "no win" issues such as abortion or aid to parochial schools—difficult issues that could cause the candidate to offend a sizeable segment of his audience.[12] In the absence of a panel, the two candidates might tacitly agree to avoid discussion of such difficult and divisive issues. For this reason, James Gannon, of the *Wall Street Journal,* a panelist for the first Ford-Carter debate, has concluded that "It's probably unavoidable to have a panel of questioners. Any other method would lead to pre-packaged speeches, with the candidates not really responding to each other."[13]

One alternative to a panel is a full direct examination format, with the candidates questioning each other face-to-face. However, this format has won little favor with either analysts or candidates. The position of the critics is best expressed by Harvey Wheeler:

> What we are after is not a spectacle of candidates for our highest office wrangling with each other. What we require is a mode of electoral competition through which the opposing candidates are induced to develop competing overall programs for dealing with the problems of our nation. . . . It is not really necessary to this process that the competing candidates ever actually interrogate each other personally or directly. What must be emphasized is not the competition between personalities, but the competition between programs and policies.[14]

Candidates, as explained in the preceding chapter, generally regard direct examination as risky. They wish neither to be trapped by a "trick" question nor to face the prospect of being perceived as too hostile, aggressive, or deferential. Image projection, then, is a central criterion for candidates in deciding whether or not to include direct examination. In 1976 Gerald Ford wanted tough questions that would bring out the best in him. Carter, although he may have been naturally prone to ask them, would probably not have done so for fear of creating backlash. As one of his advisers noted: "There is risk in having the candidates ask each other questions. . . . How will Governor Carter look questioning President Ford: small, contemptuous, irreverent?"[15] The panels gave each candidate image protection and provided Ford with an opportunity to be asked the type of questions he sought.

Thus, as long as candidates have a say in the design of their formats, it is doubtful that direct examination will become popular. And even if it did, its potential to enhance the quality of debates is limited. In close elections, candidates will probably continue to exercise extreme caution, particularly on televised debates. Direct examination is, therefore, less the key to quality debates than are the candidates' personalities, speaking ability, knowledge, and overall commitment to the debate process. Jim Karayn, who pressed for direct examination throughout the 1976 presidential debate negotiations, now concedes that it would probably have "produced more heat than light."[16]

However, in at least one recent instance, a direct examination format has led to stimulating debate. In the 1982 California senatorial campaign incumbent Governor Jerry Brown (D.) and San Diego Mayor Pete Wilson (R.) met in debates which included both a typical panel format and a direct examination segment. In their first meeting, held on August 12, both candidates displayed their best debating form in the direct examination segment. Part of their improvement may have been due to overcoming early nervousness and hitting their stride as the debate progressed; but part of the difference was also probably due to the new format. Wilson, in particular, seemed more comfortable when he could level his attacks directly at Brown, rather than having to detour them through the panelists.

Is there any way to combine the advantages of panels and direct examination while avoiding their weaknesses? One innovative format proposal was advanced in response to a 1963 study on debates conducted by the American Political Science Association. It stipulates that candidates not meet face-to-face, but rather, appear before the same panel separately to field the same questions. The questions and answers could be taped and each full taping could either be played back-to-back or each response could be spliced back-to-back. This format, according to the congressman who suggested it, would "give true and complete answers about his [a presidential candidate's] philosophy, without the temptation to vary his presentation a bit to 'sock the other guy.' "[17] Indeed, this format might accomplish the intended goal, but whether the "debate" would be more edifying without established opportunities for direct clash is highly questionable. In fact, the absence of such opportunities could increase the possibility that two candidates could take the same question in separate directions and, as a result, generate more confusion than understanding.

Bitzer and Rueter have presented four alternative formats which, they contend, would alleviate the weaknesses inherent in both the standard panel format and in direct examination. Their first format, the *news interview* format,[18] technically not a debate but rather an informal joint-interview setting, resembling familiar television programs like "Meet the Press" and "The Mac-Neil/Lehrer Report." The candidates agree upon an interviewer and the topics to be discussed, and then field alternating questions from the interviewer, with no stated provision for direct refutation of the other candidate. The candidates are pledged to avoid sharp adversarial comments; the interviewer is given the discretion to concentrate on those topics that elicit especially enlightening exchanges between the candidates. Bitzer and Rueter contend that this format would give viewers better insight into the issue positions of the candidates than can be derived from a tightly structured debate format. Political scientist Nelson Polsby, arguing for a similar, more conversational format, adds that such a format is also a better test of the candidate's personality than standard formats:

> The spontaneous capabilities of a candidate's mind can be discovered far more successfully in conversation, where entitlement to the floor is subject to tacit negotiation, moment by moment, where interruptions are possible, and where all parties to the interaction are responsible for its content, and the straightjacket of question and answer gives way to a more freely flowing discussion. Skill at this sort of conversation is far more relevant to the conduct of the presidency, because a President must stimulate and participate in this sort of interaction in order to do his job.[19]

If the candidates or sponsors insist on retaining a panel format, Bitzer and Rueter recommend a *modified Ford-Carter* format in which (1) the questions be known to the candidates beforehand, (2) the response time be lengthened, and (3) there be opportunities for rebuttals, surrebuttals, and follow-up questions. This format, they admit, would reduce somewhat the spontaneity of the debate, but they also contend that it would provide an opportunity for more polished and expansive replies.

A third alternative, the *modified Lincoln-Douglas* format, is recommended for those situations in which candidates wish to focus the debate on one particular topic. Each candidate makes a long opening statement (perhaps twenty minutes) followed by shorter rebuttals and surrebuttals and possibly by a closing statement.

The fourth format, *policy address,* requires each candidate to deliver two long addresses on a designated topic. The addresses follow each other by at least one day, to allow for adequate analysis of the opponent's prior addresses and to provide sufficient time for a well-polished statement of the candidate's position.

Bitzer and Rueter contend that these formats, despite their novelty, may be accepted by prospective debaters, because they reduce the risks associated with debate. The candidates agree beforehand on the issues to be discussed or the specific questions to be asked (in the modified Ford-Carter format), thus allowing them to set the agenda of the debate, reducing their preparation requirements, and assuring them that they will not be embarrassed by an unexpected or hostile question. Rather than being forced to provide extemporaneous statements under great pressure, the candidates will be able to deliver coherent statements on their positions in a more extended period of time.[20]

It does not follow, of course, that these features will necessarily make these debate formats more attractive to candidates. Many candidates seek a debate precisely because of the pressures and risks involved in responding to unexpected questions; they believe that they are better able to handle such situations than their opponent. Nor is the opportunity to present extended discussions of policy likely to appeal to candidates who lack the necessary speaking skills, are less informed than their opponent, or have fewer resources to research and develop issue positions. In short, the typical panel formats are probably more congruent with the goals, strategies, and resources of most candidates than are Bitzer and Rueter's alternatives. Bitzer and Rueter suggest that significant improvement in the quality of political debates depends upon the candidates' adherance to the following "elementary ground rules:"

> to speak the truth as they know it, to deal with issues squarely, to face up to problems honestly, to debate in good faith and fairness, to place the public interest in the highest position—as Plato said, to do one's best to speak so as to please the gods, if not men.[21]

If so, we cannot expect any dramatic changes in the format of political debates, for candidates speak to please men—and to win their votes.

The Panelist Selection Process

Who should serve on debate panels is another thorny issue. In presidential debates journalists have dominated the panels. The panels for the four Kennedy-Nixon debates were comprised solely of journalists, a feature that disturbed Nixon and his negotiators because they felt that the press favored Kennedy. Network officials were adamant against having newspaper, magazine, or wire service journalists on any of the four panels; the debates were their shows, they felt, and it was their prerogative to select the cast of characters. Responding to this claim in an unusual display of unity, Nixon's and Kennedy's press secretaries pressured the networks into a compromise: two print journalists would be included on panels for the second and third debates and only broadcast journalists would serve on the panels for the first and fourth debates. Moderators would be chosen by the host network from its own personnel. This decision was made in deference to the candidates, who felt that broadcast professionals would assume this responsibility more objectively than judges, college presidents, or other distinguished persons. Only journalists were panelists for the 1976 presidential debates and for the 1980 primary forums and presidential debates, although academic and nonacademic experts served as panelists for the 1976 Presidential Primary Forums.

In debates for lower-level offices there has been more variety in the composition of the panels. Panelists for nonpresidential debates have included journalists, professors, and representatives of such organizations as the League of Women Voters, Common Cause, the Chamber of Commerce, the NAACP, and the AARP.

Candidates and debate sponsors are understandably wary about including representatives of interest groups on televised debate panels. To do so would raise a problem nearly as complex as determining which minority party candidate should appear and which should not. Neither candidates nor sponsors want to enlist the ire of possibly dozens of excluded interest groups because they chose representatives from only a few. Furthermore, interest group representatives selected for debate panels have developed a reputation for serving more as advocates than as interrogators, an impression that seldom rests well with the candidates or with the electorate.

The candidate's negotiators and the sponsor are often particularly opposed to academics serving on panels. Academics, they feel, are likely to have committed themselves already to one of the candidates, prone to advance their pet hypotheses or theories, inclined to ask obtuse questions, susceptible to debating the candidate rather than questioning him, and potentially uncomfortable in a studio setting. Perhaps there is some merit to these assumptions, reinforced in no small measure by several poor quality exchanges between academics and the Democratic presidential primary contenders during the 1976 forums. However, skilled, objective academic questioners can be found *if* the process of preparing for debates is less pressured than it was before the 1960 and 1976 presidential debates. This "if" is significant, since advanced effort is required to organize debates. Such an effort should be worthwhile. It is more likely than the present, hurried approach to produce panelists well-grounded in economics, foreign relations, or whatever other subject—panelists who can detect nuances, factual inaccuracies, and fallacies not as easily understood by reporters.

Journalists are typically regarded as bringing to campaign debates a degree of expertise, objectivity, and competence as questioners less frequently found in other professions. Some critics, however, find journalists unsatisfactory as panelists. Jeff Greenfield, for example, argues that the dominance of debate panels by journalists "means that there are sharp limits to the degree of aggressiveness you can expect."[22] In his view, the journalistic norm of objectivity discourages panelists from being disrespectful or hostile. Moreover, each panelist's desire to ask his own distinctive question will "mitigate against a candidate's being battered with a series of tough questions on an issue. Rather, you can rely on an unrelated series of questions, which can be answered by a single clever response."[23] Other critics, as I shall discuss later, have been highly critical of the quality of questions from the journalists on presidential debate panels.

One interesting stereotypic notion surrounding the selection of panelists is that print journalists tend to be more penetrating in their questioning—more substance oriented—while television and radio journalists, especially well-known ones, tend to be more image-oriented. In such instances where this notion may apply, the attack-oriented candidate would normally favor the print journalist over the television or radio journalist.

The manner in which panelists are selected varies considerably, and the selection criteria or procedures are often inexact. Typically, in debates for lower-level political office, sponsors select panelists because of their reputation in the community. Thus, it is not uncommon for a high profile television anchor person whose main proficiency is reading the news to be selected over someone far more qualified to investigate and write about it.

Although the use of journalists as panelists in presidential debates has been generally accepted, the *selection process* for the panels in both the 1976 and 1980 presidential debates spawned considerable controversy. In 1960 the sixteen journalists on the presidential debate panels were chosen by lot from a pool of names of reporters covering the candidates. Searching for a better formula for the 1976 presidential debates, the League of Women Voters officials and Debate Steering Committee chairs allowed the candidates to recommend as many as forty-five journalists for each debate (fifteen print, fifteen electronic, fifteen wire service). In making the final selection, the sponsors sought specialists in the topic areas chosen for the first two debates, a woman for each panel, and a black for at least one of the four panels. They avoided journalists identified with a particular point of view. Moreover, they shied away from reporters traveling with a particular candidate because they were ostensibly too close to the candidate and not sufficiently attuned to the public's perception of them. Taking exception to this latter practice, journalists Jack Germond and Jules Witcover state:

> This fear that 'the boys on the bus' [press traveling with the candidates] would not focus enough attention on the 'important' and 'substantive' issues of the campaign is in line with the purists' desire to see votes cast solely on the basis of issue positions of the candidates. It seems to us, however, that there is just as much reason to try to gauge the character and the personality of the candidates; that is precisely what millions of voters do in deciding between the two.[24]

The League's decision to give the candidates a say in the selection of panelists evoked great controversy. Richard S. Salant, president of CBS News, considered such authority as an egregious violation of journalistic freedom. He stormed out of a negotiation session after being told to "shut up" by Steering Committee Chairman Charls Walker, and carried on in the *New York Times* a printed "debate" about the selection procedure.[25]

In the 1980 Reagan-Anderson debate, the League of Women Voters Education Fund attempted to adopt a panel selection process as far removed from candidate influence as possible; the results, however, displeased both the candidates and some members of the Fund. In July the League solicited recommendations from national journalistic organizations. For the Reagan-Anderson debate, the League selected specialists in six policy areas, including one black and one woman. The candidates had no influence over the composition of the panel. However, Lee Hanna, coordinator of the debate for the League, found it unfortunate that despite all the effort to recruit a respected, neutral panel, some of the panelists in the first debate "expressed disapproval over some of the answers" and "expressed skepticism over the positions and integrity of the candidates."[26] Representatives of the candidates were also displeased by the panel's performance. In fact, both Reagan's and Carter's negotiators, displeased by the hostility of the panel in the Anderson-Reagan debate, insisted on input into the panel selection process for their debate. The League, in response, suggested that it would supply the candidates with a list of the pool of potential panelists, with each candidate having the right of refusal on a certain number of names. Several of Reagan's advisers, who had been on the Ford team for the 1976 debates, counseled against such a method on the grounds that vetoing panelists could create enemies if word of the veto leaked, as it had in 1976. Consequently, the League's suggestion was rejected, and a different procedure adopted on the urging of both candidates' representatives. The League would provide the candidates with the list of possible panelists, each candidate would respond by recommending a short list of preferences, and the League would choose the panel from the persons common to both lists. A problem arose, however. Although both short lists contained the names of several women, no woman was named on both lists. The League, insisting that a woman must be included on the panel, eventually chose Barbara Walters of ABC News.

This selection process also attracted criticism. Some journalists assailed the League's concession of any candidate input, while several of the candidates' advisers complained about the League's violation of the agreement that only journalists on the short list of both candidates would be placed on the panel.

Two provocative recommendations for choosing presidential candidates' interrogators have been advanced by author Theodore H. White and television producer Norman Lear. White proposes that a debate be held before a joint session of Congress with principals of the opposition serving as questioners.[27] This proposal presents two major problems: first, the President has traditionally and painstakingly avoided being questioned in a public or private congressional setting, to protect the separation of powers specified within the Constitution; second, such exposure can give unfair advantage to a senator or representative who may be seeking reelection that year. Lear proposes a format consisting of, for example, "six passionate partisans, three on each side . . . arguing in the kind of freewheeling, hard hitting discussion in which personalities get ruffled, skins get pricked, and passions flow."[28] These partisans, he suggests, should consist of each presidential candidate and two of his major advisers. While such a format might be more dramatic than a typical campaign debate and possibly more revealing, it is unlikely that the candidates would want to share the limelight with their advisers, engage in an open conflict with them, be trapped by one of their opponent's advisers, or—even worse—appear less impressive than one of their own or their opponent's advisers.

The Role of the Panelist

The performance of the panelists in the 1976 and 1980 presidential debates, as well as in many other debates, has received heavy criticism from all sides, much of it justified. Some argue that the panelists toss too many easy questions at the candidates. Others claim that panelists are too hostile and aggressive, to the point of dominating the proceedings. Several persons interviewed for this study, particularly George Gallup, Jr., and Theodore H. White, contend that panelists for the 1960 and 1976 presidential debates simply were not attuned to the public's interests.[29] Researchers Robert Meadow and Marilyn Jackson-Beeck, in their study of the 1960 and 1976 debates, confirm this impression:

> Interestingly, concerns reflected in the debates were not entirely parallel to the public perception of important problems facing the country, which would make it seem that the debates were conducted somewhat outside or aside from popular concerns.[30]

The most comprehensive and thoroughly documented critique of the performance of debate panelists is made by Bitzer and Reuter in their analysis of the 1976 presidential debates.[31] They identify three major weaknesses in most of the panel's questions. First, many of the questions were inappropriate—they were irrelevant to the presidential campaign, on topics of narrow interest, likely to elicit predictable responses, based on misunderstanding of fact by the questioner, etc. Second, questions lacked clarity: they were so obscure and indirect, or so comprehensive and loaded with options, that the candidate could not conceivably answer them satisfactorily in the time allotted. Finally, many of the questions displayed hostility toward the candidate (forty-one of sixty-three), thus forcing the candidates into a contest with the panel rather than with each other.

In general, the journalists who have comprised the panels for presidential and vice presidential debates have conducted themselves in accordance with the norms of their profession. These norms include, in the words of Bitzer and Reuter, "much attention to the 'newsworthy,' dogged persistence in pursuit of answers, skepticism toward politicians, and use of adversarial and argumentative techniques of questioning."[32] Joseph Kraft, a panelist in the final Ford-Carter debate in 1976, in which he asked Ford if his record on the economy was not "rotten" and his record on the environment not "hopeless," provides a revealing picture of his conception of the panelist's role in one of his columns on the debates. He suggests that the job of the panelist is to "rip off the mask of self-awareness," to try to "yield a glimmer of spontaneity," to "find ways that break out President Ford and Jimmy Carter as human beings . . . reacting spontaneously as they would have to in the White House."[33] In Kraft's view, the relationship between panelist and candidate is an extension of the normal adversary relationship between journalist and politician.[34]

Others, however, feel that a journalist selected as a panelist should remove the journalist's mantle. They contend that the panelist is selected as a surrogate of the people—to ask those questions that are of most vital concern to them—not to search for news. Obviously, the line between one's profession and one's role as a panelist is an important one, and needs to be defined. It is hard to imagine that anyone would be satisfied if, say, a judge serving as a panelist wore robes and interrogated the candidates according to correct courtroom practice. Can we assume, then, that the normal practice of a journalist is appropriate in a campaign debate?

One of the more revealing impressions gathered from the oral history interviews I conducted was the extent to which panelists' notions about their goals varied. NBC's Richard Valeriani, a panelist for the second 1976 presidential debate, felt that questions should be developed to educate the public and to help it to "gain insight into their [the candidates'] thinking, knowledge, and character."[35] NBC's Edwin Newman saw the panelist's role as "determining the candidate's position on important issues and to test particular personality traits," adding, "if you're lucky, you'll find an answer that makes news."[36] Others, such as ABC's Frank Reynolds and the *Baltimore Sun*'s Henry Trewhitt, felt that panelists should neither test the candidate's personality nor attempt to search for news (the latter being a perennial criticism of journalists serving as panelists).[37] In one of the more typical responses, Jim Gannon of the *Wall Street Journal* stated: "I wasn't trying to dream up questions out of left field that would strike the candidates cold and score a point. I figured that voters wanted to get familiar with the candidates' views on the very basic issues."[38]

Perhaps the absence of a consensus about the proper role of a panelist is one reason why journalists (and others) serving on panels are so severely criticized. To what extent should panelists attempt to educate the viewer through the phrasing of their questions? Should they ask questions that they know the answers to (although most of their audience may not) or seek answers that make news? Should they be catalysts who merely elicit information from the candidates? Should they be prosecutors? How much confidence should they have in the critical faculties of the electorate to detect irrelevancies, misrepresentations, fallacies, and dodges? These questions are not unanswerable and should be seriously entertained by panelists, sponsors, and others concerned about campaign debates. The widespread criticism of panelists' performance reflects nothing so much as widespread, if unrecognized, disagreement about what exactly panelists should do.

Whether or not panelists should convene in advance is another issue precipitated by the uncertainty about the relationship between their roles as panelists and as journalists. Shortly before the first 1976 presidential debate, Jim Karayn suggested that the panelists convene in advance to discuss their questions and was politely rebuffed; panelists Elizabeth Drew, James Gannon, and Frank Reynolds regarded the proposed meeting as tantamount to collusion.[39] However, the panelists for the following three debates did convene to refine the phrasing of questions, eliminate duplication, tighten sequences, and trade at least one question.

Probably the least contested issue surrounding the panels is panel size. Generally, there are three or four questioners, although sometimes as many as six are included. Or there may be only one, the moderator, who reads questions submitted to him, his own questions, or both. In 1960 four panelists served on each hour-long program and asked an average of 2.7 questions; in 1976 three served on each of the ninety-minute debates (and three on the seventy-five-minute vice presidential debate) and asked an average of

4.2 questions. In the Reagan-Anderson debate, six panelists asked one question each. In the Reagan-Carter debate, four panelists asked each candidate two questions and one follow-up question. According to most panelists interviewed for this study, the larger the panel, the greater the possibility that the questioning sequences would be fragmented.

STRATEGIC AND TACTICAL IMPLICATIONS OF DEBATE FORMATS

Opening Addresses

Critics and negotiators frequently voice two objections to the use of opening addresses. First, they contend that opening addresses are often cut-and-paste rehashes of campaign speeches, offering little that is not known already and providing only the most abstract overview of what might ensue during the debate. They are, therefore, regarded mainly as a means of delaying and shortening the question period. Second, they believe that the first address affords a significant advantage, providing one candidate with too much control of the proceedings. John F. Kennedy's opening address during the first Kennedy-Nixon debate, popularly regarded as helping to turn the election tide for him, is the most noteworthy example of this. The belief that an opening address might enhance Ford's presidential image was a major reason why Carter's camp opposed opening addresses.[40]

Opening addresses often warrant the first criticism (a second principal reason, incidentally, for their exclusion from the 1976 presidential debates). On the other hand, if the electorate is not familiar with the candidates' positions, short opening addresses may be useful. As Edwin Newman, moderator of the first 1976 presidential debate, points out, opening addresses can "save time by establishing the candidates' positions on a variety of issues and questions which could then flow from those positions."[41] Negotiators cannot assume that the public is as informed as they are, especially during primaries when so many new faces are receiving their first exposure.

The second criticism also has merit. The first opening address does indeed allow a candidate to exercise some control over the issues of the debate. A candidate can, as Kennedy did in 1960, make such a striking impression on his audience by referring to issue positions with which they identify that his opponent is hard put—possibly even ill-advised—to refute him. To be effective, the candidate must, of course, be able to speak well. A less than solid performance during an opening address could impair his debate goals significantly—possibly even to the point of forcing viewers to switch channels. One way of reducing the potential impact of the first opening address is to make it shorter. Kennedy and Nixon were given eight minutes; three to five minutes has now become more customary.

Opening addresses offer the candidate several other strategic and tactical opportunities. The candidate who delivers the first address can prepare it without concern about any prior remarks by his opponent. It can, therefore, have an aggressive, positive tone. The candidate in the second position, however, must be prepared to modify his words on the spot to cope with a situation that may be wholly unexpected. Where a challenger's principal strategy is to attack, the first opening address may provide him with just that opportunity—possibly permitting him to throw his opponent off balance, which the beginning of a question period is less likely to do. Where an incumbent delivers the first opening address, not only could he sell his credentials and positions, but he could also forewarn the audience of anticipated attacks—another opportunity that may not be conveniently available during the question period.

The major tactical question for the candidate giving the second opening address is whether he wishes to engage his opponent's arguments or to separate himself from them. In short, will direct clash be more likely to help or to hurt him? This decision depends not only on his broad relational strategy but on three other factors: (1) the advantages and disadvantages of ignoring and responding to attacks, i.e., one can seem weak by avoiding an attack, too strident when responding to one; (2) issue priorities, i.e., attack or defense time may compete with the opportunity to place more important issues before the public; and (3) rhetorical skills, i.e., to respond on short notice to an address that may have been painstakingly prepared and rehearsed requires considerable skill. Many of the second opening addresses analyzed during this study were pretailored and therefore not directly responsive to the first address. This is attributable mainly to the candidates' unwillingness to take risks. A pretailored speech, they reason, will prevent them from making a serious blunder, a far more important goal than facing the risks associated with refuting the opponent's first opening address.

When the format does not include an opening address, one or both candidates might choose to insert one into the time provided for their first question. Jimmy Carter did this during his second debate with Ford in 1976, as did Reagan against Anderson in 1980, and Carter again versus Reagan in 1980. This "sneaked in" opening address has decided advantages and risks. Advantages: Like a scheduled opening address, it can help the candidate set the tone of the debate, assist him in settling down if he is more skilled in giving speeches than in responding to questions, and allow him to present positions that might not get the airing he wishes during the balance of the debate. Risks: There must be sufficient time both to make the speech and to present a respectable response to the question. In addition, the moderator or a panelist might note that the candidate has just presented a speech or is not being responsive to the question.

Rejoinders

The rejoinder consists of each candidate having the opportunity to respond to the other's opening address. The first rejoinder, usually consisting of one to two-and-a-half minutes, is presented by the speaker who gave the first opening address, followed immediately by the opponent's rejoinder. This feature has the following general implications: (1) it focuses more attention on the significance of the opening addresses; (2) it provides each candidate with an opportunity to clarify his ideological premises and to attack his opponent's; and (3) it can create a better foundation for understanding the questions asked during the debate. From the candidate's vantage point, this feature normally favors the attack-oriented challenger and especially favors the better speaker or debater, although the rejoinder, or at least major portions of it, can be tailored in advance.

Closing Addresses

Closing addresses, varying in length from one to five minutes, are more popular than opening addresses. The same strategy is applied to them as to opening addresses and to the question and answer period, unless the heat of the debate has produced a reason for a shift in strategy. Like opening addresses, closing addresses take two principal forms, memorized or manuscript and extemporaneous. The memorized or manuscript speech, the more common form, is often a collection of what are considered effective excerpts from the candidate's campaign speeches. It is frequently more abstract than what the candidate said earlier in the debate, focusing on goals, values, and visions rather than on clash. While it poses a risk that the candidate might sacrifice an important rebuttal opportunity, the memorized or manuscript speech is generally safer than an extemporaneous address for the confident frontrunner or for the candidate with weak speaking skills. The extemporaneous closing address, responsive to the ebb and flow of the debate, is especially appropriate for the more accomplished speaker, particularly one who must take risks. This, in fact, was a major reason why Carter's advisers favored closing over opening addresses for the 1976 debates. Specifically, the closing address was expected to give Carter a chance to take "questions, phrases, and sentences actually used in the debate and incorporate them in his closing statement," and thereby "demonstrate an ability to absorb and deal with issues under fire."[42] Republican campaign consultant Douglas Bailey regards the extemporaneous close as "a safety valve":

> No matter what else has happened in the debates, you get one last chance to talk on any subject that you want to, and to safeguard yourself against a mistake you made earlier or an attack by the opponent.[43]

Closing addresses can, of course, be a combination of both extemporaneous and manuscript or memorized approaches. To be effective, the candidate must be skillful in choosing what to insert extemporaneously and where to insert it, and to prevent any noticeable shift between his manuscript or memorized and extemporaneous styles. If he succeeds, as John Anderson did during the 1980 Iowa Republican Forum, he not only reduces the likelihood of being seen as programmed, an all too common perception generated by political campaign debates, but can project instead mental and verbal agility. Whatever form of close is chosen, candidates typically conclude their portion of the debate with a value-laden appeal, reinforcing the theme of their campaign:

> JOHN F. KENNEDY: And I believe it incumbent upon us to be the defenders of the United States and the defenders of freedom; and to do that, we must give this country leadership and we must get America moving again.

> RICHARD M. NIXON: And so to say this in conclusion, keep America's faith strong. See that the young people of America, particularly, have faith in God, which distinguishes us from the atheistic materialists who oppose us.

> GERALD FORD: I love America just as all of you love America. It would be the highest honor . . . for me to have your support on November second and for you to say, "Jerry Ford, you've done a good job, keep on doing it."

> JIMMY CARTER: I believe in the greatness of our country, and I believe the American people are ready for a change in Washington. We've been drifting too long. We've been dormant too long. We've been discouraged too long. And we have not set an example for our own people. . . . And with inspiration and hard work we can achieve great things. . . . But more importantly, let the people in our country realize . . . that we still live in the greatest nation on earth.

During Reagan's preparations for the debate with Carter, one of the major issues raised in discussions leading up to the format negotiations was whether Reagan would benefit more from an opening or closing address. I, quite frankly, favored the opening address because I felt that it would allow Reagan to begin the debate with his strength, speechmaking, and as a result make it easier for him to settle down to respond to questions (especially since he had gotten off to a hesitant start in Baltimore). I favored less a closing address because: (1) I felt that most closing addresses are uninspiring and (2) many viewers might not watch the closing address since the debate was to end at approximately 11:00 P.M. (EST). As it turned out, speechwriter David Gergen created for Reagan a masterful close (reminiscent of JFK's opening address in his first debate with Nixon) that persuasively focused the debate and the campaign on Carter's record, the consummation of the strategy chosen for the debate.

When opening and closing addresses are to be used, the order of the candidates' speeches must be negotiated by representatives of the candidates. Four presidential campaigns illustrate the inconsistency with which the speaking order issue has been treated. In the 1948 Dewey-Stassen Oregon primary debate Stassen, who took the affirmative in a traditional debate by arguing that the Communist Party in the United States should be outlawed, opened the debate, as would be expected, but contrary to the tradition, did not close it—that traditional right of the affirmative having been lost in the negotiations. Stassen told me some thirty-one years later that he thought this altera-tion in the format was unfair.[44] In the first 1960 presidential debate, Kennedy opened and closed the first debate and Nixon opened and closed the last. In the 1976 vice presidential debate, the only encounter of the 1976 series with an opening and closing address, Dole opened and Mondale closed. In the Reagan-Carter debate, Reagan opened (taking the first question) and closed last.

Follow-Up Questions

Optional follow-up questions were used in the 1976 and 1980 debates, although they had not been included in 1960, when negotiators for both sides wanted to limit interaction between candidates and panelists. In 1976 Ford's negotia-tors chose this feature as a means of pinning down Carter on specifics. In 1976 Carter's advisers felt that the follow-up questions would allow him "to demonstrate that he is not evasive or wishy-washy, and to show that he is cool under fire."[45] Reagan's negotiators reluctantly accepted follow-up questions for the first half of the debate.

The use of follow-up questions generated mixed reviews. Edwin Newman endorsed them: "I think that if you are a journalist, you must be able to ask follow-up questions. Otherwise, you could have a recording machine performing the function."[46] Expressing the opposite view, *Newsweek*'s Hal Bruno, a panelist for the 1976 vice presidential debate, stated:

> By the time the candidates attain national prominence they can handle the press, no matter how much follow-up you have. If they don't want to be pinned down, it winds up in the eyes of many people that the press is the villain for harassing them.[47]

Most of the nineteen follow-up questions used during the Ford-Carter debates were actually separate questions. However, Max Frankel's question to Ford that resulted in the unwitting reinforcement of his Eastern European gaffe was a true follow-up that highlighted the potential benefits of this feature to debate planners and critics alike.

Counterrebuttals

The counterrebuttal or surrebuttal is a way of resolving problems often associ-ated with follow-up questions. This feature allows the candidate who initially answers a question to speak again after his opponent's rebuttal. It, therefore, provides for more clash between the candidates (and for less between the candidates and panelists). Moreover, it can serve as a viable substitute for risk-prone follow-up questions for the candidate who tends to be general or the one who is not sufficiently informed. The candidate must, however, be reasonably quick on his feet to derive the fullest benefit from the counterre-buttal; it is not uncommon for candidates to be caught during this format segment with little or nothing to say. Finally, the counterrebuttal breaks up the long floor control period possible when a candidate follows his rebuttal in one question with his initial response to the following question. The surrebuttal feature of the 1976 vice presidential debate allowed each candidate to control the floor for no more than 2½ minutes at a time:

Response by Candidate A to his own question   2½ minutes
Rebuttal by Candidate B of A's response   2½ minutes
Surrebuttal by Candidate A of own question   1 minute
Response by Candidate B to his own question   2½ minutes

The counterrebuttal worked effectively in the 1976 vice presidential debate and the 1978 Pennsylvania gubernatorial debates, giving viewers a sense that the candidates were actually interacting with one another.

A format that combines the optional follow-up question with the counterrebuttal is likely to be too cumbersome, especially for a televised debate. If the viewers have difficulty following the ground rules, they will not only fail to appreciate the content of the debate, but may even switch channels.

Response Time

The time allotment for questions and answers has drawn considerable criticism from the academic and editorial communities. Henry Steele Commager, the eminent historian, claims that confrontations such as the Kennedy-Nixon debates "put a premium on glibness and fluency."[48] Norman Cousins, editor of *Saturday Review,* referring to the same debates, laments that they forced the candidates to be quizmasters:

> The American people are not electing an Answer Man to the Presidency; if this is what they have in mind they should examine the rosters of the discarded quiz shows. They are electing a person who can deal with the fact of change in the modern world, involving new challenges and calling for new responses.[49]

However, despite many commentators' desire for longer response times, candidates often do not use all of the relatively short periods commonly allotted to them. In 1960 Kennedy and Nixon used the entire response time available to them for only sixteen of the forty-three questions asked during the four debates. In 1976, in as many debates, Carter, Ford, Mondale, and Dole used the available time for only sixteen of fifty questions. In 1980 Anderson and Reagan used the available time for only six of their twelve opportunities. In the Reagan-Carter debate, the available time for the sixteen main responses was consumed only nine times. Clearly, candidates' responses are briefer than they need be; what isn't clear is why, or indeed, whether not consuming the full time allotted is necessarily bad. This, after all, can permit additional questions to be asked if a limit to the number of questions was not negotiated. Response length is a function of three major factors: the candidate's knowledge, his communication skill, and the amount of ground he wishes to cover during the debate.

Determining the allotted response time is often a key element in the format negotiations. In 1978 Pennsylvania Republican gubernatorial candidate Dick Thornburgh, a knowledgeable and articulate candidate, vied for longer response times largely because he and his advisers felt that his Democratic opponent, Pete Flaherty, would have difficulty sustaining a response. However, longer response times are sometimes sought even when the candidate may not be particularly knowledgeable, but has sufficient skill to give long and reasonably interesting answers. Thus, the number of questions he has to face is thereby reduced. Longer response times may also reduce the anxiety of candidates who are unsure of their ability to construct a concise, well-focused answer under the pressure of a debate. A longer response time allows a candidate to make a weak start or temporarily forget an important point, yet still have time to recover and present an effective answer.

One common practice has been to allow the candidate asked a question to have a longer response time than his opponent is given in rebuttal. This is because it is presumed that questions will be tailored to the experience or position of each candidate (e.g., "How have you, as President . . . ?"), and that it would be unfair to expect the opponent to answer at equal length, if at all. In fact, however, most questions asked in past debates seem equally suitable to both candidates (about 75 percent of the questions in 39 debates examined); thus, the main argument for unequal response time does not seem sound.

The Same Question

Each candidate being asked the same question, a format feature used in both 1980 presidential debates, has the following implications: (1) it reduces the likelihood that a question will be biased in one candidate's favor or have limited relevance to the other; (2) it limits the number of questions asked, thereby reducing the candidate's risk of being caught unprepared; and (3) it helps fix the audience's concentration on the question and, as a consequence, normally obligates the candidate to a more faithful response. In the final analysis, this feature often favors the challenger. Since normally the challenger's response opportunity when his opponent answers first is at least thirty seconds shorter, the equal time provision created by the same question feature can become a welcomed bonus.

Number of Debates

Although this issue is generally less contested than most format issues, it becomes particularly important when televised or broadcast debates are involved. Ordinarily, the confident frontrunner with ample prior exposure wants fewer debates, while his opponent wants more. Often, the number of debates sought is determined by the trailing candidate's desire to impede the frontrunner's momentum; debates are regarded as a means of distracting viewers from the opponent's media drive, forcing them to give their attention to the debates instead. According to Mike Duval, President Ford's debate coordinator, this was a major rationale behind Ford's desire to debate Carter four times, with the first debate scheduled as soon as reasonably possible after Ford's nomination.[50] Less often, both candidates may agree on to make debates a centerpiece of their campaign, with free television or radio exposure usually being a major incentive. In 1962 Max Rafferty and Ralph Richardson, candidates for the office of California's Superintendent of Public Instruction, debated forty-seven times, and in 1976 the U.S. Senate candidates from Michigan, Donald Riegle (D.) and Marvin Esch (R.) (a former college debate coach) debated forty-five times.

The candidate's ability to master the speaking skills required by the format is yet another factor in deciding the number of debates. Commenting on the impact of the number of debates issue on the 1960 presidential election, Theodore H. White states:

> The Nixon negotiators fought to restrict the number of debates—their man, they felt, was the master of the form and one "sudden death" debate could eliminate Kennedy with a roundhouse swing. They viewed the insistence of the Kennedy negotiators on the maximum possible number of debates as weakness. ("If they weren't scared," said one Nixon staff man, "why shouldn't they be willing to pin everything on one show?"). The Kennedy negotiators insisted on at least five debates, then let themselves be whittled to four. ("Every time we get them two fellows on the screen side by side," said J. Leonard Reinsch, Kennedy's TV maestro, "we're going to gain and he's going to lose.")[51]

As explained in Chapter 2, a favorable format is obviously more likely to result in a candidate's willingness to debate than an unfavorable one. However, candidates often decide on the number of debates they will engage in before they agree to a format. This is particularly true for the underdog who, applying the traditional risks-versus-rewards formula, often assumes that the exposure afforded by the debates will outweigh any possible format liabilities. The frontrunner who decides on the number of debates before knowing the format may be doing so because of public pressure; he may want to appear open and agreeable to a generally respected (and sought after) campaign practice, or to demonstrate confidence in his debating skills regardless of format. Or he may simply not be aware of the format's strategic and tactical implications.

Some commentators believe that too few debates may invite serious risks. As Lee Mitchell, author of *With the Nation Watching,* the Twentieth Century Fund's report on televised presidential debates, states:

> Fewer debates . . . unless significantly lengthened, would not allow the public sufficient opportunity to analyze the candidates and their positions carefully.

Reducing the number of debates would encourage the win/lose approach to the debate and would allow a minor "slip" by one of the candidates, or one fortuitous response to a question, to distort the entire election.[52]

More rather than fewer debates allow each candidate to become accustomed to debating in general and to debating his opponent in particular, especially since the more important debates are normally held later in the campaign. While this advantage applies to both candidates, the candidate who needs most to debate should ordinarily experience the greater advantage. In a related vein, one reason attributed to Reagan's debating success against Carter was his recent debating experience; he had debated six times during the campaign while Carter had not debated for four years.

More debates can, ironically, actually deemphasize the importance of debate in the campaign or the significance of a particular debate or series of debates. Debates can, in essence, become overexposed as a campaign medium.

Most of the principals in the 1976 presidential debates whom I interviewed approved of the number of debates in that campaign (three presidential and one vice presidential) and their sequence (the vice presidential was third, to allow the presidential to dominate the series). Journalists Jack Germond and Jules Witcover suggested that one additional vice presidential debate might be appropriate, but also warned that debates should not dominate presidential campaigns.[53]

Location of the Debate

This issue, although seldom contested, has interesting political implications. When Stephen Douglas agreed to debate Abraham Lincoln in 1858, one of the stipulations was that the two not debate in districts already canvassed by both. Douglas did not want to weaken through debate any political gains he had made in those areas. One hundred and eighteen years later, in 1976, Robert Dole's negotiators vied initially for the vice presidential debate to be held in Atlanta. This preference was based mainly on their desire to focus attention on the liberal voting record of Dole's rival, Walter Mondale, by locating the debate in the conservative South, since media coverage would naturally be greatest where the debate was being held. Since Atlanta was the home base of the Carter-Mondale campaign, this was a surprising suggestion, and Mondale's negotiator, Richard Moe, quickly agreed to it—whereupon Dole's staff had second thoughts and the negotiating atmosphere became so tense that Moe phoned Mondale at home during the session and received permission to withdraw from the debate if he saw fit.[54] Tempers were soon placated, though, and Houston was finally selected.

A noteworthy example of location making a possible difference occurred during the 1982 Massachusetts Senate race. Ray Shamie, the trailing Republican challenger to twenty-year incumbent Edward M. Kennedy, wanted the debate to be held in Boston, where local, state, and national media attention would be far greater. In addition, he preferred historic Faneuil Hall to give the event greater prestige and exposure. Predictably, Edward Kennedy wanted the debate to be held in a remote community. Eventually, both camps agreed to holding the debate in Boston College's Performing Arts Center—in effect, a potential plus for the Shamie campaign.

Length of the Debate

Televised debates seldom last more than one hour, notable exceptions being the 1976 presidential (90 minutes) and vice presidential (75 minutes) debates and the 1980 Reagan-Carter debate (90 minutes). Nontelevised and nonbroadcast debates generally last sixty to ninety minutes. The sponsor's prevailing criteria for the length of a political debate, whether live, broadcast, or televised, are its capacity to maintain audience interest and to facilitate a reasonable exchange on the issues. When the candidates have a say in the length of their debates, at least four rhetorical and political factors come into play:

1. The more informed candidate may press for longer debates to give him fuller opportunity to strike an appealing contrast with his less informed opponent. In 1976 Ford proposed two-hour debates and Carter counterproposed one-hour debates; Ford wanted to capitalize on his twenty-eight years in Washington, while Carter sought to diminish Ford's presumed advantage. Similarly, in 1980, Anderson wanted a ninety-minute debate against Reagan's preference for sixty minutes; and Carter's negotiators fought briefly for a two-hour debate, but settled for ninety minutes.
2. A longer debate increases the likelihood that a gaffe might occur, a danger for a candidate who is less informed or prone to committing gaffes. This was a concern of Reagan's advisers when they negotiated the format for the debate with Anderson, especially since Reagan had recently displayed a proclivity for gaffes.
3. The better speaker or debater might press for longer debates not only to display his own speaking skills, but also to accentuate his opponent's weaknesses.
4. A candidate who wants to discourage viewership and, as a consequence, the debate's potential impact, might press for a long debate. Although the latter possibility may have been a factor in various congressional, senatorial, gubernatorial, and mayoral debates, it had no apparent bearing on the 1976 Ford-Carter or 1980 Reagan-Carter debates. Although these debates were thirty minutes longer than the Kennedy-Nixon encounters, interest in them was sufficiently high that viewers tended to watch them in their entirety.

The extent to which anticipated audience interest should determine the length of a debate is open to question. Holding a minority view, Theodore

H. White contends that presidential debates should be no less than two hours long: the American electorate's attention span, he feels, should not be a consideration in determining length.[55] My own position is that audience interest should be a consideration, but we must be sure to allow each candidate adequate opportunity to present his positions and comment about his opponent's.

Use of Notes

Although candidates often take notes during debates, image, more than any other factor, normally governs whether or not they bring notes with them, particularly to a televised debate. The use of prepared notes can (1) misrepresent the amount of knowledge a candidate actually has stored in his mind; (2) create the impression that he is unable to think on his feet or has a poor memory, (although it can also suggest thoroughness and concern for accuracy); and (3) reduce spontaneity significantly. The extent to which these (and other) effects occur obviously depends on what the viewers actually see and to what extent notes are used. If the debate is televised, and the candidate's use of notes is not shown while his opponent is speaking (a factor that cannot be controled by the candidates), the candidate may appear to have more information than he really does. If the debate is before a live audience, the candidate may more likely appear too reliant on notes—not sufficiently informed. This is probably not a major factor, however, since live audiences usually have strong preferences and are unlikely to be significantly affected by the candidates' use of notes.

In the 1982 California Senatorial debates, Governor Jerry Brown cleverly managed to turn his use of notes into a plus rather than a negative. While debating San Diego Mayor Pete Wilson, Brown "frequently held up reference cards concerning various aspects of Mr. Wilson's record as Mayor as though they were trophies."[56]

A no-notes provision has been adopted in many debates, not only because candidates generally believe that the public will construe notes as a sign of weakness or incapacity, but also because they do not want to be victimized by any potentially dangerous surprises; e.g., the exposure of an incriminating letter or photograph by an opponent. Nixon was against the use of notes in 1960 (although Kennedy used them briefly in the third debate), and Ford and Carter agreed not to bring them to the lectern in 1976, as did Reagan and Carter in 1980. An interesting approach to the use of notes developed during the 1978 Michigan Senate race when incumbent Robert Griffin (R.) and challenger Carl Levin (D.) each agreed to bring to the debate an 8½ by 11 inch sheet of paper. Taking advantage of this provision, Levin crammed the sheet with information printed by a Xerox reduction process.

If a format contains a particularly long opening or closing address, e.g., more than four or five minutes, the less skillful speaker may be at a handicap without the use of notes. Here, a specific provision for notes during only the opening or closing address may be justified.

The Role of the Moderator

The moderator is one of the least contested features in any debate format negotiation. Unlike Lincoln and Douglas, who had no moderator, few candidates want to engage in what could turn into a free-for-all. At the very least, a traffic director is needed. Frequently, the moderator is the anchor person of a leading television station who is expected to increase debate attendance and viewership. When he is not, the role is generally assumed by a prominent journalist or official from the sponsoring organization. Prominent journalists (electronic and print) moderated the 1960 and 1976 presidential debates (although Supreme Court justices and presidents of prominent colleges were initially considered for this role in 1960).

The choice of moderator became a major issue during the negotiations for the 1982 Massachusetts Senate race debates when representatives for Democrat incumbent Edward M. Kennedy and Republican challenger Ray Shamie secured Howard K. Smith as moderator. Smith, who had moderated the first Kennedy-Nixon debate in 1960 and the 1980 Reagan-Carter debate, was too strong a choice for Kennedy's advisers, who vied for a low profile debate and, as a consequence, "uninvited" him. Shamie, with understandable indignation and characteristic campaign flair, hired planes to fly over Massachusetts, carrying banners which read, "Teddy—What's wrong with Howard K. Smith?"

More frequently controversial is the scope of authority the moderator should have beyond opening the debate, explaining the ground rules, introducing the candidates and panelists, announcing overtimes, and closing the debates. In some debates moderators are permitted to ask questions. However, this role was not assigned to the moderators for the 1960, 1976, and 1980 presidential debates, possibly because it might have encumbered the format, given too much responsibility to the moderator, or both. In other debates, the moderator asks a lead-off question that normally results in a short opening address by each candidate, and then leaves the remainder of the questioning to the panel. Less frequently, the moderator, acting alone, questions the candidates, using his own questions, the audience's, or both. This latter approach was employed with apparent success during the 1980 Illinois and Texas primary forums with Howard K. Smith as moderator. Its major advantage is that it diminishes any distractions the panels might create for the candidates. Also, candidates might expect a single moderator to provide less hostile questions than a panel, owing to his need to appear neutral.

Even more contested is the authority a moderator should have in interrupting a nonresponsive candidate. Few moderators want to risk projecting themselves as anything less than neutral, particularly when chairing a televised debate. Reinforcing this stance, Frank Reynolds, who has moderated several noteworthy televised debates, contends that the moderator should not interrupt a candidate (except to announce time limits); instead, his opponent should expose the weakness.[57] Other moderators and critics in general agree that the American public can judge the weaknesses of the candidate's responses without the moderator's intrusion. In contrast to these positions, as the 1976 vice presidential debate was about to begin, moderator Jim Hoge stated: "I should mention at this point that I will intervene if a candidate is not addressing the question that has been posed to him." (Although occasionally tempted, Hoge did not find it desirable to interrupt either candidate.)[58] Edwin Newman argues that the moderator's intervention "could have too much effect on the outcome"; this could be particularly likely when the moderator is well known.[59] And, quite to be expected, candidates generally do not want the moderator to have the authority to interrupt. As Henry Trewhitt stated, "If a moderator could interrupt, you wouldn't find a candidate to participate in a debate."[60]

Audience Questions

Audience questioners used with and without panelists have been particularly popular in nontelevised debates and, to a lesser extent, in televised ones. The questioning can take three forms: direct, quasi-direct, or indirect. Direct questions are posed instead of or following the panelists' questions, with the moderator designating questioners without foreknowledge of what the questions will be. The major assets of this method, used successfully in the 1980 Des Moines and Manchester forums, is its ability to fulfill the audience's need to participate, add to the integrity of the event, and place the candidate in close contact with the public. However, this method poses the risks that the person selected may issue a statement instead of a question, debate one or more of the candidates, be unduly biased, engage in a struggle for control with the moderator, or pursue an irrelevant or overly repetitious line of inquiry. Quasi-direct questioning is the solution to such problems. Here the audience members submit questions in advance for screening by a moderator or neutral panel. If the question is approved, the moderator calls upon the audience member to read it. A version of this method was successfully used during the 1976 presidential forums. A modest adaptation of the quasi-direct question is the indirect question. This involves the same submission and screening process except that the question is asked by a moderator or panelist who generally identifies the author. The questions can be submitted by the live audience or be mailed in advance as they were during the 1960 Kennedy-Humphrey West Virginia primary debate.

Audience Reaction Shots

Few issues brought to the negotiating table are as hotly contested as the use of audience reaction shots.[61] These shots involve the television camera focusing on one or more audience members during the debate as frequently as the director chooses. Candidates normally protest these shots, contending that the reaction of an audience member in the live debate setting could influence viewers' perceptions of the candidates. Moreover, candidates also feel that the reaction shots can constitute unwanted distractions while the candidate is saying something which may be potentially persuasive. Debate sponsors and television directors often insist on reaction shots from a professional journalistic point of view, contending that the audience is an integral part of the event.

Prohibition of reaction shots has raised an intriguing legal issue regarding the proper interpretation of Section 315, the "equal time" provision of the Federal Communications Act of 1934 and various related rulings handed down since. Debates, according to current communications law, are supposed to be inherently newsworthy events, regardless of television coverage. Television coverage, therefore, should not be a necessary or sufficient condition for their newsworthiness. When reaction shots are prohibited, the debate, critics argue, becomes more a television event and less an independent news event covered by television. While there is some, if not considerable, merit to this position, the candidates in the 1960, 1976, and 1980 presidential debates and in countless lower level debates have won their way by securing agreements forbidding reaction shots. The Federal Communications law continues to perpetuate a subterfuge—if not a sham—since televised debates would normally pale into insignificance, if not oblivion, if they were not televised.

Formats for Three or More Candidates

The appearance of more than two candidates often poses significant format problems, especially when additional candidates seek inclusion in a debate after two have already agreed to a format, as was the case with the 1980 Nashua Republican primary debate. Since a loosely constructed format can give a third party considerable exposure, a tight format is usually insisted on by the original debaters. However, a loose format might be desirable to one candidate if the third candidate could become either an overt ally through his debate conduct and positions or an implicit ally by drawing more votes from the original opponent than from the candidate himself. As discussed earlier, this latter reason prompted Carter's advisers to discourage him from debating Ronald Reagan and John Anderson since they felt that Anderson would draw more support from Carter than from Reagan.

A typical questioning sequence developed for a three-candidate debate was used during the Philadelphia mayoralty contest in 1979:

1. Candidate A responds to question   1½ minutes
2. Candidate B responds   1 minute
3. Candidate C responds   1 minute
4. Candidate A counters   30 seconds

This sequence gives Candidate A time equivalent to the total of his opponents' time and the last word to balance out attacks against him or his positions. While all four steps are desirable in most cases, the time breakdowns may require adjustment. For a skillful, concise, and articulate candidate, thirty seconds for a counterrebuttal may be adequate, but for a less endowed candidate, it would probably be a tight squeeze, especially since candidates tend to consume rebuttal time more fully than initial response time.

The most satisfying format for a debate of four or more candidates is to have each candidate answer each question for the same amount of time. Such a format was used in the 1980 Republican primary encounters in Des Moines (Iowa), Manchester (New Hampshire), and Columbia (South Carolina). Obviously, great pains should be taken to prepare questions appropriate for all candidates. A question tailored to a particular candidate's interests is unfair to all candidates, and usually results in a string of meaningless and time-consuming responses from the others. Response time in debates of three or more parties is generally shorter than it is in two-party debates; as a consequence, pressure is placed on candidates to be concise.

Multi-candidate debate formats remain problematic, despite the length of response opportunities. Normally, candidates alternate in answering each question first, often progressing from audience left to right. Thus, while the candidate to the audience's right may be blessed with more thinking time and with greater refutational opportunities, particularly in debates with more than three candidates, he must also present an interesting answer once his turn comes. In addition, once he has the first response opportunity, it may be so late in the debate that he and the other candidates could have lost a fair percentage of their audience. In the final analysis, then, seating order can be strategically and tactically significant.

COMMENT

Political campaign debates are bound to persist with few, if any, structural modifications, despite carping by journalists and scholars who criticize formats for their emphasis on glibness and images rather than on issues. And while there may be at least partial merit to their indictments, not only do they demonstrate seemingly willful insensitivity to the strategic and tactical implications of the formats and to the magnitude of the stakes facing the candidates, but they also reflect the most uncritical notions about how debates can be designed to serve better the public interest.

Clearly, the format used during the Lincoln-Douglas debates, venerated by all too many critics, is not necessarily ideal. It places great emphasis on the candidates' debating skills and requires debating a question of great import about which the candidates differ. But the former is not necessary for political office and the latter not present in every campaign.

It is, moreover, incorrect to conclude that the candidate's and the public's interests are necessarily at odds. For instance, the candidate's unwillingness, for politically expedient reasons, to engage in cross examination does not *ipso facto* deprive the electorate of an edifying contest. Nor, as the preceding discussion suggests, do panels necessarily favor the candidate's interests over the electorate's.

Since the candidate's personal interest—his concern for political success— is ordinarily equivalent in his mind to what would best suit the public interest, it is not difficult to understand why a debate format tailored to his own capabilities would seem eminently justified to every candidate. Moreover, it would seem naïve to criticize a candidate for taking all reasonable steps to get elected. A candidate is no more guilty of deception when he insists on a particular debate format than when he insists that his campaign photographs show him in the most favorable profile. Debate formats are likely to continue to meet the needs of candidates—at least until someone devises a fair standard format, hardly a likely prospect.

NOTES

1. Edwin Erle Sparks, ed., *Lincoln-Douglas Debates of 1858* (Springfield, Illinois: Illinois State Historical Library, 1908), pp. 6–7.

2. Ibid.

3. *With the Nation Watching*, Report of the Twentieth Century Fund Task Force on Televised Presidential Debates (Lexington, Massachusetts: D.C. Heath, 1979), pp. 6–7.

4. Interview, Mitchell Rogovin, July 2, 1981.

5. J. Jeffery Auer, "The Counterfeit Debates," in *The Great Debates: Kennedy vs. Nixon, 1960*, ed. Sidney Kraus (Bloomington, Indiana: Indiana University Press, 1962), pp. 147–148.

6. Memorandum, Samuel Popkin to Carter campaign staff, August 30, 1976.

7. Interview, Michael Hemsley, campaign manager for David Marston, October 6, 1979.

8. Richard Nixon, *Six Crises* (New York: Doubleday, 1962), p. 324.

9. Interview, Barry Jagoda, television adviser to President Carter, December 16, 1977.

10. Lloyd Bitzer and Theodore Rueter, *Carter vs. Ford: The Counterfeit Debates of 1976* (Madison, Wisconsin: The University of Wisconsin Press, 1980), p. 187.

11. Ibid., p. 246.

12. Lee M. Mitchell, "Background Paper," in *With the Nation Watching*, p. 96.

13. Interview, James Gannon, February 3, 1978.

14. Cited in Lee M. Mitchell, "Background Paper," p. 94.

15. Memorandum, Popkin, August 30, 1976.

16. Interview, James Karayn, November 17, 1978.

17. American Political Science Association, *Report of the Commission on Presidential Campaign Debates* (Washington, D.C., 1964).

18. The four alternative formats are discussed in Bitzer and Rueter, *Carter vs. Ford: The Counterfeit Debates of 1976*, pp. 225–250.

19. Nelson Polsby, "Debatable Thoughts on Presidential Debates," in *The Past and Future of Presidential Debates*, ed. Austin Ranney (Washington, D.C.: American Enterprise Institute, 1979), p. 185.

20. Bitzer and Rueter, *Carter vs. Ford: The Counterfeit Debates of 1976*, pp. 227, 245–247.

21. Ibid., p. 250.

22. Jeff Greenfield, *Playing to Win: An Insider's Guide to Politics* (New York: Simon & Schuster, 1980), p. 204.

23. Ibid.

24. Jack W. Germond and Jules Witcover, "Presidential Debates: An Overview," in Ranney, *The Past and Future of Presidential Debates*, p. 200. The phrase "boys on the bus" is taken from a book by Timothy Crouse, *The Boys of the Bus* (New York: Random House, 1973).

25. *New York Times*, September 18, 1976, p. 1; September 19, 1976, p. 10; September 21, 1976, p. 29.

26. Interview, Lee Hanna, August 6, 1981. For Hanna's views on other aspects of debate formats, see "Hanna Criticizes Candidates' Influence in Debate Set-up," *Broadcasting* (February 16, 1981), pp. 76–78.

27. Interview, Theodore H. White, February 21, 1978.

28. *With the Nation Watching*, Report of the Twentieth Century Fund Task Force on Televised Presidential Debates, p. 16.

29. Interview, George Gallup, Jr., January 2, 1978; interview with Theodore H. White.

30. Robert G. Meadow and Marilyn Jackson-Beeck, "A Comparative Perspective on Presidential Debates: Issue Evolution in 1960 and 1976," in *The Presidential Debates: Media, Electoral, and Policy Perspectives*, eds. George F. Bishop, Robert G. Meadow, and Marilyn Jackson-Beeck (New York: Praeger, 1978), p. 57.

31. Bitzer and Rueter, *Carter vs. Ford: The Counterfeit Debates of 1976*, pp. 39–77.

32. Ibid., p. 40.

33. Joseph Kraft, "A No-Win Debate," *Washington Post*, September 26, 1976, p. C7.

34. Interview, Joseph Kraft, January 27, 1978. Kraft did not use these words, but the statement is consistent with the positions he expressed in the interview.

35. Interview, Richard Valeriani, February 17, 1978.

36. Interview, Edwin Newman, February 21, 1978.

37. Interview, Frank Reynolds, March 3, 1978; interview, Henry Trewhitt, July 14, 1978.

38. Interview with James Gannon.

39. Interview, Elizabeth Drew, February 3, 1978; interview with James Gannon; interview with Frank Reynolds.

40. Memorandum, Popkin, August 30, 1976.

41. Interview with Edwin Newman.

42. Memorandum, Popkin, August 30, 1976.

43. Interview, Douglas Bailey, November 18, 1978.

44. Interview, Harold Stassen, April 17, 1979. For an interesting discussion of this debate, see Robert F. Ray, "Thomas E. Dewey: The Great Oregon Debate of 1948," in *American Public Address*, ed. Loren Reid (Columbia, Missouri: University of Missouri Press, 1961), pp. 245–267.

45. Memorandum, Popkin, August 30, 1976.

46. Interview with Edwin Newman.

47. Interview, Hal Bruno, June 12, 1978.

48. Henry Steele Commager, "Washington Would Have Lost a TV Debate," *New York Times Magazine,* October 30, 1960, p. 13.

49. Norman Cousins, "Presidents Don't Have to be Quiz Masters," *Saturday Review* (November 5, 1960), p. 34.

50. Interview, Michael Duval, December 20, 1977.

51. Theodore H. White, *The Making of the President 1960* (New York: Atheneum, 1961), p. 283.

52. Lee Mitchell, "Background Paper," in *With the Nation Watching,* Report of the Twentieth Century Fund Task Force on Televised Presidential Debates, p. 100.

53. Germond and Witcover, "Presidential Debates: An Overview," pp. 198–200, 203.

54. Interview, Richard Moe, August 18, 1978.

55. Interview with Theodore H. White.

56. *New York Times,* August 14, 1982, p. 8.

57. Interview with Frank Reynolds.

58. Interview, Jim Hoge, June 29, 1978.

59. Interview with Edwin Newman.

60. Interview with Henry Trewhitt.

61. The possibility of televised audience reaction shots influencing millions of viewers understandably troubled the Task Force on Televised Presidential Debates sponsored by the Twentieth Century Fund. Their solution: "We recommend, subject to legal requirements, against an immediate audience that might by its behavior inject its own partisan feelings into the proceedings." *With the Nation Watching,* Report of the Twentieth Century Fund Task Force on Televised Presidential Debates, p. 11.)

6

Metadebating

Political candidates, like the rest of us, have their private goals and public postures. In contemplating whether or not to debate, these can often conflict. Many candidates conclude that a debate is not in their interest; but most candidates also believe that rejecting a debate invitation can be politically damaging. Thus, a candidate may feel obligated to insist publicly on his willingness to debate, while hoping to avoid such an eventuality. When the private campaign goals (to avoid debate) conflict with the public posturing ("I want to debate"), a metadebating situation occurs. Metadebating, or "debate about debates," is a psychological game played by candidates and their surrogates through the media to influence the public. The essence of metadebating is to clothe decisions made on the basis of self-interest with the mantle of the public interest, and to shift to the opponent the blame for any delay or complication in the debate planning process.

The candidates' metadebating performance can influence significantly the public's perception of them. Depending on how it is approached, metadebating can generate greater interest in the debates or can turn voters off. A candidate's image can be injured if he is perceived during the metadebating as an unwilling participant in debate (especially if his behavior during the debate reinforces this perception), or it can be bolstered if he is perceived as eager to debate. The image a candidate projects in the metadebate may affect the public's perception of the debate itself. As Scott suggests, a voter who believed that Jimmy Carter was acting "unfairly" in refusing to debate Ronald Reagan early in the 1980 campaign may have been more likely to perceive Carter's attack in the debate as similarly "unfair".[1] Finally, in some cases metadebating can become more significant than the debates themselves, the most prominent example being the 1980 Nashua "metadebate" which will be discussed later in this chapter.

Candidates rarely engage in metadebating themselves. Rather, they prefer to insulate themselves to preserve an aura of dignity more compatible with the office they seek than with hard political campaigning. The metadebate is carried out instead by the candidates' spokesmen, or surrogates, who work the media to create a favorable perception of their candidate. Metadebate activity is often particularly prominent between early summer, when media coverage of the fall election begins to build, and Labor Day, when candidates traditionally emerge from isolation to begin their public campaign.

In general, metadebating is most intense in close elections where each candidate has much to gain or lose from both the actual debate and the public's perceptions of his maneuvering prior to the debate. In these circumstances, candidates may find it necessary to engage in metadebating on any or all of the following six issues: (1) Will there be a debate? (2) Who will participate? (3) What will be the format? (4) How many debates will there be? (5) When will the debate(s) occur? (6) Where will the debate(s) be held? Critical metadebating questions can arise at any time in the campaign, from the initial decision to issue or respond to a debate challenge, until election day. In this chapter I discuss the following stages of the metadebate: the ploys associated with issuing, refusing, or accepting a challenge; the subsequent defense in the media of the candidate's decision; various metadebating options available in the debate itself; and finally, the need to shape public perceptions following the debate.

THE CHALLENGE

Challenges to debate can be classified as either sincere (reflecting an actual desire to debate) or insincere (issued principally to achieve a political effect). To differentiate between the two is often difficult if not impossible, for candidates whose challenges are less than sincere are understandably chary about revealing their actual intent.

The Sincere Challenge

As explained in Chapter 2, there are many reasons why a candidate may be eager to debate. Ordinarily, the sincere challenge is issued by the trailing candidate who feels that both the exposure and the opportunity to be contrasted with his opponent during one or more debates might change his fate.

If a candidate is eager to debate an opponent who might be willing (but not anxious) to debate, he must be sensitive to the implications of the timing of his challenge. If he issues his challenge early in the campaign and the opponent either openly refuses or ignores it, he may be able to use the time to generate public pressure for debates. On the other hand, the challenge might be accepted with the proviso that the debates take place sooner than he had hoped. Douglas Bailey, a leading consultant to Republican candidates, often advises his clients to "get them [debates] out of the way early." In Bailey's view, events occurring late in the campaign have much more weight than those near the beginning, so it is often better to accept some early damage from a debate than to have one's failure to debate remaining an issue until election day.[2] However, this principle, like most, has its exceptions. When Gerald Ford proposed that the 1976 presidential debates begin within three weeks after he challenged Carter, his goal was to establish their primacy in the campaign as soon as possible to pare down Carter's 20-plus point lead.

A far less obvious benefit of debating early is that the preparatory effort for the debate, systematically and thoroughly approached, can add immeasurably to the clarity of the candidate's issue positions, his skill in presenting speeches and in appearing before the media as well as to his overall confidence level. Indeed, in so many instances not only can "candidates make debates," but "debates can also make candidates."

On rare occasions, a candidate who desires a debate may nevertheless choose not to issue a challenge. He may feel that the challenge would acknowledge his opponent's credibility, or even communicate desperation on his own part, an impression more likely to surface if a wide margin separates him from his opponent. If he is fortunate enough to have in his constituency a respected group with a tradition of sponsoring debates (for example, the League of Women Voters), it may be expedient to wait for it to issue a debate invitation.

Moreover, not every trailing candidate who issues a challenge is sincere. When Wendell Wilkie challenged FDR to debate in 1940 he was sincere, according to Harold Stassen, one of his closest advisers, although Wilkie did not expect FDR to accept.[3] But Barry Goldwater's challenge to Lyndon B. Johnson in 1964 was apparently not sincere despite Goldwater's public statements to the contrary. While Goldwater might have relished a debate with Johnson, he told me that he neither expected nor really pushed for one.[4] Hubert Humphrey's challenges to Nixon in 1968 were apparently not especially sincere either; if they were, Humphrey would probably have lobbied for a suspension of the equal time amendment and removed the condition that George Wallace join him and Nixon in a three-way debate. George McGovern's challenge to Nixon in 1972 may have been in earnest, but again with little hope that Nixon, maintaining at least a 23-point lead throughout the campaign, would debate.

The Insincere Challenge

Insincere challenges are normally issued by candidates who do not actually want to debate, but feel confident that their opponent will refuse the invitation. The insincere challenger wants to enjoy the psychological fruits of being the challenger without the requisite responsibilities; he hopes to project himself as open, aggressive, and strong, while forcing his opponent to appear evasive, weak, or even arrogant. An insincere challenge may also come from a reluctant candidate who tries to get his challenge out before an expected challenge from his opponent. The challenge may protect his image while he calculates whether or not he can avoid a debate entirely.

The candidate who issues an insincere challenge has several tactics available to reduce the likelihood of an acceptance by his opponent. The challenge can be issued late in the campaign, making it difficult for the opponent to change his schedule and to prepare for a debate. More commonly, the challenge can be issued with stipulations that the opponent is unlikely to accept. The possibilities for this tactic are nearly endless: candidates can insert unacceptable demands about format, the number of debates, time and location, etc. Negotiations over these items can be drawn out for weeks, and if the candidate is successful in his metadebating, blame for the failure to debate can be placed on his opponent. A final, but embarrassing, option for an insincere challenger who finds his challenge accepted is simply to reverse his field and search for a reasonably credible basis for refusing to debate.

THE RHETORIC OF REFUSAL

If a candidate is hesitant or unwilling to debate, he has three major options available when challenged: (1) to refuse flatly, (2) to accept with stipulations, or (3) to ignore the challenge. The effectiveness of these options depends largely on situational factors: which candidate is leading; the personalities involved; the amount of public interest in the election and public pressure favoring debates; the manner in which the refusal or stipulated acceptance is announced, i.e., who releases it; etc.

Collectively, these factors help condition a major form of metadebating, the rhetoric of refusal. For example, a flat refusal or a stipulated acceptance might communicate evasiveness, weakness, or arrogance if the challenger is respected, the election is expected to be close, and the candidate being challenged holds unpopular positions or has behaved in a manner considered improper by his intended constituents. However, if the challenge were especially unpopular, then the candidate being challenged might be able to refuse, accept with stipulations, or ignore the challenge entirely without suffering adverse consequences.

Ignoring a challenge, the least common response, is tantamount to renouncing metadebating. A candidate who decides to ignore a challenge does so only if he is sufficiently confident that the public will not react adversely to this tactic. When Lyndon Johnson initially ignored Goldwater's debate challenges in 1964, he was also ignoring Goldwater himself. Such a strategy is mainly feasible in political campaigns where one candidate is significantly ahead of the other; the frontrunner may conclude that he communicates greater confidence in his campaign not only by avoiding debates (or "debates" about debates), but also by avoiding any reference to his opponent.

Many candidates may prefer to avoid a debate, but few want openly to refuse one. A candidate who refuses to debate may be perceived as being arrogant, afraid of meeting his opponent, or heedless of the public's desire for debate. An open refusal may have considerable costs, and is thus most appropriate when a candidate has a wide lead. When FDR flatly refused to debate Willkie in 1940, he was shielded not only by his incumbency, but also by public opinion; slightly more than half the Americans surveyed by Gallup in late August recommended that Roosevelt not accept Willkie's challenge.[5] LBJ's flat (although delayed) refusal of Goldwater's half-hearted challenge in 1964 and Nixon's of McGovern in 1972 were no less confident; LBJ enjoyed at least a 28-point lead over Goldwater throughout the campaign while Nixon, as mentioned earlier, savored at least a 23-point margin during the same period eight years later.

A candidate who refuses a challenge typically will provide a public justification to minimize the negative impact of his decision. The four most popular forms of the rhetoric of refusal found by the 1978 CDS were: (1) "My opponent wants to debate because he's afraid he's going to lose"; (2) "I don't need to debate; I have conducted an open campaign"; (3) "My opponent has been responsible for a breakdown in the negotiations over format which demonstrates that he didn't want to debate in the first place"; (4) "The duties of my office make it inadvisable for me to debate my opponent at this time." On this last point, the late adjournment of the 95th Congress during the 1978 Congressional campaign (October 14) provided a convenient excuse for incumbents not to debate. Although this excuse may have had greater currency for Congressmen living considerable distance from Capitol Hill, it was often used by those who could reach their districts within a few hours. Surely, many of them would have debated had they regarded debates to be politically expedient. As these examples illustrate, a candidate who refuses a debate often tries to shift the blame by attacking his opponent for unreasonable demands or unethical campaign tactics. During the summer of 1982, for example, Senator John Heinz (R. Pa.) refused to debate his challenger Cyril Wecht (D.) until Wecht stopped what the Heinz camp called personal attacks and distortions of Heinz's record.[6]

Joseph Napolitan, a leading consultant to Democratic candidates, regards refusal an ill-advised strategy:

> If I had a candidate who was a clear favorite, I'd try to keep him off TV debates. But I would never openly refuse to debate. If challenged to a debate, you say, "Yes, sure. How about my campaign manager meeting yours at 4 P.M. on Thursday?" Then at five to four on Thursday, you call and say, "We've had a real crisis here, can we make it on Saturday?" And on Saturday You put it off till next Wednesday . . . and so on.[7]

Napolitan feels that the favored candidate can lessen or avoid altogether those aspects of metadebating potentially damaging to his opponent and thereby preclude mounting public pressure for debates. Whether this objective can be consistently accomplished in this manner is questionable. When negotiations become delayed, public interest in the election may increase, and so may the persuasive potential of the metadebating waged by the candidate who sincerely wants to debate.

ACCEPTANCE

Accepting with Stipulations

Attaching stipulations to a debate acceptance is not a particularly popular tactic. Modest stipulations, such as Nixon's insistence in 1960 that the debates "should be conducted as full and free exchanges of views without prepared notes and without interruption,"[8] and Carter's call in 1976 for "tough cross-examination by representatives of the news media,"[9] not only communicate the candidate's sincerity in debating (even if he is not sincere) but can imply that his opponent is either less than earnest or less than open. However, a particularly confining stipulation or a large number of stipulations can raise serious doubts regarding the candidate's sincerity. During the 1964 New York Senate race between challenger Robert F. Kennedy and incumbent Republican Kenneth Keating, both candidates raised several format stipulations, prompting serious doubts about their sincerity in wanting debates. Keating proposed two different formats—one involved each candidate fielding questions from three young Republicans or young Democrats; the other required that each candidate deliver five-minute opening speeches, twenty-minute outlines of their positions, and five-minute closing statements. Kennedy rejected both proposals, and accused Keating of trying to "prevent the debate by creating a controversy over ground rules."[10] Kennedy, who may not have wanted to debate at the time because he was ahead in the polls (which he denied), proposed a format involving direct interaction, which Keating rejected. And interestingly, as each side was vying for advantage, neither had apparently made a sincere effort to negotiate privately with the other.

A new twist in the stipulation strategy occurred in the 1982 Pennsylvania gubernatorial race between well-known incumbent Dick Thornburgh and a little-known challenger, Allen Ertel.[11] As early as March 25, Ertel was calling for a debate; Thornburgh's spokesman replied that he would not even consider debating until the fall. On June 16, a letter from Thornburgh's campaign manager suggested that the two candidates could communicate their positions to the voters "without engaging in formalized, staged debate," and that for Thornburgh even to consider a debate, certain conditions would have to be met. Notably, Ertel would have to abandon his rumored search for a debate coach. Referring to Thornburgh's 1978 gubernatorial campaign, his campaign manager wrote:

> When Gov. Thornburgh debated Mayor Flaherty, he did so without the use of any slick props, fancy debate tricks or professional training in theatrics. . . . Accordingly, I am suggesting that you now pledge that you will not utilize the services of debate coaches and consultants whose specialty is to turn debates into matters of theater, histrionics, form and gimmickry.

An Ertel aide replied that not only was Ertel not searching for a debate coach, but that he did not even know such people existed. He then concluded:

The Thornburgh people have a penchant for the bizarre, but at bottom their response is right out of the textbook. They keep just pulling reasons out of left field to justify their decision not to debate.[12]

An equally interesting set of onerous stipulations was issued during the 1982 debate negotiations between Congressman Joseph Moakley (D. Mass.) and State Representative Deborah Cochran (R.). Moakley's aides presented an extensive list of provisos, including forty-eight hour notification for all questions. In the second stage of negotiations Moakley's campaign demanded that Cochran sign a "Code of Fair Campaign Practices" that was unrelated to the contested debate. Moakley, of course, had already signed it, while Cochran's aides insisted that their candidate would comply if Moakley would agree that an unlimited range of subjects be debated. Surprising few who followed the proceedings, Moakley's people broke off negotiations, wasting little time to announce that Moakley wouldn't debate anyone who refused to sign the "Code."

Accepting (For Now)

The candidate not willing to debate may accept an invitation or challenge without stipulations, intending to withdraw from the negotiations later. John F. Kennedy's and Gerald Ford's representatives feared this possibility; they were not confident of Nixon's or Carter's commitment to debate when negotiations began for the 1960 and 1976 presidential debates. Kennedy's negotiators were highly agreeable during the negotiations, particularly during the early stages, exercising every caution to avoid giving Nixon an excuse to back out. In 1976, Ford's negotiators were less pliant, apparently confident that they could make a persuasive case to the American people if Carter reneged on a commitment to debate the President of the United States.

Candidates who renege on an earlier commitment to debate usually blame their opponents for making "unreasonable" or "impossible" demands in the private format negotiations. They hope that the voters, confused by all the charges and countercharges, will not be able to assign responsibility for the breakdown of negotiations. It is indeed often difficult for the voter (or even the opponent) to determine if a candidate is intentionally avoiding a debate. For example, House incumbent Robert Edgar (D., Pa.), an experienced and effective debater, took the offensive by issuing a debate challenge to his 1982 Republican opponent, Steve Joachim, thirty minutes after the polls closed on primary day. Edgar proposed two debates with no specified subject matter, unlimited length of answers, and audience participation. Joachim soon replied with his own proposal: four debates, each limited to a specific topic (crime, the economy, busing, and foreign policy), questions from a panel of reporters, and time limits on the answers. There followed the usual round of charges from both sides that their opponent had proposed a debate format tailored to his own strengths (true in both cases) and had never seriously intended to debate at all (perhaps true, perhaps not). Then both sides issued their idea of a compromise: Joachim announced he would accept Edgar's idea of two debates, but could not accept his format, and Edgar announced that he would accept Joachim's plan for four debates, but not *his* format. As of this writing Joachim has pronounced himself "encouraged" by Edgar's response (for reasons that elude me), while Edgar's negotiator is both insisting on his eagerness to debate and saying that Joachim could "fall on the sword and bleed all over the place for all I care."[13] If Edgar and Joachim never do debate, how is a citizen to know who is to blame?

An alternative to strangling a debate in negotiations is to announce that due to unforeseen and unfortunate circumstances, a debate has become inappropriate. The most notable recent example of this ploy was Jimmy Carter's withdrawal from the Iowa Democratic Primary Forum in January 1980, scheduled to pit him against Edward Kennedy and Jerry Brown. Carter had agreed to participate when public opinion polls showed him badly trailing Kennedy. Even at the time, however, there was considerable doubt among political analysts that Carter would actually appear. Then, on November 4, 1979, the U.S. Embassy in Iran was seized and 53 hostages taken. Largely as a result of positive public reaction to Carter's handling of the crisis, he went from trailing Kennedy in the Gallup poll 54% to 20% on the day of the seizure to leading him 48% to 40% on December 12, the largest jump in presidential approval ratings since the poll was founded in 1935. As Carter's ratings improved, his participation in the forum became increasingly doubtful. On December 27, White House sources announced that Carter might not debate because of the increasing international tension provoked by the Soviet Union's invasion of Afghanistan that very day and by the seizure of the U.S. Embassy in Tehran on November 4. Carter's official withdrawal, expressed the following day in a telephone call and telegram, was attributed to his unwillingness both to leave Washington during the international crisis and to appear at political events while seeking nonpartisan support for his approach to the Iranian hostage situation. The sponsors then attempted to salvage the debate by offering to hold it in Washington before the National Press Club and to ban discussion on the Iranian crisis. Kennedy and Brown acceded, but Carter held firm.

Carter's withdrawal was widely perceived by the press as politically motivated. Suspicions regarding his stated reasons for avoiding the debate were heightened by extensive telephone campaigning he was conducting from the White House with hundreds of Iowa Democrats. The White House admitted he was making between 15–20 two- to three-minute calls per evening, aided by small cue cards identifying the names of the family members of the person being called and other information to personalize the call.

To soften the impression that the withdrawal was politically expedient, Jody Powell, Carter's Press Secretary, released in generous quantities to the press a confidential internal White House memo. It sought to corroborate an allegation by key Carter campaign advisers Hamilton Jordan, Robert

Strauss, Stuart Eizenstat, and Powell himself that they wanted Carter to debate while Secretary of State Cyrus Vance and National Security Adviser Zbigniew Brzezinski reportedly felt that it would be counterproductive to a constructive approach to the Iranian and Afghanistan crises. Powell contended that Carter could not risk being perceived as running from the debate. He further argued that withdrawal would set a precedent that would preclude Carter from campaigning for the duration of the crisis. The memo represents Kennedy's initiatives in Iowa as further justification for Carter's participation in the forum:

> A debate in this format places you in the strongest position and EMK [Kennedy] in the weakest. He has shown signs of late that he is perfecting his stump speech, but there is no reason to believe that he is able to handle a tough give-and-take.
>
> Since there is little chance that you will be able to personally campaign in Iowa, the debate is your chance to have a personal impact before the first round of caucuses. EMK is practically living in the state and his continued presence will help him.[14]

The memo generated immediate suspicion and pointed editorial comment, particularly from Richard Reeves of the *Washington Star:*

> Carter and Powell are perfecting a new political art form: the public memo. The things are being released to wire services . . . at just about the same time as they go into the Oval Office.
>
> The one last Saturday concerning the president's decision to quit a televised Iowa debate with Kennedy and Jerry Brown is not the first public memo from the White House, but it's the best so far. Carter answered it with a scrawl across the bottom: "I can't disagree with any of this; but I cannot break away from my duties here which are extraordinary now and ones which only I can fulfill. . . ."
>
> If I believed all that and believed that this is the way Carter talks to Powell in private—to the young man the president describes as "like my son"—then I would stay up tonight and wait for the tooth fairy.[15]

THE PSYCHOLOGY OF METADEBATING

Metadebating has only begun when the candidates make their decisions to challenge, ignore, accept, or refuse. The candidate and his surrogates will continue the metadebate until election day, if necessary, to facilitate the desired image of their candidate. Their task, in essence, is to convince the media, and through them the public, that their position on the proposed debate serves the public interest, while their opponent's position is imbued with crass self-interest.

"I am being fair to my opponent"

The first metadebating priority of most candidates is to have their position perceived as the "fair" one. There is no better example of the importance of "fairness" than the 1980 presidential election. The primary metadebating issue was who should debate, and Reagan and Carter both explained their positions in terms of what would be fair. Reagan argued that the fair way to deal with a third-party campaign like John Anderson's was to get all the contenders face-to-face, at one time, in one place. As James Baker, coordinator of Reagan's debate task force, put it, "We do not want to be a party to any agreement that would serve to exclude any viable challenger."[16] Carter, on the other hand, argued that Anderson did not deserve a place in a debate, because he was "primarily a creation of the press" and not a serious contender for the office; moreover, only months earlier he had been competing in Republican primaries. In Carter's words, "I see no reason why I should debate against two Republicans who have been active in the Republican Party, who have held positions of leadership in the Republican Party, who have a Republican voting record."[17] Media coverage was heavily critical of Carter on this issue, largely because, in the words of Professor Robert Scott, "Carter seemed to be avoiding or seeking advantage to a much greater degree than did Reagan. Especially after Reagan and Anderson debated, Reagan's apparent concern for fairness eclipsed Carter's."[18] Scott argues that this not only hurt Carter at the time, but also influenced perceptions of the debate itself. The image of "unfairness" created in the metadebate led viewers to expect Carter to seek unfair advantage in the debate. In Scott's view, "Carter lost the election . . . in the debate but . . . the impetus that made the contrast between himself and Reagan so dramatic was largely fixed in the debate about the debate."[19]

"My opponent is afraid to debate"

The defense of oneself as being fair is often complemented with an attack on one's opponent as being afraid to debate. The "you're afraid" tactic can accomplish three objectives: (1) it accuses the opposition of ducking a debate, in itself a negative all candidates try to avoid; (2) it projects the accuser as a confident and open candidate; and (3) it increases the pressure on a reluctant opponent to debate.

The fear alibi surfaced constantly in the metadebate in the 1980 presidential election. Jody Powell, speaking for Carter, suggested that "The Reagan campaign's real goal is to avoid a one-on-one situation,"[20] a theme echoed by John White, Democratic National Chairman: "It's remarkable how Ronald Reagan is afraid to debate President Carter one-on-one without hiding behind Congressman Anderson."[21] Carter, attempting to draw as starkly as possible the contrast between his openness and the opponent's reluctance, stated that

"Governor Reagan has not chosen to accept the one-on-one debate. I am very eager to pursue this idea and have no concern at all about the location or time except that I want it to be anywhere in this nation and as frequently as possible."[22]

Reagan, meanwhile, was charging that Carter was afraid to debate ("He wouldn't debate Kennedy during the primaries and now he seems to be afraid of Mr. Anderson."); that he had good reason to be afraid ("He wouldn't win a debate if it were held in the Rose Garden before an audience of administration officials with the questions asked by Jody Powell."); and that he was shirking his responsibility to the public ("It looks as though he prefers his office and the Rose Garden to the kind of debate that is overwhelmingly desired by the American people.")[23] In an effective combination of the fear and fairness themes, Reagan asserted that, "I've said from the very beginning that if Anderson is a viable candidate he should be a part of the debate. I can't for the life of me understand why Mr. Carter is so afraid of him."[24]

One of the more imaginative efforts to embarrass a candidate into debating was unfolded during the 1982 Massachusetts Senate race when Republican challenger Ray Shamie posted a $10,000 reward "to any person or nonpartisan organization, not related to Edward M. Kennedy or his staff, who was able to get the senator to schedule a one-on-one debate . . . for a statewide, prime-time audience." This ploy, which attracted significant media attention throughout Massachusetts, was complemented by airplanes carrying banners throughout Massachusetts which read, "$10,000 Reward—Get Ted Kennedy to Debate Ray Shamie."

The ploy worked. Two months after the reward was announced, Kennedy, a 20-year incumbent, enjoying at least a 30-point lead in the polls and savoring the incalculable advantages of the Kennedy name, agreed to debate. Shamie, wanting to prevent Kennedy from reneging, donated the $10,000 the next day to a charity of Kennedy's choosing, a media event in its own right.

"You're not kidding me or the public"

A candidate who wants to debate and believes his opponent's public acceptance is insincere will attempt to communicate this perception to the public. The key here is to convince the media of the opponent's reluctance, then rely on the media to expose the opponent and impute publicly that his reasons are smokescreens hiding his political advantage in not debating. At best, the opponent may be forced into a debate to refute the charges; at worst, he will bear full responsibility if a debate fails to materialize.

Here, as elsewhere in the metadebating context, winning the favor of the media is critical. Most media representatives have a strong preference for campaign debates, sustained by both their own self-interest and a conception of the public interest that places a high priority on candidate confrontations over policy issues. A candidate who can convince the media of his sincerity in calling for a debate is therefore likely to receive much more favorable press than his opponent. In 1980, for example, Carter was cast as the heavy for avoiding a three-way debate with Reagan and Anderson, and his motives for doing so were subject to considerable scrutiny by the media. For example, Tom Wicker of the *New York Times* said the President was "needlessly arrogant" and "presumptuous," and displayed "open contempt for the wishes of the public." Responding to Carter's argument that Anderson was not a serious rival for the presidency, but rather "a creation of the press," Wicker replied that Carter might be fairly called the "first real media president."[25] Meanwhile, the equally self-interested motives of Reagan and Anderson in seeking a debate were subject to little comment. They were represented as serving the public interest, while Carter was pursuing his own advantage.

"I'm not trying to kid anyone"

Candidates, as we have seen, often try while metadebating to project an image that bears little resemblance to reality. Self-interested decisions to debate are couched in terms of the public interest. Formats designed to highlight a candidate's strong points are defended as the only ones consistent with a "wide-open, free-wheeling debate." Suggestions that debating success requires certain skills at image projection, and that candidates may require some training at these skills, are rejected out of hand. Candidates may even be reluctant to admit that they are preparing for a debate. In the 1980 presidential campaign, for example, there was, for a while, great concern among Reagan's advisers not to let the press know that Reagan was practicing in a garage that had been converted into a television studio. When the press corps arrived to interview him, the practice sessions were brought to a halt, the garage was locked, and Reagan nonchalantly greeted the press on his patio overlooking the Blue Ridge Mountains.

Occasionally, however, the public posture of a candidate may accurately reflect his private goals. Sometimes a debate is clearly so advantageous to a candidate that he and his advisers will be open about their reasons for seeking an encounter. John Anderson in 1980 made the ritual comments about the public interest, but he also admitted that he wanted a debate because his chances would be hopeless without one. At other times a candidate's lead may be so great that he can be unabashedly open about his motives for refusing to debate.

At times there may be two levels of metadebating going on at once, one for general public consumption and the other for the benefit of the more politically sophisticated. In the 1980 presidential campaign, the general public was being swamped by both the candidates and the media with the usual clichés about fairness and the public interest. At the same time, however, a realistic defense of the candidates' actions was being sent to a more select audience. Robert Strauss, Carter's campaign manager, admitted that Carter could "look like a bum" for refusing to join Reagan and Anderson, but explained, "We have our selfish interests. Reagan has his selfish interests. We all have our selfish interests. Don't let's kid ourselves."[26]—thus placing Carter's refusal of a debate on the same plane as Reagan's and Anderson's acceptance. James Baker was equally open in discussing Reagan's position after the Anderson debate: "We still have the option of debating the president, but the numbers are such that we don't feel that way now. We'll keep an eye on the polls and keep that tactical option open. We could change our minds."[27] Baker thus conceded that the decision to debate was being made on self-interested grounds, a revelation which could hardly have shocked the sophisticated, as he communicated his real message—that Reagan held the superior position in the campaign and would consider debating Carter if it became necessary.

DEBATES AND NONDEBATES

A candidate whose challenges have been rebuffed has two extreme ploys available to him—the "empty chair" debate and the "cut and paste" debate. In the "empty chair" the challenger appears before a live audience or on television, directing his arguments to an empty chair which symbolizes his opponent's unwillingness to debate. This ploy is advisable only when the public clearly perceives the missing candidate to be responsible for the lack of a real debate; otherwise, the risk of being charged with unfair campaign tactics may be greater than the possible gains from the "debate." This is especially true if the missing opponent devises a strategy to counter the challenger's move.

The 1964 New York Senate race between Republican incumbent Kenneth Keating and Democratic Robert F. Kennedy featured a now-famous "empty chair" debate, the culmination of a month of haggling between the candidates' representatives.[28] In a final attempt to nail down commitments from both men, CBS sent them invitations on October 24 to a one-hour debate to be held three days later. Keating accepted immediately, but Kennedy did not respond since he was both ahead in the polls and fearful of the appeal the grandfatherly Keating might generate in contrast to his own boyish looks. On the morning of the debate, CBS wired Kennedy that he had until 3:30 in the afternoon to accept. Kennedy refused, claiming that the format had not been resolved. Keating then purchased that evening's 7:30 to 8:00 time slot to debate an empty chair, whereupon Kennedy's advertising agency bought the 8:00 to 8:30 slot.

At 7:29 P.M., Kennedy arrived at Keating's studio, pointed a finger at one of Keating's staff members and said, "Kindly inform Senator Keating I am here and ready to go on the air." CBS officials prohibited his appearance, contending that the time belonged to Keating. Keating, seated throughout the "empty chair" debate with Jacob Javits, his Senate colleague, spent a large portion of the program decrying Kennedy for not showing up. However, the impact of this performance was quickly blunted half an hour later when Kennedy, appearing on his own show, took every advantage to diminish Keating's strategy. Six days later Kennedy handily won the election by 720,000 votes.

The 1962 Pennsylvania gubernatorial race featured a "not-so-empty" chair, another effective defensive ploy.[29] Democrat Richardson Dilworth, a former mayor of Philadelphia, and Republican William Scranton, Sr., a Congressman, met in a televised debate on September 17, during which Dilworth challenged Scranton to three more encounters and threatened to debate an empty chair if Scranton failed to show. Scranton ignored the challenge until the evening of the debate, October 20, when shortly before the studio doors were locked and to Dilworth's complete surprise he took his "empty chair" only a few seconds before air time. Accenting this drama, he placed on the table a whitewash bucket and brush to symbolize Dilworth's "whitewashing graft and corruption in Philadelphia and in the administration of Governor David L. Lawrence." Dilworth lost both his temper during the debate and the election two weeks later by a 470,000 vote landslide.

At one point in the format negotiations for the 1980 Reagan-Anderson debates the League of Women Voters suggested that an empty lectern be placed on the stage to symbolize Carter's absence. Reagan's and Anderson's representatives initially agreed, then began to consider whether such a tactic might not communicate too much disrespect for the President. Eventually, the League withdrew its own suggestion, and the possibility of the first-ever presidential "empty chair" debate dissipated, although Carter's absence was nonetheless pronounced.

Political consultants are sometimes quick to discredit the "empty chair" tactic as hackneyed. However, it need not be; its effectiveness depends on the extent to which public opinion supports debates between the challenger and his opponent, plus the quality of the candidate's performance, particularly his composure, the cogency of his arguments, and his fairness toward his missing opponent. In this latter regard, the candidate's audience (which in the "empty chair" situation generally consists of his own supporters) might nevertheless discredit the willing debater if he apparently took unnecessary advantage of his absent opponent.

A related form of the "empty chair" is what I call the "cut and paste debate." Here a candidate eager to debate an unwilling opponent refutes excerpted portions of his opponent's speeches and statements using actual voice cuts and film footage. Senator Arthur Vandenberg got presidential campaign debating off to an unhealthy start with a cut and paste debate in 1936, when he responded on CBS radio in Alf Landon's behalf to selected recorded excerpts from President Franklin Delano Roosevelt's 1932 and 1933 speeches and from his oath of office. CBS banned the "debate" before it was broadcast by several of its affiliates and shortly after other affiliates had done so, prompting a heated public exchange involving CBS, Vandenberg, and the leaders of the Republican and Democratic parties. The tenor of the debate is reflected in the following excerpt:

> ROOSEVELT: Let it be from now on the task of our party to break foolish traditions and leave it to the Republican leadership, far more skilled in that art, to break promises.
>
> VANDENBERG: Which of our "traditions" do you consider "foolish"? How about "traditions" of free enterprise and free men? How about the "traditions" of checks and balances in government set up to save us from the tyrannical dictations of "government by Executive decree"?[30]

In 1972, George McGovern had been unsuccessfully challenging Richard Nixon to a debate from the beginning of the campaign. In a final desperate effort, Larry O'Brien, Chairman of the Democratic National Committee, suggested staging a McGovern-Nixon debate with film clips of each candidate. McGovern initially opposed the idea, fearing that it might be considered unfair, much as the earlier Vandenberg-Roosevelt radio "debate" had been. O'Brien reassured him and the film was prepared, but never shown. At a preview screening McGovern's major advisers agreed that the debate had been too fair: Nixon had won the "debate."[31] And on November 7, 1972, Nixon would win the election by 23 points, the second largest plurality in presidential campaign history.

In the early months of the 1980 Democratic primaries, Senator Edward Kennedy was pushing hard for a campaign debate with President Jimmy Carter. After Carter withdrew from a scheduled debate in the Iowa primary Kennedy became more desperate. He tried unsuccessfully to appear with Carter on NBC's "Meet the Press" only to enlist Jody Powell's terse refusal: "It's really sort of ridiculous for candidates to say 'Oh, the President is being interviewed. I want to be interviewed, too.' "[32] On January 30, Kennedy wrote Carter, proposing that they confront each other on February 6, before the Consumer Federation of America in Washington. The White House declined, claiming that such a "partisan event" would impair the President's ability to enlist bi-partisan support for his handling of the Iran and Afghanistan crises.[33] Kennedy then responded with a letter proposing that the debate be limited to "nonpolitical, noncampaign matter," and suggested further that it be restricted to the contents of a pamphlet, "The Record of President Jimmy Carter," a widely disseminated White House publication.[34]

Kennedy's unheeded challenges resulted in one of the more dramatic moments in his weakening campaign. On February 6, he debated a voice cut from Carter's press conference before 1,500 members of the Consumer Federation of America, who had invited both him and Carter to debate. Only moments earlier Carter had addressed the same body in one of his rare campaign appearances, stipulating upon his acceptance of the engagement that he would not debate Kennedy.

After the abbreviated "debate" was over, Kennedy launched into a lengthy, forceful diatribe against Carter's refusal to debate. A few representative excerpts:

> The most important single issue before the country in 1980 is the need for a full and fair debate on consumer issues. A silent campaign is a form of consumer fraud. It makes of our democracy a defective product, where voters cannot check the truth behind a candidate's carefully packaged labels. . . .
>
> The President pleads that he cannot give a minute or even an hour to partisan activities. In fact this is sheer hypocrisy—and Jimmy Carter knows that, and so does the national press, and so does everybody in this room. . . . He does not have an hour to debate, but he has hours upon hours to phone voter after voter in Maine and New Hampshire. In a single weekend he makes a hundred calls. . . .[35]

The ultimate "cut and paste" debate was John Anderson's 1980 cable television "debate" with Carter and Reagan. Piqued at being excluded from the second presidential debate, Anderson and his advisers devised a complicated media hook-up which allowed him to respond live from a Washington, D.C. television studio to the points debated by Carter and Reagan in Cleveland. Unfortunately for Anderson, the broadcast was marred by severe technical problems.

THE DEBATE ABOUT THE METADEBATE

Metadebating not only creates a context in which campaign debates are waged; it can also intrude into the actual debate itself. The most dramatic example of this is the 1980 Nashua (N.H.) Republican Forum. This debate, or more precisely, the metadebating preceding the actual debate, was, according to David Nyham of the *Boston Globe,* "the most controversial, uproarious and important event of the Republican Presidential campaign."[36] Held on February 23 before 2,700 persons seated in a Nashua high school auditorium and broadcast throughout the state three days before the primary, the debate grew out of a challenge that Ronald Reagan had extended to George Bush in late January. The *Nashua Telegraph,* with Reagan's and Bush's cooperation and approval, had carefully spent the preceding seven weeks planning it. The five other Republican contenders were excluded by the *Telegraph* "given the prevalent wisdom that Mr. Reagan and Mr. Bush are the frontrunners. . . ."[37] Indeed, the *Telegraph's* aim seemed reasonable: The seven candidates had participated only three days earlier in the Manchester debate; furthermore, having seven candidates engaged in a political debate is seldom conducive to a searching examination of the issues.

The *Telegraph's* executive editor and debate coordinator, Jon Breen, formerly an assistant press secretary with the President Ford Committee, had until approximately five hours before the debate full agreement with both Bush and Reagan that the exclusion was satisfactory. At that point, the news broke that Reagan had succumbed to pressure exerted by other Republican presidential hopefuls Robert Dole, Howard Baker, John Anderson, and Philip Crane (John Connally had stepped out of the matter to campaign in South Carolina) and invited them to debate without the *Telegraph's* or Bush's foreknowledge or approval.

In fact, John Sears, then Reagan's campaign manager, and Jim Lake, a Reagan aide, had been talking to the other candidates for several days about a possible change in the debate format, and called them the morning of the debate to invite them. Anticipating the possibility that debate moderator Breen might leave the gymnasium in protest of this unilateral action, Sears also quietly arranged for George Roberts, Speaker of the New Hampshire House of Representatives, to replace him if necessary.

The reason behind the invitation, however, was not pressure from the other candidates so much as it was changing calculations within the Reagan camp. Earlier, Sears had been eager for a two-man debate with George Bush, certain that Reagan would outperform his leading rival. After seeing Wirthlin's figures on the impact of the Manchester debate, Sears concluded that a one-on-one debate with Bush would present more risks than benefits. Reagan had shown in Manchester that he could do well in a multi-candidate debate. Why, then, should he participate in a two-man debate, which would present far more opportunities for a major mistake and antagonize the other candidates? In addition, Sears calculated that inviting the other candidates would present Reagan as a champion of open debate, thus neutralizing some of the adverse effects of his refusal to debate in Iowa, and would put Bush in an unexpected situation that he might not respond to effectively.[38]

Reagan apparently felt that he was entitled to extend the invitation: he had agreed to underwrite the debate ($3,500) after the Federal Election Commission, responding to complaints filed by Dole, Anderson, and Baker three days earlier, advised the *Telegraph* that, in effect, it would be making an illegal corporate contribution if it held "any debate for primary, caucus, or convention candidates [that would] promote one candidate over another."[39] Bush's organization refused to share the debate expenses, arguing that Reagan had issued the challenge.

The five hours before the debate were tension-filled. They involved separate discussions between the *Telegraph's* management and representatives of Reagan's and Bush's campaign. At no point, however, did the *Telegraph* consider including the other candidates. As Breen told me, "We felt all along that we had made a moral commitment to a one-on-one debate—one more important than what went on before [Manchester]. Including all of them would have been a rerun of the Manchester debate."[40] Reagan himself was unaware of Sears' actions in the days prior to the debate. Although he later said he was "uncomfortable" about excluding the other candidates, he was informed by Jim Lake only an hour before the debate that Dole, Baker, Anderson, and Crane would be coming. Minutes before the debate, Reagan met with his four rivals while his aides tried unsuccessfully to win Bush's agreement to open up the debate. After toying with the idea of walking out on the debate entirely if the others were not included, Reagan finally decided to take the stage. As he walked to the stage, his advisers were still unsure what he would do. Reagan's reaction to these unexpected and unsettled circumstances would have to be spontaneous.[41]

From the moment the debate began, Sears' invitation to the excluded candidates was translated into one of the cleverest and possibly most underhanded tactics ever employed in a presidential campaign. As Herman Pouliot, the *Telegraph's* publisher, announced amid heavy audience booing that Dole, Anderson, Baker, and Crane could make statements only at the end of the debate, and then began to introduce Breen, the moderator, Reagan tried to speak. Shortly after Breen introduced the panelists, Reagan interrupted again, whereupon Breen asked that Reagan's microphone be turned off. In a display of righteous indignation that would be filmed and featured on the network news, Reagan then shouted, "I am paying for this microphone." The microphone was not turned off and Reagan retained command of the situation: "I volunteered to have our campaign pay for this debate. I felt that as technical sponsor of the debate, I had some right. I felt we should make it a debate of all the candidates."[42] The lively crowd seated in the bleachers cheered Reagan loudly; he had projected a sense of fair play to the hilt and a large percentage of those who watched him loved it.

Dole, standing behind Bush with Baker, Crane, and Anderson, then requested that the excluded candidates make their statements "now," whereupon Breen told him to wait until the end of the program. The excluded candidates then left the stage, but not before shaking hands with Reagan, though not with Bush, who initially tried to ignore what was happening.

But Bush couldn't ignore the situation for long. Having unwittingly created the impression that he was as responsible for excluding the four candidates as the *Telegraph,* he requested and was granted an opportunity to speak. He explained to little apparent avail that he had been challenged by Reagan to a one-on-one debate, that there would be another debate including all competing candidates in the South Carolina primary the following week, and that he had just found out that afternoon about Reagan's invitation to the others. Breen then spoke in defense of the *Telegraph* (and, in effect, for Bush's position) explaining that he had learned at only two o'clock that afternoon that Reagan wanted to change the rules, and stressing that the *Telegraph* was the debate's sponsor.

Unfortunately for Bush, both his own and Breen's statements failed to include important points that they had previously agreed to make. Bush did not know for certain that the other four candidates would appear until his campaign manager, Jim Baker, spied them in a room with Reagan minutes before the debate. He did, of course, know that their appearance was a possibility, and had devised a plan to deal with the situation. Bush was to state that he had accepted the invitation of the *Nashua Telegraph* and would be pleased to debate in any format it thought proper, thus divesting himself of responsibility for excluding his fellow candidates. Breen was to point out the simple truth that Reagan was attempting to change the rules in the middle of the game (in fact, at the very end of the game), and was failing to live up to his commitment to the *Telegraph.* Breen also agreed to restate the point that Bush was willing to appear in any format the sponsor chose, including a multi-candidate debate, and that the *Telegraph* was solely responsible for excluding the other candidates. However, Breen never did make this point, and even more surprisingly, neither did Bush. Instead, by arguing that he had to honor his commitment to the *Telegraph,* Bush put himself in the position of defending the exclusion of four rivals.[43]

As Bush and Breen were justifying their positions, the excluded candidates were conducting an informal press forum of their own to denounce Bush roundly. Baker called the exclusion "the rawest political act I've seen in fifteen years." Dole said it was "the sorriest episode in American politics," and Anderson, for once agreeing with Dole and Baker, asserted that "George Bush shot himself in the leg."[44] Reagan, who had been the bad guy for not participating in the Des Moines debate, had suddenly and dramatically replaced Bush as the good guy. And Reagan's metadebating ploy, many political analysts argue, destroyed Bush's chances for receiving his party's nomination.[45]

INFLUENCING AUDIENCE PERCEPTIONS

When metadebating becomes a prolonged part of a campaign, it can influence audience expectations of what will occur during the actual debate. The press plays a part in this, because metadebating is a good story, and therefore involves much speculation of each party's motives. But the candidates also attempt to condition or to prepare the press and public to react to the debate in a manner beneficial to them.

Ironically, part of this process involves downplaying the skills of one's own candidate and praising the opponent. A candidate should appear confident about the debate, but he should not encourage the expectation that he will be an easy winner. If expectations of a candidate's performance are too high, a debate in which he does not clearly outclass his opponent may be seen as a "loss." Accordingly, a common strategy is keeping expectations "reasonable." This requires that the candidate publicly acknowledge his opponent's skills and say he hopes to "do well" in a debate. If this is said often enough, the debate audience may be satisfied with something less than a one-sided victory. Both candidates' 1980 metadebating strategy recognized this. Carter's spokesmen were constantly reminding voters of Reagan's acting background, thus suggesting that he should do well in a debate while the Reagan camp was quite willing to concede that Carter was a seasoned campaigner and skillful debater.

Attempts to influence the public's perceptions continue even after the debate. Immediately following the debate, a well-organized campaign will have supporters of the candidate ready to express to the media their satisfaction with the candidate's performance and to explain why they thought he won. These explanations are not always spontaneous. Rather, before the debate even occurs, a candidate's staff often will compile an analysis of the debate's "outcome" consistent with the candidate's overall strategy, and share it with the surrogates, those expected to be approached for comment. Jeff Greenfield suggests that the proper attitude to convey is one of "restrained celebration," since a too-obvious display of jubilation might be perceived as gloating.[46] Surrogates will also be available to explain away a candidate's gaffe, "clarify" an unfortunate statement, or magnify the opponent's mistakes. It has become standard procedure in at least presidential debates to have a research team closely monitoring the debate for factual errors or omissions by the opponent which should be called to the media's attention. The campaign may also have supporters standing by to call in their votes on a post-debate "instant poll," to ensure that their candidate is reported the "winner" before the viewing audience turns off their television sets.

The metadebate continues in the succeeding days as the candidates and their surrogates interpret the event to the public. This usually takes the form of focusing attention on any unfortunate statements or gaffes by the opposition. Gerald Ford's misstatement that "There is no Soviet domination of Eastern Europe" in his second 1976 debate with Jimmy Carter remained the center of editorial commentary on the debate for several days. Although Ford's aides explained that he had not meant to say that the Soviets do not control Eastern Europe, but rather that they had not crushed the spirit of the Eastern European people, Ford could not be convinced to repudiate his remark. Carter took full advantage of the opportunity. He suggested that Ford had been "brainwashed" on his trip to Eastern Europe and that Ford's statement reflected his "inaccessibility" and his "lack of knowledge" about the attitudes of ethnic Americans. Pulling out all stops, Carter concluded: "I think Mr. Ford showed confusion about our people, about the aspirations of human beings, about human rights, about liberty, about simple justice."[47]

Occasionally, the conduct of the debates also becomes a metadebating issue. For example, after the third Kennedy-Nixon debate in 1960, Nixon complained vigorously that Kennedy had violated their pre-debate agreement by using notes to quote several public figures. Whether or not this agreement was actually reached is uncertain; no evidence has been uncovered during oral history interviews with the negotiators that it was, although Nixon did insist on "no notes" when he accepted the original invitation to debate. Characterizing the Vice President as "more disappointed than angry," his press secretary, Herbert Klein, insisted that the rule be clarified before the next debate, and said that Nixon would argue for no notes, "But if Senator Kennedy insists he needs notes, then we should know about it in advance." Kennedy's press secretary, Pierre Salinger, denied that there was a no-notes agreement, and said "the Senator feels that when he quotes the President of the United States, he wants to quote him accurately. . . . He feels it would be advantageous to all candidates if they quoted the record accurately."[48]

Metadebating may also occur over whether additional debates should be held. The night of their fourth and final debate in 1960, Kennedy handed Nixon a telegram challenging him to a fifth debate. Two days later, Nixon wired his response:

> I find it difficult to understand your continued public statements to the effect that I am afraid to meet you in debate. Such a statement is sophomoric and not worthy of one who is running for the highest office in the land. Furthermore, you know it is untrue.[49]

Later in the telegram he proposed that they debate the question, "What should the United States Government do about Cuba?" In his reply, Kennedy agreed to "discuss the whole of Cuba" but also chided Nixon for not being willing to discuss "our relations with the Soviet Union, the problem of Latin America, Asia and Africa" and "open the domestic issues which you and the Republican Party seem to wish to bury during this campaign. . . ."[50] After five days of negotiations between their subordinates brought no agreement, Kennedy called Nixon's unwillingness to debate "incomprehensible" and issued an ultimatum: "If agreement is not forthcoming . . . the American people will know where to place the responsibility."[51] A Nixon aide countered: "There can be no further negotiations unless Senator Kennedy apologizes to the charge of 'bad faith' which he has made and withdraws his ill-advised ultimatum."[52] The Nixon camp may have had the last word, but a week later their candidate lost to Kennedy by .17 of a point.

COMMENT

Metadebating is largely an image game. To the voters the game is often confusing. The political motivations of the candidates are complex and hidden behind a strategically-selected public posture. A candidate's public statements can fall anywhere on the scale of truth, and will usually be contradicted by statements from the opposition.

For the candidates, the impact of their metadebating may be unclear, but the game must be played. The media have a fascination with political debates, and often an antipathy toward candidates who may be avoiding them. Few candidates will allow their opponent to blame the breakdown of debate negotiations on them without a metadebate.

The major defect of metadebating is the extent to which it can promote distortions or outright lies. The redeeming values of metadebating may be its inherent capacity to encourage interest in campaign debates or to force a reluctant candidate to participate.

NOTES

1. Robert Scott, "You Cannot Not Debate: The Debate Over the 1980 Presidential Debates," *Speaker and Gavel* 18 (Winter 1981), pp. 28–33.

2. Interview, Douglas Bailey, November 18, 1978. Bailey's view that debates occurring early in the campaign have little lasting impact is reflected in the advice of another consultant, who says that "if your opponent makes a mistake early in the campaign, let it sit for a while and then beat him to death with it in the final two weeks." See Hank Parkinson, "Topical Techniques," *Campaign Insight: An Overview of Political Techniques* 8 (February 1, 1979), p. 14. Napolitan expressed similar sentiments in an interview, January 10, 1979.

3. Interview, Harold Stassen, April 18, 1979.

4. Interview, Barry Goldwater, July 13, 1978.

5. American Institute of Public Opinion, *The Gallup Poll: Public Opinion 1935–1971, Volume One 1935–1948* (New York: Random House, 1972), p. 240.

6. *Philadelphia Inquirer,* July 12, 1982, p. 8.

7. Napolitan as quoted in Robert MacNeil, *The People Machine: The Influence of Television on American Politics* (New York: Harper & Row, 1968), pp. 174–175. Napolitan expressed similar sentiments in an interview, January 10, 1979.

8. *New York Times,* August 1, 1960, p. 9.

9. *The Presidential Campaign: Volume Three, The Debates* (Washington, D.C.: United States Government Printing Office, 1979), p. 2.

10. *New York Times,* October 19, 1964, p. 1.

11. *Philadelphia Inquirer,* July 12, 1982, p. 8.

12. I do not know if I am more amused by Ertel's expressed surprise at learning of the existence of debate coaches or Thornburgh's manager principled denunciation of the species. I served as a debate consultant to Thornburgh in 1978 with Frank Ursomarso, advance man to President Nixon and Ford and head advance man for Ford for the 1976 presidential debates.

13. *Philadelphia Inquirer,* July 12, 1982, p. 8.

14. Memorandum, Jody Powell to President Carter, n.d.

15. *Washington Star,* January 4, 1980, p. 15.

16. *Baltimore Sun,* August 27, 1980, p. A1.

17. *Washington Post,* June 1, 1980, p. A4.

18. Scott, "You Cannot Not Debate: The Debate Over the 1980 Presidential Debates," p. 30.

19. Ibid., p. 31.

20. *Baltimore Sun,* August 28, 1980, p. A1.

21. *Baltimore Sun,* August 24, 1980, p. A1.

22. *New York Times,* September 19, 1980, p. B5.

23. *Baltimore Sun,* September 10, 1980, p. A1; September 17, 1980, p. A11.

24. *New York Times,* September 9, 1980, p. D18.

25. *New York Times,* September 12, 1980, p. A23.

26. Strauss made this statement on the NBC "Today" show. "The MacNeil/Lehrer Report" of September 3, 1980 presented a fascinating discussion of the positions of the three candidates by Strauss, James Baker, and Mitchell Rogovin. See Transcript, MacNeil/Lehrer Report, September 3, 1980 (New York: Educational Broadcasting Corporation, 1980).

27. *Washington Star,* September 25, 1980, p. 4.

28. *New York Times,* October 25, 1964, p. 72; October 28, 1964, pp. 1, 36; October 29, 1964, pp. 24, 25.

29. *Philadelphia Inquirer,* October 21, 1962, pp. 1, 25.

30. *New York Times,* October 18, 1936, p. 31.

31. Lawrence F. O'Brien, *No Final Victories* (New York: Ballantine, 1975), pp. 338–339.

32. *New York Times,* January 13, 1980, p. 28.

33. *New York Times,* February 2, 1980, p. 7.

34. Ibid.

35. *New York Times,* February 7, 1980, pp. 16, 17.

36. *Boston Globe,* June 1, 1980, p. 1.

37. Letter, Jon L. Breen (Executive Editor of the *Nashua Telegraph*) to Gerald Carmen (Senior Consultant, Northeast Division, Ronald Reagan for President Committee), February 7, 1980.

38. Jack W. Germond and Jules Witcover, *Blue Smoke and Mirrors* (New York: Viking, 1981), pp. 125–126.

39. Letter, Charles N. Steele (General Counsel to the Federal Election Commission) to the *Nashua Telegraph,* February 19, 1980.

40. Interview, Jon Breen, March 28, 1980.

41. Germond and Witcover, *Blue Smoke and Mirrors,* pp. 126–128.

42. Tape recording of the Nashua debate, February 23, 1980.

43. Interview, James Baker, March 9, 1981. For the *Telegraph*'s analysis of these events, see *Nashua Telegraph,* February 28, 1980, p. 4.

44. *Washington Post,* February 28, 1980, p. 2.

45. *Boston Globe,* June 1, 1980, p. 1; Germond and Witcover, *Blue Smoke and Mirrors,* pp. 129–131. James Baker, campaign manager for Bush, and Richard Wirthlin, pollster and strategist for Reagan, agree that the impact of Nashua has been overestimated, giving more credit to Reagan's performance during the Manchester debate, held three days earlier. For Wirthlin's view see *Washington Post,* February 28, 1980, pp. A1, A8.

46. Jeff Greenfield, *Playing to Win: An Insider's Guide to Politics* (New York: Simon & Schuster, 1980), p. 215.

47. *New York Times,* October 8, 1976, p. A18.

48. *New York Times,* October 14, 1960, p. 1.

49. *New York Times,* October 24, 1960, p. 18.

50. *New York Times,* October 24, 1960, p. 19.

51. *New York Times,* October 30, 1960, p. 1.

52. Ibid.

Epilogue

Campaign debates have become increasingly popular in recent years, and there is every reason to expect this trend to continue. The ongoing decline of party loyalty in the electorate, the growing reliance on television as a news source, and the appearance of a generation of articulate, image-conscious politicians will likely create greater demand for debates by the public and greater willingness to debate by the candidates. The rise in campaign debating is just one facet of a seemingly irreversible change transforming American elections, namely, the replacement of party-dominated election campaigning by individualistic, media-dominated campaigning. The various aspects of this transformation feed off each other. As cable television spreads, for example, the frequency of debates on lower levels of American politics is likely to increase; and with this will probably evolve increased public expectations for debates at all levels.

Already, the political process has reached a point where candidates who would prefer to avoid debates often feel they have no choice but to accept. Public pressure, when it is strong, seems to be an effective catalyst for encouraging debates. Thus, all the onus for a failure to debate should not be placed solely on a candidate or candidates; it might be attributable to the electorate for not feeling the need for debates or not knowing how to express that need.

"Equal Time": An Obstacle to Debate?

It is ironic that until recently one of the chief obstacles to political debate has been a statute ostensibly aimed at ensuring the free and fair interchange of ideas in political campaigns. Section 315 of the Communication Act of 1934 requires a broadcaster who sells or donates time to a political candidate to provide equal time for any other legally qualified candidate for the same office. The "equal time" clause from its inception has, in fact, discouraged political debates. Major party candidates typically refuse to debate with minor party or independent nominees. And broadcasters refuse to air debates solely featuring the major candidates, wanting to avoid burdensome claims for free "equal time" from each excluded candidate.

Congress attempted to break the twenty-six-year-old stalemate in 1959, by legislating that broadcasters were exempt from the equal time provision under four circumstances: (1) the appearance of the candidate in a "bonafide newscast," (2) a "bonafide news interview," (3) a "bonafide news documentary," and (4) "on-the-spot coverage of bonafide news events." However, the Federal Communications Commission, charged with administering the legislation, has since interpreted these terms so narrowly as to negate the intended impact of the legislation.

Real change finally occurred in 1975. The FCC, reversing its former position in response to a petition from the Aspen Institute, a public interest foundation, ruled that broadcasters would be exempt from the equal time provision, providing that the events to be aired met five criteria: (1) be arranged by a third party not associated with the broadcaster (to prevent broadcasters from both making and covering the news); (2) take place outside the broadcaster's studios (to prevent conflict of interest); (3) be covered live (to protect their newsworthiness); (4) be covered in their entirety (to prevent biased editing); and (5) be based on "good faith journalistic judgment of the newsworthiness of the event" and not for serving the political interest of one of the candidates.

Subsequently, even these standards have been relaxed. In 1976 and 1980, the FCC accepted the legal fiction that the networks were merely covering on-the-spot presidential debates staged for the benefit of the live audience. In 1978, the requirement of live coverage was relaxed to allow a delay of up to twenty-four hours. And in 1981, broadcasters were allowed to air debates produced in their own studios "as a matter of technical convenience" as long as a qualified sponsor had arranged the event. By 1982, the FCC was further considering rulings that would allow broadcasters to sponsor debates themselves, permit rebroadcast of a debate after the twenty-four-hour period, and liberalize the rules for a candidate's appearance in documentary programs.

Indeed, the obstacles posed to debates have been reduced dramatically since 1975. One might, in fact, ask whether the relaxation of Section 315 has gone too far too fast. Has the FCC adequately protected the rights of the minor party and independent candidates? If the League of Women Voters had decided in 1980 to exclude John Anderson entirely from the debates, he would have had no legal grounds for complaint under the Aspen ruling. Should private sponsoring organizations be allowed to wield such power in election campaigns, or should a test of eligibility be written into law? Clearly no easy legislative solution is attainable. For this reason, the issue will probably be treated on a campaign to campaign basis, dependent in large measure on the judgment and good faith of the sponsoring organizations, and, of course, ultimately on the willingness of the major party candidates to participate when minor party or independent candidates are deemed eligible.

Should Presidential Debates Be Mandatory?

Several parties have proposed that presidential debates be made mandatory. They contend that since incumbent presidents, left to their self-interested calculations, will rarely agree to debate, debates must be institutionalized by law. This position, of course, rests on the assumption that debates are potentially valuable to the electorate. While I essentially support this assumption, I nevertheless contend that mandatory debates would be bad public policy. The decision to enter a debate, like all other strategic campaign decisions, should be left to the candidate's discretion. Debates are simply one form of campaign communication among many; if a candidate prefers to rely on the other means of communication, that should be his right.

Proposals for mandatory presidential debates are not only misguided theoretically, they are flawed practically. Political scientist Malcolm Moos proposes that Congress require the networks to provide specific time slots for debates, regardless of whether either or both candidates are willing to participate. If one is willing, then he would be granted the allocated time, a factor which would most likely prompt his opponent's reluctant participation. Section 315 would, of course, have to be modified or suspended to make this recommendation feasible. James Karayn, coordinator of the 1976 debates for the League of Women Voters, and journalists Jack Germond and Jules Witcover recommend that debate participation be made a prerequisite for receiving publicly-financed campaign funds. Both of these approaches, however, would almost surely be ruled a violation of a candidate's First Amendment rights, which embraces the choice not to speak.

How Can Debate Formats Be Improved?

Whether or not debate formats are truly problematic is itself debatable. Despite oft-heard claims that the formats are, in essence, security blankets for the candidates—means by which they can protect themselves against fatal flaws—there is no reason to assume that the candidate's concern for self-protection is ipso facto contrary to the public interest.

Since the stakes of political debating are often so great, especially at higher levels, candidates should retain the right to negotiate their own formats. Imposition by a third party sponsor can either prevent debates, limit their effectiveness, or result in political injury to one or more candidates. While one or more standardized formats is neither desirable nor attainable, formats, regardless of their specific design, should provide for each candidate adequate and equal opportunity for refutation. The absence of this provision is clearly a disservice to both the candidates and the electorate. The candidate's opportunity to attack, defend or sell is notably stifled, as is the electorate's opportunity to make coherent comparisons of the candidate's positions.

One of the more promising ways to improve political debates involves the panelists and their conduct. If the panel survives, as presumably it will, then it is imperative for the panelists' role to be defined. Is it to shed insights into the candidates' character and personality? Is it to expose weaknesses in the candidates' positions? Is it to throw the candidate off balance? Is it to make news? Panelists, I contend, should be exclusively concerned with asking questions to facilitate responses which can help the electorate compare the candidates' positions on significant issues. In this regard, the following specific recommendations, if adopted, should enhance the role of panels:

1. Panelists need not necessarily be journalists. Experience has demonstrated that journalists hold no special claim to questioning skill.
2. Panelists should, before their questions are prepared, consult as a group with experts and pollsters to assess the inherent quality of their questions, to determine appropriate answers, and to give greater assurance that the subject of the question is of sufficient relevance to the electorate.
3. Candidates need not have a say in the selection of panelists, particularly if a nonpartisan, blue ribbon commission assumes this role.
4. For presidential debates, the panel selection process, including the preparation of questions, should not be hurried, as it normally is. Systematic advance preparation, regardless of whether or not the candidates have committed themselves to debating, should yield high caliber questions.

Finally, as critics indict political debate formats for not being conducive to an enlightening exchange regarding the issues, so too must they examine the entire process of political communication. In fact, should such an educational burden even be placed on debates? The candidates' culpability for superficiality or undue attention to image must be evaluated in relation to electoral responsibility. If the public habitually practices being uninformed, candidates are ill-advised to communicate on a level which the electorate cannot comprehend. Indeed, no surer route to political defeat could be found.

Should the Media's Role in Debates Be Altered?

Absolutely. The media, despite its good intentions, has not yet demonstrated sufficient commitment to educate the electorate. Nightly news coverage and occasional campaign-related programming should be supplemented by a series of briefings on the major issues on the public agenda. These briefings should provide the electorate with a reasonably solid basis for understanding the ebb and flow of debates. Moreover, the briefings can diminish any undue attention by the electorate to image factors which may interfere with the rationality of its decision-making process.

The media has the added responsibility to cease and desist from its horse-race orientation to debates. Telling the viewers in postdebate commentaries and superficial polls who "won" or "lost" diminishes the substance of the debates. Moreover, it constitutes a violation of the citizens' right to react to the candidates on the merits of their performance rather than on the merits as hastily gleaned and expressed by some commentator.

Should a National Debate Commission Be Established?

James Karayn, drawing on his experience as coordinator of the 1976 presidential debates for the League of Women Voters, proposes that Congress charter and fund a blue-ribbon National Debate Commission to be permanent sponsor of the presidential debates. The Commission, he recommends, should include journalists, political figures, business and union officials, civic leaders, and debate experts. This idea has considerable merit. A National Debate Commission might not only assume the heavy logistical burden of staging presidential debates, as Karayn recommends, but also could serve as a clearinghouse for information about campaign debates at all levels. Further, it could cooperate with the networks in producing informative briefings covering the issues likely to arise in the debates.

My only objection to Karayn's proposal is that it would give full responsibility to the commission for choosing the schedule, format, and agenda of the presidential debates. In my view, as I have stated previously, these issues should be negotiated with the candidates, not dictated to them.

How Can Candidates Contribute to More Informed Debate?

I stated earlier that "not only do candidates make debates" but "debates also make candidates." Yet in nearly every campaign in which I have been involved, debates are treated with last minute haste which places monumental stress on the candidate and his campaign—stress which can result in a debate of far less quality than otherwise possible.

Few if any campaign exercises are as edifying or as capable of producing confidence as quality debate preparation. It allows the candidate to address the issues in speeches and media appearances more articulately and authoritatively; it reduces the likelihood of gaffes and of being caught ill-informed; it can ultimately strengthen not only the candidate's confidence but campaign morale as well. Thus, the sooner campaign advisers realize that the value of debate preparation far transcends the debate itself, the greater will be the benefit to candidates, campaigns, and the electorate.

A Final Note

The destiny of the political process in general and debates in particular is rooted in human understanding. A campaign debate is the result of merging self interests—the candidates', the sponsors' and the electorate's and, therefore, includes the willingness to compromise. If debates are to occupy a prominent position on the political landscape, then the interested parties must appreciate each other's vantage point—the nuances, the constraints, the complexity. This book has been inspired by the desire to further that end.

Selected Bibliography

BOOKS

Agranoff, Robert. *The Management of Election Campaigns.* Boston: Holbrook Press, 1976.

Agranoff, Robert, ed. *The New Style in Election Campaigns.* Boston: Holbrook Press, 1972.

Angle, Paul M., ed. *Created Equal? (The Complete Lincoln-Douglas Debates of 1858).* Chicago: University of Chicago Press, 1958.

Bailey, Thomas A. *Presidential Greatness (The Image and the Man From George Washington to the Present).* New York: Appleton-Century-Crofts, 1966.

Bishop, George F., Meadow, Robert G., and Jackson-Beeck, Marilyn. *The Presidential Debates (Media, Electoral, and Policy Perspectives).* New York: Praeger, 1978.

Bitzer, Lloyd, and Rueter, Theodore. *Carter vs. Ford (The Counterfeit Debates of 1976).* Madison, Wisconsin: University of Wisconsin Press, 1980.

Bloom, Melvyn H. *Public Relations and Presidential Campaigns (A Crisis in Democracy).* New York: Thomas Y. Crowell Company, 1973.

Blumer, Jay, G., and McQuail, Denis. *Television in Politics (Its Uses and Influences).* Chicago: University of Chicago Press, 1969.

Boorstin, Daniel. *The Image (A Guide to Pseudo-Events in America).* New York: Harper Colophon Books, 1964.

Chester, Edward W. *Radio, Television and American Politics.* New York: Sheed and Ward, 1969.

Chester, Lewis, Hodgon, Godfrey, and Page, Bruce. *An American Melodrama (The Presidential Campaign of 1968).* New York: Viking Press, 1969.

Chisman, Forrest P. *Attitude Psychology and the Study of Public Opinion.* University Park, Pennsylvania: The Pennsylvania State University Press, 1976.

Clotfelter, James, and Prysby, Charles L. *Political Choices (A Study of Elections and Voters).* New York: Holt, Rinehart, and Winston, 1980.

Devlin, L. Patrick. *Contemporary Political Speaking.* Belmont, California: Wadsworth, 1971.

DeVries, Walter, and Tarrance, V. Lance. *The Ticket-Splitter (A New Force in American Politics).* Grand Rapids, Mich.: Wm. B. Eendmans Publishing Co., 1972.

Diamond, Edwin. *The Tin Kazoo (Television, Politics and the News).* Cambridge, Mass.: MIT Press, 1975.

Drew, Elizabeth. *American Journal (The Events of 1976).* New York: Random House, 1977.

_____. *Portrait of an Election (The 1980 Presidential Campaign)*. New York: Simon & Schuster, 1981.

Fenno, Richard F., Jr. *Home Style (House Members in Their Districts)*. Boston: Little, Brown and Company, 1978.

Fiorina, Morris P. *Congress (Keystone of the Washington Establishment)*. New Haven: Yale University Press, 1977.

Ford, Gerald R. *A Time to Heal (The Autobiography of Gerald R. Ford)*. New York: Harper & Row, 1979.

Germond, Jack W., and Witcover, Jules. *Blue Smoke and Mirrors*. New York: Viking, 1981.

Gilbert, Robert E. *Television and Presidential Politics*. North Quincy, Massachusetts: The Christopher Publishing House, 1972.

Greenfield, Jeff. *Playing to Win (An Insider's Guide to Politics)*. New York: Simon & Schuster, 1980.

Hart, Gary Warren. *Right from the Start (A Chronicle of the McGovern Campaign)*. New York: The New York Times Book Company, 1973.

Hargrove, Erwin C. *Presidential Leadership (Personality and Political Style)*. New York: Macmillan, 1966.

Heckman, Richard A. *Lincoln vs. Douglas (The Great Debates Campaign)*. Washington, D.C.: Public Affairs Press, 1967.

Hershey, Marjorie Randon. *The Making of Campaign Strategy*. Washington, D.C.: Heath & Company, 1974.

Jennings, M. Kent, and Ziegler, Harmon. *The Electoral Process*. Englewood Cliffs, New Jersey: Prentice-Hall, 1966.

Kelley, Stanley, Jr. *Political Campaigning (Problems in Creating and Informed Electorate)*. Washington, D.C.: The Brookings Institution, 1960.

Kraus, Sidney. *The Great Debates (Kennedy vs. Nixon, 1960)*. Bloomington, Indiana: Indiana University Press, 1962.

_____. *The Great Debates (Carter vs. Ford, 1976)*. Bloomington, Indiana: Indiana University Press, 1976.

Ladd, Everett Carll, Jr., and Hadley, Charles D. *Transformations of the American Party System (Political Coalitions from the New Deal to the 1970's)*. Second Edition. New York: W. W. Norton & Company, Inc., 1978.

Lang, Kurt, and Lang, Gladys E. *Politics and Television*. Chicago: Quadrangle Books, 1968.

Levin, Murray B. *Kennedy Campaigning (The System and the Style as Practiced by Senator Edward Kennedy)*. Boston: Beacon Press, 1966.

McGinniss, Joe. *The Selling of the President, 1968*. New York: Trident Press, 1969.

MacNeil, Robert. *The People Machine (The Influence of Television on American Politics)*. New York: Harper & Row, 1968.

Mann, Thomas E. *Unsafe at Any Margin*. Washington, D.C.: American Enterprise Institute, 1978.

May, Ernest R., and Fraser, Janet, ed. *Campaign '72 (The Managers Speak)*. Cambridge, Massachusetts: Harvard University Press, 1973.

Mayhew, David R. *Congress (The Electoral Connection)*. New Haven: Yale University Press, 1974.

Mayo, Earl, ed. *The Great Debates*. Santa Barbara, Calif.: Center for the Study of Democratic Institutions, 1962.

Mendelsohn, Harold, and Crespi, Irving. *Polls, Television, and the New Politics.* Scranton, Pennsylvania: Chandler, 1970.

Mickelson, Sig. *The Electric Mirror (Politics in an Age of Television).* New York: Dodd, Mead, 1972.

Minow, Newton N., Martin, John Bartlow, and Mitchell, Lee M. *Presidential Television.* New York: Basic Books, Inc. 1973.

Napolitan, Joseph. *The Election Game (And How to Win It).* New York: Doubleday & Company, 1972.

Nie, Norman H., Verba, Sidney, and Petrocik, John R. *The Changing American Voter.* Cambridge, Massachusetts: Harvard University Press, 1976.

Niemi, Richard G., and Weisberg, Herbert F., eds. *Controversies in American Voting Behavior.* San Francisco: W. H. Freeman & Company, 1976.

Nimmo, Dan. *Politican Communication and Public Opinion in America.* Santa Monica, California: Goodyear Publishing Co., 1978.

Nimmo, Dan. *The Political Persuaders (The Techniques of Modern Election Campaigns).* Englewood Cliffs, New Jersey: Prentice-Hall, 1970.

Nixon, Richard M. *Six Crises.* New York: Doubleday & Co., Inc., 1962.

———. *RN: The Memoirs of Richard Nixon.* New York: Grosset & Dunlap, 1978.

Novak, Michael. *Choosing Our King (Powerful Symbols in Presidential Politics).* New York: Macmillan, 1974.

O'Brien, Lawrence F. *No Final Victories: (A Life in Politics—From John F. Kennedy to Watergate).* New York: Ballantine Books, 1974.

Page, Benjamin I. *Choices and Echoes in Presidential Elections.* Chicago: University of Chicago Press, 1978.

Polsby, Nelson W., and Aaron Wildavsky. *Presidential Elections (Strategies of American Electoral Politics).* New York: Charles Scribner's Sons, 1976.

Ranney, Austin, ed. *The Past and Future of Presidential Debates.* Washington, D.C.: American Enterprise Institute, 1979.

Reid, Loren, ed. *American Public Address (Studies in Honor of Albert Craig Baird).* Columbia, Missouri: University of Missouri Press, 1961.

Report of the Commission on Presidential Campaign Debates. American Political Science Association. Washington, D.C., 1964.

Ritter, Kurt W., ed. "The 1980 Presidential Debates." *Speaker and Gavel* 18. Winter, 1981.

Ross, Irwin. *The Loneliest Campaign (The Truman Victory of 1948).* New York: New American Library, 1968.

Rubin, Bernard. *Media, Politics, and Democracy.* New York: Oxford University Press, 1977.

Rubin, Bernard. *Political Television.* Belmont, California: Wadsworth Publishing Company, 1967.

Sanders, Robert E. *The Great Debates.* Columbia, Missouri: University of Missouri Freedom of Information Center, 1961.

Schlesinger, Arthur M., Jr., and Israel, Fred L., eds. *History of American Presidential Elections, 1789–1968.* 4 volumes. New York: Chelsea House, 1971.

Schram, Martin. *Running for President 1976 (The Carter Campaign).* New York: Stein & Day, 1977.

Simons, Herbert W. *Persuasion (Understanding, Practice, and Analysis).* Reading, Massachusetts: Addison-Wesley, 1976.

Sparks, Edwin Erle, ed. *Lincoln-Douglas Debates of 1858.* Springfield, Illinois: Illinois State Historical Library, 1908.

The Mass Media. Aspen Institute Guide to Communication Industry Trends. New York: Praeger, 1978.

The Presidential Campaign 1976, Volume III (The Debates). Washington: United States Government Printing Office, 1979.

The Presidential Election and Transition, 1960–61. Washington, D.C.: The Brookings Institution, 1961.

Thompson, Wayne N. *Quantitative Research in Public Address and Communication.* New York: Random House, 1967.

White, Theodore H. *The Making of the President 1960.* New York: Atheneum, 1962.

————. *America in Search of Itself (The Making of the President 1956–1980).* New York: Harper & Row, 1982.

Witcover, Jules. *Marathon (The Pursuit of the Presidency 1972–1976).* New York: The Viking Press, 1977.

With the Nation Watching. Report of the Twentieth Century Fund Task Force on Televised Presidential Debates. Lexington, Massachusetts: D.C. Heath, 1979.

Wykoff, Gene. *The Image Candidates.* New York: Macmillan, 1968.

INTERVIEWS

Persons Interviewed for the 1960 Presidential Debates

Senator John F. Kennedy's Advisors and Negotiators

Myer Feldman. Issues advisor to John F. Kennedy. September 14, 1977.

Henry M. Jackson. Chairman, Democratic National Committee in 1960; adviser to John F. Kennedy. June 12, 1978.

Larry O'Brien. Campaign Manager for Senator John F. Kennedy's campaign for the presidency in 1960. March 15, 1979.

David F. Powers. Aide to John F. Kennedy. January 16, 1979.

J. Leonard Reinsch. Head of John F. Kennedy's debate negotiating team and his media adviser during the 1960 presidential campaign. May 23, 1977.

Theodore Sorensen. Issues adviser, speechwriter, and negotiator for John F. Kennedy. June 23, 1977.

William F. Wilson. Technical adviser to John F. Kennedy and debate negotiator. September 9, 1977.

Vice President Richard M. Nixon's Advisors and Negotiators

Leonard Wood Hall. Chairman, Nixon for President Campaign, 1960. September 14, 1978.

Herbert Klein. Press Secretary to Vice President Nixon and debate negotiator. August 23, 1977.

Edward A. (Ted) Rogers. Television adviser to Vice President Nixon and debate negotiator. August 23, 1977.

Fred C. Scribner, Jr. Head of Vice President Nixon's negotiating team. August 31, 1977.

Candidates

Henry Cabot Lodge. Headed Eisenhower's presidential campaign in 1952; Richard Nixon's running mate in 1960. March 11, 1978.

Network Officials and Participants

Julian Goodman. Producer of the second debate (NBC). July 7, 1977.
Don Hewitt. Producer of the first debate (CBS). August 23, 1977.
Sig Mickelson. Chief negotiator for CBS. August 23, 1977.
Edward P. Morgan. Panelist for second debate (ABC). June 21, 1977.
Howard K. Smith. Moderator for the first debate (CBS). June 21, 1977.
Frank Stanton. Former president of CBS and host for first debate. July 7, 1977.

Persons Interviewed for the 1976 Presidential Debates

League of Women Voters Representatives

James Karayn. Coordinator for the debates. November 11, 1977; November 7, 1978; and December 7, 1978.
Peggy Lampl. Executive Director, League of Women Voters. December 16, 1977 and August 21, 1978.
Rita Hauser. Attorney, Co-Chair of the 1976 Presidential Debates Steering Committee. February 21, 1978.
Newton Minow. Co-Chair of the 1976 Presidential Debates Steering Committee. March 4, 1978.
Charls E. Walker. Co-Chairman of the Steering Committee. March 4, 1978.
Theodore H. White. Member of the Steering Committee. February 21, 1978.
George Gallup, Jr. Member of the Steering Committee. January 2, 1979.

Moderator and Panelists, First Debate, September 23

Edwin Newman. Moderator (NBC). February 21, 1978.
Elizabeth Drew. Author and correspondent, *New Yorker*. March 8, 1978.
James Gannon. Reporter, *Wall Street Journal;* presently managing editor, *Des Moines Register,* February 3, 1978, March 13, 1980.
Frank Reynolds. Reporter/commentator, ABC. March 3, 1978.

Moderator and Panelists, Second Debate, October 6

Pauline Frederick. National Public Radio, moderator (letter). January 27, 1978.
Max Frankel. Associate Editor of the *New York Times.* February 7, 1978.
Henry Trewhitt. Foreign correspondent for the *Baltimore Sun.* July 14, 1978.
Richard Valeriani. Diplomatic correspondent, NBC. February 17, 1978.

Moderator and Panelists, Vice Presidential (Third) Debate, October 15

James Hoge. Editor *Chicago Sun Times,* moderator. June 29, 1978.
Marilyn Berger. NBC correspondent. August 23, 1978.

Hal Bruno. Political correspondent with *Newsweek.* June 12, 1978.
Walter Mears. Special correspondent for the Associated Press. June 12, 1978.

Moderator and Panelists, Fourth Debate, October 22

Joseph Kraft. Syndicated columnist. January 27, 1978.
Jack Nelson. Washington Bureau Chief, *Los Angeles Times.* June 12, 1978.

Governor Jimmy Carter's Advisers and Negotiators

Barry Jagoda. Formerly the president's media adviser. December 16, 1977.
Jerry Rafshoon. Campaign adviser and debate negotiator for President Carter. March
    9, 1978.

President Ford's Advisers and Negotiators

Dean Burch. Negotiator. July 14, 1978.
William Carruthers. Media adviser to President Gerald Ford during the 1976 presiden-
    tial campaign, March 22 and 25, 1978.
Richard Cheney. White House Chief of Staff during the 1976 presidential campaign.
    November 18, 1977.
Michael Raoul Duval. Debate coordinator and negotiator. December 11 and 20, 1977.
Robert Teeter. President Ford's pollster. January 11, 1978.
Frank Ursomarso. Head advance man for the debates. November 20, 1977 and October
    8, 1979.
Don Penny. Speech adviser to President Ford. January 4, 1979.
Melvin Laird. Adviser to President Ford. March 2, 1979.

Senator Dole's Advisors and Negotiators

Senator Ted Stevens, (R., Alaska). Co-negotiated format for 1976 Vice Presidential
    Debate. September 28, 1978.

Senator Walter Mondale's Advisors and Negotiators

Roger Coeloff. Responsible for preparation of briefings and strategy. August 25, 1978.
Richard Moe. Negotiator. August 18, 1978.
Dr. Joseph Peckman. Brookings Institution. Briefed Senator Mondale on economic
    and taxation matters. August 25, 1978.

Candidates

President Gerald Ford. March 24, 1978.
Ronald Reagan. Republican Presidential Primary Candidate, 1976. September 25,
    1978.
Milton J. Shapp. Former Governor of Pennsylvania. Democratic presidential primary
    candidate, 1976. December 21, 1978 and February 8, 1979.
Senator Robert Dole. Vice presidential candidate, 1976. January 25, 1979.
Vice President Walter Mondale. Vice presidential candidate, 1976. July 7, 1979.
Senator Barry Goldwater. Republican presidential candidate, 1964. July 13, 1978.

Other Resource Persons

Douglas Bailey. Political consultant to Republican candidates. November 18, 1978.

Charles Benton. Prime supporter for the 1976 presidential forums and presidential debates. November 17, 1978.

W. Averill Harriman. Former Governor of New York, unsuccessful presidential contender (1948) and Ambassador. August 12, 1978.

Joseph Napolitan. Political consultant for Democratic candidates. January 10, 1979.

Dean Rusk. Secretary of State during the Kennedy Administration. September 13, 1978.

Joseph Lelyveld. Columnist, *New York Times.* February 21, 1978.

Bill Connell. Administrative Assistant to Senator Hubert Humphrey, 1968. June 8, 1978.

Frank Manciewicz. Press Secretary to Senator Robert F. Kennedy, 1968. Press Secretary to Senator George McGovern in 1972. June 8, 1978.

Jeff Smith. Executive Assistant to Senator George McGovern during 1972 presidential campaign. June 8, 1978.

Harold Stassen. Republican presidential candidate 1948. April 18, 1979.

Chris Lindsay. Associated Press, panelist for Nashua Debate. May 24, 1980.

Jon Breen. Managing editor *Nashua Telegraph,* moderator for Nashua debate. March 28, 1980.

Persons Interviewed for the 1980 Presidential Debates

Governor Ronald Reagan's Advisers and Negotiators

James Baker III. Head of Debate Task Force and negotiations. March 9, 1981.
David Gergen. Head of debate briefing preparations. March 10, 1981.
Mark Goode. Media adviser to Governor Reagan. July 8, 1982.
Frank Ursomarso. Head advance man for 1980 presidential debates. June 11, 1982.
Richard Wirthlin. Pollster and strategist. March 10, 1981.

Congressman John Anderson's Advisers and Negotiators

Clifford Brown, Jr. Political Director. July 4, 1980.
Mitchell Rogovin. Legal counsel and debate negotiator. July 2, 1981.
Robert Walker. Campaign Director. July 9, 1981.

President Jimmy Carter's Advisers

Stuart Eizenstat. Domestic policy adviser. October 6, 1981.
Samuel Popkin. Debate adviser. July 8, 1981.

League of Women Voters Representatives

Lee Hanna. Debate coordinator. August 6, 1981.
Ruth Hinerfeld. League president. July 1, 1981.

DEBATES AND FORUMS ANALYZED

Presidential Debates and Forums

Harold Stassen and Thomas Dewey, Oregon Primary, May 17, 1948.

John F. Kennedy and Hubert Humphrey, West Virginia Primary, May 3, 1960.

John F. Kennedy and Richard M. Nixon, The 1960 Presidential Debates, September 26, and October 7, 13, and 21, 1960.

Hubert Humphrey and George McGovern, California Primary, May 28 and 30, 1972.

George McGovern, Hubert Humphrey, Sam Yorty, Taylor Hardin (for George Wallace), and Shirley Chisholm (ABC's "Issues and Answers," preceding California primary), June 4, 1972.

Birch Bayh, Jimmy Carter, Fred Harris, Henry Jackson, Milton Shapp, Sargent Shriver, and Morris Udall, New England Forum (Boston), February 23, 1976.

Jimmy Carter, Henry Jackson, and Milton Shapp, The Southern Forum, (Miami), March 1, 1976.

Jimmy Carter, Frank Church, Fred Harris, Henry Jackson, and Morris Udall, The Mid-Atlantic Forum (New York), March 29, 1976.

Morris Udall and Frank Church, The Midwest Forum, (Chicago), May 3, 1976.

Gerald Ford and Jimmy Carter, The 1976 Presidential Debates, September 23, October 6 and 22, 1976.

Robert Dole and Walter Mondale, October 22, 1976.

Philip Crane, Howard Baker, John Anderson, John Connally, Robert Dole, and George Bush, The Republican Presidential Debate, (Des Moines, Iowa), January 5, 1980.

John Anderson, John Connally, Philip Crane, George Bush, Robert Dole, and Ronald Reagan, The 1980 Presidential Forum (Manchester, New Hampshire), February 20, 1980.

George Bush and Ronald Reagan, The Nashua (New Hampshire) Primary Debate, February 23, 1980.

Ronald Reagan, George Bush, John Connally, and Howard Baker, South Carolina Primary Debate, (Columbia), February 28, 1980.

John Anderson, George Bush, Philip Crane, and Ronald Reagan, The 1980 Presidential Forum, (Chicago), March 13, 1980.

Ronald Reagan and George Bush, The 1980 Presidential Forum (Houston), April 23, 1980.

Ed Clark, (Libertarian Party) and Barry Commoner (Consumer Party) (Ann Arbor, Michigan), August 3, 1980.

Ronald Reagan and John Anderson, The 1980 Presidential Debate, (Baltimore), September 21, 1980.

Ronald Reagan and Jimmy Carter, The 1980 Presidential Debate, (Cleveland), October 28, 1980.

Senate Race Debates

John F. Kennedy and Henry Cabot Lodge, (Waltham, Massachusetts), September 16, 1952.

Jacob Javits and Robert F. Wagner, Jr., (New York City), September 20 and October 28, 1956.

Robert Packwood and Wayne Morse, (Portland, Oregon), October 25, 1968.
Bill Bradley and Jeff Bell, (New Jersey), September, 1978.
Charles Percy and Alex Seith, (Illinois), October, 1978.
Carl Levin and Robert Griffin, (Michigan), October, 1978.
Arlen Specter and Peter Flaherty, (Pennsylvania), May 3, June 3, September 15 and
    October 12, 1980.
Pete Wilson and Jerry Brown, (California), June 9, August 12, and October 6, 1982.
Ray Shamie and Edward M. Kennedy, (Massachusetts), October 24, 1982.

Gubernatorial Debates

Richard Thornburgh and Peter Flaherty (Pennsylvania) October 10 and 25, 1978.
John Sears and Michael Dukakis (Massachusetts), October 23, 1982.

Congressional Debates

Robert Edgar and Dennis Rochford, (7th District Pa.), September 27, 1980, October
    23, 1980.

Mayoral Debates

William Green and David Marston, (Philadelphia), July 26, 1979.
William Green, David Marston, and Lucien Blackwell, August 29, October 5, 24,
    1979.

Index